CAMBRIDGE STUDIES IN NINETEENTH-CENTURY
LITERATURE AND CULTURE 27

TESTIMONY AND ADVOCACY
IN VICTORIAN LAW,
LITERATURE, AND
THEOLOGY

CAMBRIDGE STUDIES IN NINETEENTH-CENTURY
LITERATURE AND CULTURE

General editor
Gillian Beer, *University of Cambridge*

Editorial board
Isobel Armstrong, *Birkbeck College, London*
Terry Eagleton, *University of Oxford*
Leonore Davidoff, *University of Essex*
Catherine Gallagher, *University of California, Berkeley*
D. A. Miller, *Columbia University*
J. Hillis Miller, *University of California, Irvine*
Mary Poovey, *New York University*
Elaine Showalter, *Princeton University*

Nineteenth-century British literature and culture have been rich fields for interdisciplinary studies. Since the turn of the twentieth century, scholars and critics have tracked the intersections and tensions between Victorian literature and the visual arts, politics, social organisation, economic life, technical innovations, scientific thought – in short, culture in its broadest sense. In recent years, theoretical challenges and historiographical shifts have unsettled the assumptions of previous scholarly syntheses and called into question the terms of older debates. Whereas the tendency in much past literary critical interpretation was to use the metaphor of culture as 'background', feminist, Foucauldian, and other analyses have employed more dynamic models that raise questions of power and of circulation. Such developments have reanimated the field.

This series aims to accommodate and promote the most interesting work being undertaken on the frontiers of the field of nineteenth-century literary studies: work which intersects fruitfully with other fields of study such as history, or literary theory, or the history of science. Comparative as well as interdisciplinary approaches are welcomed.

A complete list of titles published will be found at the end of the book.

TOURNAMENT BETWEEN THE PRESS AND THE BAR.

This illustration from *Punch* depicts the animosity between the Bar and the press in 1845: *Punch* 9 (London, 1845), 128. By permission of the Syndicate of Cambridge University Library.

TESTIMONY AND ADVOCACY
IN VICTORIAN LAW,
LITERATURE, AND
THEOLOGY

JAN-MELISSA SCHRAMM

CAMBRIDGE
UNIVERSITY PRESS

CAMBRIDGE UNIVERSITY PRESS
Cambridge, New York, Melbourne, Madrid, Cape Town, Singapore, São Paulo

Cambridge University Press
The Edinburgh Building, Cambridge CB2 2RU, UK

Published in the United States of America by Cambridge University Press, New York

www.cambridge.org
Information on this title: www.cambridge.org/9780521771238

First published 2000
This digitally printed first paperback version 2006

A catalogue record for this publication is available from the British Library

Library of Congress Cataloguing in Publication data
Schramm, Jan-Melissa.
Testimony and advocacy in Victorian law, literature, and theology / Jan-Melissa Schramm.
p.   cm. (Cambridge studies in nineteenth-century literature and culture; 27)
Based on the author's dissertation.
Includes bibliographical references and index.
ISBN 0 521 77123 4 (hardback)
1. English literature – 19th century – History and criticism. 2. Law and literature.
3. English literature – 18th century – History and criticism. 4. Evidence, Criminal, in literature.
5. Witnesses in literature. 6. Theology in literature. 7. Trials in literature. 8. Narration
(Rhetoric) I. Title. II. Series.
PR468.L38S37   2000
820.0′355 – dc21   99–37798 CIP

ISBN-13 978-0-521-77123-8 hardback
ISBN-10 0-521-77123-4 hardback

ISBN-13 978-0-521-02635-2 paperback
ISBN-10 0-521-02635-0 paperback

For Chris

[I]t is a settled rule at common law, that no counsel shall be allowed [to] a prisoner upon his trial, upon the general issue, in any capital crime, unless some point of law shall arise proper to be debated. A rule which . . . seems to be not at all of a piece with the rest of the humane treatment of prisoners by the English law. For upon what face of reason can that assistance be denied to save the life of a man, which yet is allowed him in prosecutions for every petty trespass?

William Blackstone, *Commentaries on the laws of England*, 4 vols. (Oxford: Clarendon Press, 1765– 1769), vol. IV, pp. 349–350.

If an honest man is to be bullied in a witness-box, the barrister is instructed to bully him. If a murderer is to be rescued from the gallows, the barrister blubbers over him, as in TAWELL'S case; or accuses a wrong person, as in COURVOISIER'S case. If a naughty woman is to be screened, a barrister will bring Heaven itself into Court, and call Providence to witness that she is pure and spotless, as a certain great advocate and schoolmaster abroad did for a certain lamented QUEEN CAROLINE.

[W. M. Thackeray], 'War between the Press and the Bar: Mr Punch to the Gentlemen of the Press', *Punch* 9 (1845), 64–65.

Contents

Preface

This study has a particularly interdisciplinary genesis. Most Australian universities offer a combined Arts/Law degree programme which enables a student to pursue parallel studies in literature and law over the course of five or six years. Tutorials on the admissibility of confessional testimony in criminal trials could then be followed by a close study of *Tom Jones* or *Adam Bede*, for example, enabling the two discourses to enjoy what Daniel Kornstein in *Kill All the Lawyers?* has called a peculiarly dynamic 'synergism'. Within this context, there are several educational experiences which have shaped the unusual interface of interests pursued in this text. As an undergraduate student in the Department of English at the Australian National University in Canberra, I was privileged to undertake the course entitled 'Faith and Doubt in Victorian Literature' taught by Stephen Prickett, which placed the reception of Biblical narratives and the impact of German higher criticism firmly at the forefront of any engagement with Victorian fiction. The image of John Henry Newman's eponymous heroine, Callista, giving evidence at her trial, with or without the assistance of supernatural inspiration, has been seminal to my subsequent preoccupation with the status and reliability of human testimony before a secular tribunal.

But my interest in the more formal operation of rules of evidence in the courtroom only arose at a later date when, as a junior practitioner in a common law jurisdiction, I gained some experience in criminal litigation. My work often involved arguments about the admissibility of material which I hoped to tender to the court or which prosecution counsel wanted to adduce in evidence, and such tests of inclusion or exclusion invariably shaped the findings of the court. The practice of the law produced insights into the manipulation and presentation of evidence which could not be gained at Law School.

The final impetus for this study was the response of the general public to the representation of those accused of crime. Whenever I was asked what sort of legal practice I was engaged in, this question always came back at me: 'So how can you justify defending people whom you know to be guilty?' I would always raise some combination of the following issues in reply – that it is the task of the judge to decide upon the guilt or innocence of the accused on the basis of reasoned argument put forward by the representatives of both parties, that the burden of proof in a criminal case rests upon the prosecution, that an accused may have committed the criminal act but may still lack criminal responsibility, or have a defence which must legitimately be put to the court (such as insanity), that an accused may not have committed the crime with which he has been charged (even though he has been guilty of something else which the public would classify as 'wrong-doing'), or that much of my legally-aided work involved the presentation of pleas in mitigation after the possibility of a defence had been explored and discarded. But my listeners usually remained unconvinced, and it seemed to be the one topic which aroused public fears of the law's rhetorical excesses. Does the representation of suspected criminals by lawyers obfuscate truth and generate erroneous or even fraudulent verdicts, and if not, why is the work of criminal lawyers perceived in this way? As I began post-graduate research on changes in the idea of testimony in the nineteenth century, I had little idea that these three interests – in the testimony (either of witnesses or of martyrs) given at trial, in the exclusion of evidence, and in the replacement of the narratives of the accused by the stories of defence lawyers – could intersect so richly in an exploration of nineteenth-century fiction and the conventions of formal realism. Given that law and literature share authoritative (and competing) claims for the representation of 'reality', the questions 'who can speak in a court of law?', and 'what is the ambit of their licence to speak?' become critical for literary theorists as well as legal historians. This study explores the way in which literature positions itself in relation to the law – the way in which fiction seeks to generate assent in the reader and to bolster its claims to authenticity by its appropriation of evidentiary paradigms, but also the way in which fiction must make space for itself by denigrating the narrow, exclusionary emphasis of the law and seeking to recover those stories which the law ignores as inadmissible or irrelevant. In this way, the presentation of testimony in courts of law and in fictional courts illuminates some of the most important issues in nineteenth-century epistemology.

Acknowledgements

My greatest thanks are due to Gillian Beer for the tireless assistance and inspiration she provided over the course of the doctoral research which served as the foundation of this study. I would also like to offer special thanks to Adrian Poole for the thoughtful assistance he has provided in the course of the text's completion. In addition, I have benefited from the invaluable criticism and encouragement of legal and literary colleagues; John Beer, David Cairns, Stefan Collini, Jonathan Grossman, Stephen Prickett, and Ian Ward have all either read portions of this work or heard various sections at conferences and the text has been enriched by their input. Any errors or omissions which remain are mine alone.

My research at the University of Cambridge was made possible by a scholarship from the Cambridge Commonwealth Trust and additional funding from the Overseas Research Students Awards Scheme. I would like to acknowledge both these institutions for their generosity in facilitating my studies. I am also grateful to Lucy Cavendish College, Cambridge, for electing me into the Alice Tong Sze Research Fellowship which rendered possible the post-doctoral revision of this text. Of the Fellows at Lucy, I would especially like to thank Louise Tee for her advice and her example.

It has been a delight to work with Linda Bree at Cambridge University Press and I am grateful for the work of the external readers, including Alexander Welsh, who commented on the text and suggested various improvements. At the very conclusion of this project I benefited from participation in an inspirational Law and Literature Colloquium organised by Michael Freeman and Andrew Lewis at University College London. Some material from Chapter 3 has appeared in *Current Legal Issues: Law and Literature* 2 (1999), a collection of papers given at the conference, edited by Michael Freeman and Andrew Lewis, and published by Oxford University Press.

To Andrew Rae, James Crotty, and to the staff and the judiciary of the Hobart Court of Petty Sessions and the Supreme Court of Tasmania I owe thanks for instruction in court procedure during my time as a lawyer in Tasmania. In addition, a number of treasured family members, friends, and colleagues both in Australia and in Cambridge have offered me the benefit of their instructive conversation over the years, particularly Sally Bushell, Lil and Garry Deverell, Kylie van Dijk, Emma Gunn, Kate Quirk, Leah Price, Jeanine Willson, and my parents Margaret and Mervyn Turner. Jan Caldwell's friendship has been a support to me at every stage in the composition of this study. I would also like to thank my husband, Chris, for his wonderful sense of humour and for all his good cooking! Without his continuing love and encouragement, the adventures of study and travel which have generated this text would not have been possible.

Abbreviations

Throughout this text, I make numerous references to three seminal articles by the legal historian John H. Langbein: 'The Criminal Trial Before the Lawyers', *University of Chicago Law Review* 45 (1978), 263–316; 'Shaping the Eighteenth-Century Criminal Trial: A View from the Ryder Sources', *University of Chicago Law Review* 50 (1983), 1–136; and 'The Historical Origins of the Privilege Against Self-Incrimination at Common Law', *Michigan Law Review* 92 (1993–1994), 1047–1085. For reasons of brevity, these articles are referred to in the text as Langbein I, II, and III respectively. Frequent reference is also made to *Strong Representations: Narrative and Circumstantial Evidence in England* (Baltimore: Johns Hopkins Press, 1992) by Alexander Welsh, and, where possible, page numbers have been included in the text.

Unfortunately, Kieran Dolin's work *Fiction and the Law: Legal Discourse in Victorian and Modernist Literature* (Cambridge University Press, 1999) appeared at too late a stage for Chapter 1 of this text to be able to engage with his arguments.

Definition of legal terms

Throughout the text reference is made to the English Bar, a body of legal practitioners who, on instruction by attornies or solicitors, were able to speak on behalf of lay clients in court. Some of those who practised (either exclusively or in part) in the criminal jurisdiction of the common law courts were nicknamed 'Old Bailey pleaders'. The term 'felony' refers to that class of crime which was regarded as more serious than mere misdemeanours (for example, crimes of violence and crimes against property), which rendered an accused liable to harsh punishment upon conviction. Historically, such penalties included forfeiture of land and goods, and/or capital punishment.

Introduction: justice and the impulse to narrate

The English criminal trial at common law is a fact-finding model which has long been dependent on the testimony of witnesses. Those who give evidence to a common law court have traditionally had to 'be *un oyant et veyant*, a hearer and seer . . . one who could say, as the witnesses to courts in older times always had to say, *quod vidi et audivi*; it must not be testimony at second hand'.[1] The testimonial evidence of the credible eye-witness induces some kind of assent in the minds of the jurors who are to decide upon the facts, an assent which may amount to either 'certainty' or at least the degree of conviction required to acquit or condemn the accused:

A Jury of twelve men are by our laws the only proper Judges of the matter in issue before them. As for instance,
1. That Testimony which is delivered to induce a Jury to believe, or not to believe the matter of Fact in issue, is called in Law EVIDENCE, because thereby the Jury may out of many matters of Fact, *Evidere veritatem*, that is, *see clearly the truth*, of which they are proper Judges.[2]

As Geoffrey Gilbert, author of one of the earliest treatises on evidence in English, has noted, what is at stake in the presentation of competing witness narratives is a claim to the reconstruction of 'reality' itself; in response to the presentation of credible and probative testimony, 'the Mind equally acquiesces therein as on a Knowledge by Demonstration, for it cannot have any more Reason to be doubted than if we ourselves had heard and seen it'.[3]

Hence, the presentation of evidence in a court of law has often served authors of fiction as a coherent and influential model of 'reality', and writers have long imitated the strategies of persuasion privileged by legal forensic methodology. Michael McKeon has rightly implicated the generation of assent in the definition of genre; romance narratives invariably fail to persuade, and '[b]y an easy transference, credulity in the auditor is mendacity in the speaker'.[4]

His approach is also central to this study; he too asks '[w]hat kind of authority or evidence is required of narrative to permit it to signify truth to its readers?'[5] We see these issues well illustrated in Wilkie Collins's analysis of his own impetus to create. In his exploration of the relationship between the case of *R* v. *Palmer* (1856) and the genesis of *The Woman in White*, John Sutherland draws attention to this passage in Nuel Pharr Davis's biography of Collins:[6]

> One day about 1856 [Collins] had found himself at a criminal trial in London. He was struck by the way each witness rose in turn to contribute a personal fragment to the chain of evidence. 'It came to me then . . . that a series of events in a novel would lend themselves to an exposition like this . . . one could impart to the reader that acceptance, that sense of belief, which was produced here by the succession of testimonies . . . The more I thought of it, the more an effort of this kind struck me as bound to succeed. Consequently when the case was over I went home determined to make the effort'.[7]

As a number of critics have pointed out, Collins's assertion that this imitation of the trial format, with its particular emphasis on the presentation of personal testimony, was a new species of writing was at best a little naive. It is more accurate to see Collins as part of a long tradition of English writers, including Daniel Defoe, Samuel Richardson, Henry Fielding, Charles Dickens, and George Eliot, who felt the need to ground their fictional endeavours in the conditions or sanctions which govern the telling of truthful tales in a court of law.

Although legislative provision was made as early as the sixteenth century for the recording of testimony in certain circumstances, for example, in the pre-trial examination of the accused before a magistrate,[8] it is oral evidence – the stories of witnesses – which is of particular significance to English legal procedure.[9] Common law litigious practice was unique in its emphasis upon the presentation of eye-witness testimony at trial, and long-cherished notions of judicial fairness required that the tribunal hear both sides of a dispute before proceeding to judgement. The narratives of those eye-witnesses who could meet certain qualifications of competence and credibility were thus intimately associated with the discovery of facts and the just assessment of action and intent.

An analysis of the relationship between evidence and the generation of assent in courts of law and in acts of reading must examine the role of eye-witnesses in the reporting of an 'event'. Does their act of perception create meaning or does meaning reside in facts external to the witness? The Christian faith, which underpinned Victorian ideas of civilisation and culture, depended upon the reliability of testimonial evidence, and, in the mid-nineteenth century, the impact of German higher criticism rendered the paradigm of the evangelist as eye-witness particularly vulnerable to these competing anxieties. The role of the witness in twentieth-century historiography is well-established; the rise of the news media has produced a journalism obsessed with obtaining access to the true 'facts' of an 'event' and there is a corresponding emphasis on the value of the stories of individual lives told by the participants 'in their own words'. For scholars of testimony, such as Richard Weisberg, Shoshana Felman, and Dori Laub, the current reliance on eye-witness testimony arises in part from responses to the horrors of the Second World War, particularly to the Holocaust. Both Weisberg and Felman see contemporary history as 'an Era of Testimony'; 'testimony has become a crucial mode of our relation to events of our times'.[10] In Elie Weisel's words, '[i]f the Greeks invented tragedy, the Romans the epistle and the Renaissance the sonnet, our generation invented a new literature, that of testimony. We have all been witnesses and we all feel we have to bear testimony for the future'.[11] Scholars of Holocaust literature define testimony in this context in broad terms, to include both factual accounts of war-time atrocities and fictionalised responses which can also 'bear witness' to cultural upheaval and genocide. For Weisberg, the characteristic feature of this post-modern emphasis on individual narrative is its 'tendency to undermine "authoritative" testimony' generated by those in power:

[T]he most prescient story-tellers of our generation . . . were far less sceptical of individual eye-witness accounts than of the manner in which institutional forces ignored, warped and distorted them for their own purposes . . . [I]n the context of our own generation, the eye-witness gains credibility just as the political or institutional or cultural account is precisely devalued.[12]

For Felman and Laub, the Holocaust may be understood as 'a radical historical crisis of witnessing, and as the unprecedented, inconceivable, historical occurrence of "an event without a witness" – an event eliminating its own witness'.[13] The most famous example of this extinction of the voice of the witness is perhaps the conclusion to Anne Frank's *Diary of a Young Girl*; there is no first-person narration of a redemption from her captivity, only the closure wrought by an editor's hand – 'Anne's diary ends here'[14] – which confirms, and is premised on, the silencing of Anne's own voice.

Reliance on testimony thus carries great ethical weight. The narrative of the eye-witness often records the experiences of people expelled from their own communities by those who wield power and privilege. For Paul Ricoeur, as for Weisberg, narrative construction should not shirk issues of ethical responsibility; the impulse to narrate is intimately associated with the lost voices of the oppressed and the disempowered:

> We tell stories because in the last analysis human lives need and merit being narrated. This remark takes on its full force when we refer to the necessity to save the history of the defeated and the lost. The whole history of suffering cries out for vengeance and calls for narrative.[15]

These observations are particularly applicable to the genre of autobiography and the need to document 'real' accounts of individual experience. Autobiographical writing can also testify to the forces or influences which have shaped an author's intellectual life, and there are many examples of such narratives in the period I discuss, such as Fielding's *Journal of a Voyage to Lisbon* (1754) and John Henry Newman's *Apologia pro Vita Sua* (1856). In his *Biographia Literaria* (1817), Samuel Taylor Coleridge attributes the genesis of his exculpatory first-person narrative in part to a response to public criticism, thus associating the generation of testimony with personal trial. And there are many fictional imitations of this form, with its emphasis on the justification of individual action, such as Charlotte Brontë's *Jane Eyre* (1847) or Dickens's *David Copperfield* (1850). In such texts as these, the value of autobiographical testimony as a narrative model is implicit. But third-person narrative (whether 'realistic' or otherwise) may also be said to 'bear witness' to the author's perceptions of his or her era or to his or her own imaginative transfiguration of experience.[16] In fictional texts where formal accusations of guilt are made and subsequently proven or rejected in a legal forum, we see a particular sensitivity to many of the most important epistemological issues of the age. Hence, I focus on narratives where the self-reflexive assessment of the trial format invokes the fictional representation of testimony as a means of proof, not simply as a subjective and unfalsifiable account of an individual's 'life'.

Like its autobiographical counterpart, the representation of testimony in imaginative fiction can also serve to recover evidence of suffering. In *Expulsion and the Nineteenth Century Novel: The Scapegoat in English Realist Fiction*,[17] Michiel Heyns draws attention to the plight of those expelled from the cosy world of Victorian domesticity as a consequence of perceived transgression – such as fallen women, the poor, the insane, or the criminal – and he explores the society against which such scapegoats are defined. The nature of their alleged offence determines whether such scapegoats can be 'rehabilitated'; for some, such as Arthur Donnithorne in *Adam Bede*, reconciliation is possible – at a price – whilst for others, such as Hetty in the same novel, the expulsion is final and complete. In this study I argue that the provision of testimony in nineteenth-century narrative is frequently represented as the voice of the oppressed or persecuted – those accused of crime or on trial for their lives in the work of Henry Fielding, William Godwin, George Eliot or Charles Dickens, or those shunned for their religious convictions in the work of John Henry Newman or Robert Browning.

For this is the essential ambiguity of the term 'testimony' – that it not only encompasses narratives of experience which need lay no immediate claim to issues of truth or falsehood, but that it seeks to be regarded as a species of evidence. Seen as evidence, testimony serves as a vehicle for the attestation of the 'real' because of its roots in ancient notions of legal and religious authority. In his analysis of Augustan attitudes towards the demonstrative knowledge of the high sciences ('*scientia*') and the non-deductive proof of the 'low sciences' (the realm of physico-theology), Douglas Lane Patey has revealed the epistemic foundation of literature's commitment to probabilistic representations.[18] And, as Barbara Shapiro has demonstrated in her detailed studies of seventeenth-century thought, English scientific empiricism and natural philosophy have long regarded the testimony of credible witnesses to the realm of the probable as capable of generating 'fact' or knowledge rather than simply opinion.[19] In legal or religious testimony, the purpose of eye-witness narrative is to persuade the listener of the probable truth or 'moral certainty' of an event, not merely to entertain. The aim of this enquiry is to trace the fictional, legal, and religious antecedents of the contemporary reliance on testimony in narrative and to use imaginative literature to explore the role of eye-witness representations in the proof of 'fact'.

Central to my study is the claim that the representation of

testimony in nineteenth-century English realist fiction is often closely allied to proof of innocence rather than guilt. That Victorian authors felt compelled to prove a protagonist's innocence in the face of unjust accusation places the act of literary construction in a peculiarly symbiotic relationship to legal history, where the emphasis has traditionally been on the proof of guilt. It is arguable that the history of the realist novel is also a history of strategies of acquittal, and later in this study I suggest some reasons why the comparatively late appearance of defence lawyers in trials for felony may have afforded authors the imaginative space to explore narratives of exculpation. This emphasis on acquittal is partly a response to literary convention which required the heroic protagonist to demonstrate his or her innocence of any possible taint of criminal culpability in order to be worthy of the earthly and spiritual rewards invariably conferred by narrative closure. It is also partly a response to the daily administration of justice in the criminal courts which often required some declaration of innocence on the part of the accused if he wished to escape condemnation; in Jeremy Bentham's words, 'innocence claims the right of speaking, as guilt invokes the privilege of silence'.[20]

As legal historians have established, the presumption that the prosecutor bore the burden of proof in a criminal trial emerged during the mid-eighteenth century, but in practice, unless an accused person could adequately explain the evidence marshalled against him or her, s/he was unlikely to be acquitted. This placed the story of accused persons at the heart of the criminal trial and gave the court access to their own descriptions of their own behaviour or their intentions. The legislative expansion of the work of the Bar in the early nineteenth century helped alleviate the injustices of a harsh legal system (which had previously denied full legal representation to those accused of felony), but the gradual appearance of defence counsel created other problems for the representation of just adjudication in narrative. As I discuss in subsequent chapters, the speeches of the lawyers replaced the prisoners' own accounts of events, leaving public opinion (particularly as voiced in the periodical press) suspicious of verdicts founded only on technicalities or on the power of rhetoric divorced from more substantive ideas of truth. Anxieties about the ethics of professional representation also inform fictional texts such as Dickens's *Posthumous Papers of the Pickwick Club* (1837), *Bleak House* (1851), Eliot's *Felix Holt* (1866), Elizabeth Gaskell's

Mary Barton (1848), and Anthony Trollope's *Orley Farm* (1862), and for a time the activities of defence counsel served as the standard against which the moral purposes of realistic literature could be articulated and defined. The testimony of the prisoner enjoys a privileged position in criminal trials at common law as it provides the only direct evidence of the accused's intention at the time an allegedly felonious act was committed. It is thus crucial to the enquiry as to whether or not a particular act merits punishment as a crime – an enquiry of interest to both the courts and authors of fiction – and the novelists were reluctant to follow the courts in the procedural suppression of stories told by represented felons. In nineteenth-century narrative, characters are rarely subject to judgement without the reader being offered their personal testimony of guilt or innocence, and thus realist fiction represents itself as capable of reaching the truths of human behaviour to which the bench was now denied access. To extend the analyses of John Bender and John Zomchick, a prisoner's story is the point of intersection between personal responsibility and public accountability; testimony is important to the representation of the protagonist as a criminal juridical subject because it posits a consistency between criminal responsibility (or the interiority of conscience) and the public act of adjudication, which the law can reach towards but never guar-antee.[21] But there is also a way in which the very emergence of the novel in the eighteenth century can be seen as an imaginative imitation of the lawyers' skills in the manipulation of evidence, and hence the relationship between the two professions remains uncom-fortably ambiguous.

LAW, LITERATURE, AND THE MANIPULATION OF EVIDENCE

Throughout this study, I will be exploring this creative alignment of literature and the laws of criminal evidence. Does fiction follow the law, imitating legal procedure and invoking legal authority for its representations of reality? In many ways, the answer to this question is yes; for example, a number of notorious trials have generated fictional commentary, and authors are often keen to argue that their tales would satisfy tests of evidentiary probity. Like witnesses in a court of law, authors wish to be 'taken at their word'; they are afraid of allegations of perjury and they resist an over-reliance on hearsay material. 'My Lord, this is clearly not evidence', said counsel for the defendant to the bench in respect of certain hearsay material in the famous trial of *Norton* v. *Melbourne* on 22 June 1836,[22] and Charles Dickens was the man who reported the exchange for *The Morning Chronicle.* We see this concern surface in Dickens's later fiction, just as it informs Wilkie Collins's strategies of persuasion in *The Moonstone.* As Gabriel Betteredge states,

I am forbidden to tell more in this narrative than I knew myself at the time . . . In this matter of the Moonstone the plan is, not to present reports, but to produce witnesses. I picture to myself a member of the family reading these pages fifty years hence. Lord! what a compliment he will feel it, to be asked to take nothing on hearsay, and to be treated in all respects like a judge on the bench.[23]

Many commentators have noticed that authors, like lawyers, must be able to argue a case, to master the manipulation of evidence, and the similarities between the construction of fictional and of legal narratives are now well documented. Attention has been drawn to the ways in which narrative closure may be likened to a judicial verdict and it is recognised that the aims and purposes of the criminal trial impact upon narrative form as well as content. As Alexander Welsh has noted, '[t]he trial, which must end in conviction or acquittal, confers the idea of completeness upon that of connectedness',[24] and these qualities are in turn implicated in the construction of realist narrative.

There has been some debate amongst contributors to the 'law and literature movement' whether such similarities are more apparent than real. Richard Posner has argued that 'legal matter in most literature on legal themes is peripheral to the meaning and significance of the literature', and that 'law as depicted in literature is often just a metaphor for something else that is the primary concern of author and reader'.[25] Posner concedes that 'this is in general, not in every case',[26] but he is nevertheless criticised by jurists such as Robin West and Richard Weisberg, both of whom stress the value of literary texts as a medium of jurisprudential debate. They accept that fiction may be preoccupied with legal procedure and the assessment of evidence in a structural and thematic way; indeed, Weisberg suggests that in post-Providential analysis, legality has emerged as 'the controlling principle in modern society'.[27] As a consequence:

[S]erious fiction has never used law as merely a source of satire or even of social criticism. In each period, law has drawn the attention of the literary

artist because of its similarities to narrative art, not its differences. Law's
manner of recreating and discussing reality strikes the artist as close (and
where misguided or erroneous, threateningly close) to what story-tellers
themselves are in the business of doing.[28]

In the period under analysis in this study, it is the legal representation afforded to accused felons which both appeals to, and simultaneously repulses, the authors of realist fiction. The narration of
facts, and the discussion of character and intention in a criminal
court, where the penalty for guilt may be death, did indeed seem to
'strike' such authors as 'threateningly close' to their own activities,
although authors chose to imitate the advocacy of their legal
counterparts as well as to criticise it. A comparison of these
competing yet related strategies of representation reveals, and in
turn depends on, the ethical agenda of both types of discourse. The
role of literature as 'an ethical laboratory where the artist pursues
through the mode of fiction experimentation with values' has been
articulated since ancient times,[29] and both West and Weisberg
presuppose the effectiveness of what Ricoeur calls 'the heuristic
force of fictions' – 'their capacity to open and unfold new dimensions
of reality by means of our suspension of belief in an earlier
description'.[30] C. R. B. Dunlop summarises this type of claim as he
promotes 'the power of literature to move and discomfit the reader
in a way that philosophy or law simply cannot do'.[31] This approach
is somewhat naive; Dunlop's assertion that '[a]fter a lawyer or law
student reads Charles Dickens's *Bleak House*, he can never again be
completely indifferent or "objective" towards the client across the
desk'[32] is both over-generalised (in that the responsiveness of a
reader is neither predictable nor quantifiable) and idealistic (in that,
as West cautions, the complicity of literature with the power
structures which also inform the law may mean that fiction is not
always well placed to redeem or recover the stories of the oppressed).[33] But the assumption that literature can serve as an ethical
supplement to the law receives some support from Ricoeur's belief
that 'the practice of narrative lies in a thought experiment by means
of which we try to inhabit worlds foreign to us'. Thus, 'reading also
includes a moment of impetus' and 'becomes a provocation to be
and to act differently'.[34]

But if the narrative arts of authors and barristers are closely
related, it must also be acknowledged that, in other ways, fiction is
shaped by its very dissimilarity to the act of adjudication. As West

has observed '[t]he analogy of law to literature . . . although fruitful', confuses textual interpretation with acts of imperative power imposed by the courts.[35] The criminal trial has a purpose (to find facts and to determine guilt according to certain established standards of proof) and a concomitant power to impose state-enforced sanctions in the event of a finding of culpability. This purpose and power cannot be separated from other more narrative-oriented aspects of trial procedure; it alters, for example, the act of reading a criminal statute or of composing a statement of facts or a plea of guilty. This is not to deny that interpretative communities wield some power in preferring one reading of a text over another,[36] but it is usually in the law that the perpetrators of such exclusory readings are most equipped to enforce their judgements with the penal powers of the state. Authors of fiction also respond to this sense of the law's distinctness; for example, a number of narratives begin where the laws of evidence define a piece of information as relevant to the cause in hand, but inadmissible, or obtainable only by paralegal means, and the resolution of many a narrative lies in the fact that, for all its indebtedness to the evidence-based generation of assent, the novel is not a trial. Authors are thus liberated by artistic licence to snatch a protagonist from the gallows, to reverse judgements at will or to act on the basis of information which would not have been available to a court. The exclusionary rules of evidence in force in England in the early nineteenth century, which impacted upon both witness competence and the admissibility of evidence, provided much material for criticism in the press. If this witness had been allowed to give evidence, what would he or she have said? If this piece of evidence had been available to the jury, would they have reached a different decision? It is equally arguable that authors of fiction share this interest in what falls outside the law, that they somehow require a legal lacuna in order to find their own imaginative space in which to pursue their own quest for justice.

Hence, law and literature circle warily around their representations of each other's discourses, leaving authors to construct an image of their own ethical activities from their opposition to the work of lawyers as well as from a sense of their shared role as culturally-preferred story-tellers. Often authors choose to engage with, and manoeuvre around, the public power of legal discourse in order to find a legitimate space for their tale. This reading is perhaps to concede that the law had certain institutionalised advantages in its claims to the privileged presentation of 'reality' – the antiquity of its practices, the wealth and respect attached to the court system by the state, the self-interested professionalism of its exponents and, in the public sphere, the power to punish the authors of certain narratives deemed illegal or offensive, as studies of the laws of blasphemy and libel have revealed.[37] Jonathan Grossman has argued that the quest of fictional authors for status and respectability in the early nineteenth century necessarily entailed a confrontation with the other profession which placed rhetoric in the service of profit – that it is no coincidence that Charles Dickens had to depict (and, I would argue, discredit) – the activities of lawyers in his first novel (*The Posthumous Papers of the Pickwick Club*) in order to make the requisite space for his own fictional endeavours.[38] Coral Lansbury sees formal techniques of legal pleading employed as a similar creative foil in the works of Trollope,[39] and R. D. McMaster has also drawn attention to Trollope's interest in the history and satirical analysis of forensic advocacy.[40] And I believe that this creative engagement – between the forensic advocacy of the courtroom and the narrative advocacy of fiction – influenced not only the ways in which authors conceived of their professional standing, but also the very material that they chose to address in their narratives and the formal way in which such material was rendered.

It is a common fictional device for an author to explain why his or her tale could not be heard in a court of law or why the protagonists were seeking literary recognition rather than a judicial remedy. For example, the alternative narrative presentation of the plot of *Clarissa* is the prosecution of Lovelace on a charge of rape in a court of law; Richardson draws upon evidentiary procedure whilst discarding the legal option (and hence the male-dominated, public gaze of the courtroom) as a viable vehicle for the treatment of his heroine's tale. Clarissa is too modest and too charitable to prosecute Lovelace in public, freeing Richardson to act as advocate for the Crown in revealing and punishing his villain's perfidy. And the providential resolutions of a number of works rely upon the recovery of paralegal evidence, a technique which must invoke the law and simultaneously reveal it as flawed. Perhaps the clearest example of this ambiguity is to be found at the very beginning of Collins's *The Woman in White* (1860). The text opens with a declaration that the evidence which its story contains would satisfy a Court of Law – '[a]s the Judge might once have heard it, so the Reader shall hear it now. No circumstance

of importance, from the beginning to the end of the disclosure, shall
be related on hearsay evidence'[41] – and hence its narrative form is
intimately associated with forensic techniques of persuasion and
conviction. Each character can only 'speak to the circumstances
under notice from their own knowledge':

> Thus the story here presented will be told by more than one pen, as the
> story of an offence against the laws is told in Court by more than one
> witness – with the same object, in both cases, to present the truth always in
> its most direct and most intelligible aspect; and to trace the course of one
> complete series of events, by making the persons who have been most
> closely connected with them, at each successive stage, relate their own
> experience, word for word. (p. 5)

But, as Victor Sage has noted, *The Woman in White* reveals a
paradoxical attitude to the role of evidence in the discovery of
truth.[42] More than that, the *telos* of the plot is generated by its very
dissimilarity to a trial; the conception of law as foil in turn liberates
fiction to pursue its own idea of justice. For, unlike the discourse of
law which is characterised as untrustworthy because it remains 'the
pre-engaged servant of the long purse', the language of fiction is
independent and enquiring (p. 5). So the narrative is indebted to the
techniques of the courtroom, but also to the very limitations of the
law; for this tale can only be told in fiction when the law has refused
to claim it as her own.

The Woman in White thus seeks to achieve the restitution of Laura
Fairlie's lost identity by paralegal means. When Walter Hartright
places all the evidence he has collated before the family's lawyer, Mr
Kyrle, he is told that he has 'not the shadow of a case' (p. 450). Mr
Kyrle argues that he has no proofs suitable to go before a jury and
Hartright concedes that 'the facts appear to tell against us' (p. 451):

> 'But you think those facts can be explained away', interposed Mr Kyrle.
> 'Let me tell you the result of my experience on that point. When an English
> jury has to choose between a plain fact, on the surface, and a long
> explanation under the surface, it always takes the fact, in preference to the
> explanation. For example, Lady Glyde (I call the lady you represent by that
> name for argument's sake) declares she has slept at a certain house, and it is
> proved that she has not slept at that house. You explain this circumstance
> by entering into the state of her mind, and deducing from it a metaphysical
> conclusion. I don't say the conclusion is wrong – I only say that the jury
> will take the fact of her contradicting herself, in preference to any other
> reason for the contradiction that you can offer' (p. 452)

The jury of laymen in a common law trial is seen to be suspicious of careful reasoning, preferring instead the plain fact which 'speaks for itself' and which requires no act of interpretation to serve as a clear and effective piece of evidence. This is a deliberate misrepresentation or simplification of Victorian forensic analysis, formulated to enhance the ethical profile of the novel which can then lay claim to a more sophisticated ability to unravel secret truths: it also suggests the naivety of laymen in comparison to the careful inductive practices of legal (and by implication) literary professionals.[43] At the same time, however, the standard of proof which Hartright must satisfy is that which would be operative in a contemporary court of law. When all the testimonial narratives are collated, they can be endorsed by the legally-trained Mr Kyrle – he 'declared, as the legal adviser of the family, that [their] case was proved by the plainest evidence he had ever heard in his life' (p. 635). For Hartright, poverty had effected his salvation by forcing him to act for himself, to assert his agency in the face of the law's impotence and to refuse to abdicate his responsibilities to the lawyers who professionalise and weaken moral discourse (p. 636). This ambiguity both venerates the law as the established discourse of justice and suggests the role of fiction in the resolution of hard cases which lie outside the ambit of usual trial procedure. In this way fiction launches a half-hearted critique of law's evidentiary blindnesses; on the one hand, the perceived limitations of the administration of justice are revealed to the scrutiny of the reader (e.g. the law serves those who are rich, and legal procedure could not have generated the evidence which was required to see justice done), but at the same time the narrative affirms unproblematically the law's indebtedness to a patriarchal value system which marginalises Laura's own story and enables an indignantly protective male to recover her identity for her.

If law and prose narrative in the late eighteenth and early nineteenth centuries saw themselves as competing for the right to provide an authoritative account of the 'facts' of an event, the question must be asked 'what did authors see fiction bringing to the task that the law could not?', a question which implicates not only the authors' conception of their own role as ethical commentators but which also acknowledges the subjectivity of their representations of the law. For example, both William Thackeray's Arthur Pendennis and Dickens's David Copperfield represent the law in utilitarian, reductionist terms in order to confirm their own 'higher' calling to the work of journalism or creative authorship. In the *History of Pendennis*

(1848–1850) the protagonist and his friend Warrington share chambers in the Temple with a diligent law student called Paley:

[Paley] has not been throwing himself away: he has only been bringing a great intellect laboriously down to the comprehension of a mean subject, and in his fierce grasp of that, resolutely excluding from his mind all higher thoughts, all better things, all the wisdom of philosophers and historians, all the thoughts of poets; all wit, fancy, reflection, art, love, truth altogether – so that he may master that enormous legend of the law, which he proposes to gain his livelihood by expounding. . . . He could not cultivate a friendship or do a charity, or admire a work of genius, or kindle at the sight of beauty or the sound of a sweet song – he had no time, and no eyes for anything but his law-books. All was dark outside his reading-lamp. Love, and Nature, and Art (which is the expression of our praise and sense of the beautiful world of God) were shut out from him.[44]

On the other hand 'the man of letters can't but love the place [the Temple] which has been inhabited by so many of his brethren, or peopled by their creations as real to us at this day as the authors whose children they were'; in the narrator's nostalgic memory, Samuel Johnson and Henry Fielding share pride of place with Sir Roger de Coverley and Mr Spectator.[45] 'Gradgrindian', mechanistic fact is thus opposed to sensitive imaginative fancy. But the promulgation of this binary model of utilitarian law and creative perception was not disinterested, and whilst authors claimed to be monitoring the morality of the legal profession they were also exploring their own progress towards salaried self-sufficiency and social respect. Hence, it is no surprise that criticism of the Bar intensified during the so-called 'War between the Bar and the Press' which erupted in 1845 when two regional disciplinary bodies of the Bar (the Oxford and Western Circuits) prohibited their members from reporting for the newspapers. Albany Fonblanque's *Examiner* responded by castigating the false pride of the Bar, thus betraying in turn the offended honour of the press as a consequence of this perceived snub.[46] In such circumstances, it was convenient to allege that barristers were little better than thieves, that they suppressed true evidence and generated false evidence in the service of their client, that lawyers were effectively (and etymologically) 'liars' who would say anything for a fee. Perhaps so too would professional writers, those who created imaginative works loosely grounded on 'real' trials to meet the public demand for endless accounts of genuine crimes and executions (which was in turn generated by the press and their predecessors, the authors of criminal broadsheets and biographies).[47] Such incestuous generic interdependence prompted combative statements of ethical intent. Authors could claim that fiction represented a higher court of appeal than the Old Bailey; journalists could assert that newspapers exposed all relevant evidence to the gaze of public opinion; and in response, lawyers could argue that writers were irresponsible in their treatment of evidence – that they were prepared to exaggerate procedural injustice in the interests of a good story or a sentimental plot.

What fiction sought to claim as its own, what it saw as marginalised by the post-enlightenment, scientific language of the common law, was emotion, the discourse of passion and of bodily sensation.[48] Time and time again in Victorian fiction we see the law ridiculed for its reductionism, for its legalese, for its callous failure to acknowledge that behind the language of rights, duties, and sanctions lies a seething world of emotional turmoil and physical experience which defies easy categorisation or description. These defects of the law are identified by authors with enthusiasm; the legal profession's semiotic weaknesses legitimise the authors' own representations of the 'real'. Law and literature thus seem to be grappling for the right to represent most truthfully whatever 'fact' is in contention in a given case or to construe most accurately the 'identity' of parties to a cause. The law adopts the ritualised discourse of rights and, as John Barrell and Peter Goodrich have suggested, it seeks to silence any competing discourse which would threaten its strategies of representation.[49] Goodrich in particular has sought to uncover the texts which lie hidden in the silences of the law, and he questions the self-evident authority of the law to repress other representations of the 'real'. Goodrich then seeks to 'listen to what [law] does not wish to address . . . to attend to the slight indications, the symptoms or lapses, which hide that which law seeks to forget'.[50] In a sense this study also proceeds in the interstices of fiction's debt to the authority of the law and its ambivalent, ambiguous critique of the law's exclusionary powers. We can identify specific Victorian anxieties about the techniques of repression deployed by the law, such as its self-arrogated power to define the relevancy of the facts in issue and to reject those which it deems irrelevant, its refusal to consider evidence which is inadmissible, either because the witness is incompetent to give it or because the evidence is itself 'flawed', and finally its choice to ignore issues of policy behind the enactment of existing laws or the need for reform. And fictional narrative can thus represent itself as providing for the exploration of the repressed material. An example of this combative delimitation of discourse is the legal approach to death or bodily suffering,[51] as, for example, in Richardson's *Clarissa* (1747–1748). Here, Lovelace salaciously reads a licence for pre-marital sexual conquest into the business document which contains the terms of his marriage settlement:

I offered to read to [Clarissa] the old deed while she looked over the draft; for she had refused her presence at the examination with the clerk: but this she also declined.

I suppose she did not care to hear of so many children, first, second, third, fourth, fifth, sixth, and seventh sons, and as many daughters, *to be begotten upon the body of the said Clarissa Harlowe.*

Charming matrimonial recitativoes! – Though it is always said *lawfully begotten* too – as if a man could beget children *unlawfully* upon the body of his own wife – But thinkest thou not that these arch rogues the lawyers hereby intimate, that a man may have children by his wife *before* marriage? – This must be what they mean. Why will these sly fellows put an honest man in mind of such rogueries?[52]

Dickens bequeaths to us a memorable expression of this experiential division as he ponders the bodily incarceration of impoverished debtors to Chancery in *The Posthumous Papers of the Pickwick Club* (1837): 'The body! It is the lawyer's term for the restless whirling mass of cares and anxieties, affections, hopes, and griefs, that make up the living man.'[53] In *The Woman in White*, Fosco suggests to Percival Glyde that it is but a short step from the cold legal language of testamentary contingencies to the contemplation of murder; ' "I speak of your wife's death as I speak of a possibility. Why not? The respectable lawyers who scribble-scrabble your deeds and your wills, look the deaths of living people in the face. Do lawyers make your flesh creep? Why should I?" ' (p. 334). Given the choice that Fosco posits for Laura – either she signs her fortune over to Glyde or she discharges his debts with her death – to adopt the terminology of the law is to quash the emotional and the sensate, to normalise murder and the extinction of the self.

So, one preoccupation of this study is narrative treatment of testimony and the ways in which lawyers and authors manipulate this evidence in the competition to provide an authoritative reading of events. The legal interrogation of witnesses tests certain empirical conclusions and assumptions which authors can also draw on in their representations of the 'real', but equally significant in the English history of ideas is the Christian belief that testimony can reach to the divine, to the supernaturally 'real' or absolute. There is a rich literary tradition which seeks to draw on the derivation of the word 'witness' from its Greek root 'martyr', and the idea of the privileged role of the eye-witness in the discovery of truth in criminal matters was closely allied to Protestant beliefs and methods of enquiry. Critical exploration of the knowledge of eye-witnesses was important to theological as well as legal investigation; in the period I address, the legitimate scope of a witness's testimony was a topic of debate for jurists and theologians alike, and the contentious status of testimony illuminates cross-disciplinary issues of epistemology and religion as well as courtroom advocacy. To what extent was the representation of eye-witness testimony in fictional narratives affected by developments in religious and jurisprudential thought? This turns on the exploration of two inter-related issues. Who can be a witness of the truth in religious or legal investigations? And once those initial qualifications of competence are established, what are the limits of a witness's licence to speak? It seems that shifts in the idea of evidence interacted with metaphors and methods in fiction as authors engaged with contemporary changes in religious and legal thought.

FICTION AND THE REPRESENTATION OF LAW AND RELIGION

The fiction of each generation inevitably absorbed changing interpretative strategies as authors experimented with new representations of the 'real' or the absolute. The central issue for the author, the jurist, and the theologian was the limits of man's knowledge; fiction provided a medium for the exploration of issues of proof and moral certainty. All were concerned with the demarcation between questions of faith and questions of reason, and the extent to which language can convey apprehensions of the 'real' or the 'infinite'. That this was an important debate of mid-Victorian times can be seen in the contrasting theories of Henry Mansel and Benjamin Jowett. In the Preface to his Bampton Lectures of 1858, Mansel cites with approval Professor Fraser's observation that ' "the theological struggle of this age, in all its more important phases, turns upon the philosophical problem of the limits of knowledge and the true theory of human ignorance" '.[54] Adopting the cautious tones of Bishop

Joseph Butler's *Analogy of Religion* which stressed man's incapacity to
judge the fitness of revelation, Mansel argues that all attempts to
conceive of the absolute (either mystically or rationally) must fail;
and without a philosophy of the absolute, '[t]here can be no such
thing as a Speculative theology'. Revelation, then, 'represents the
infinite God under finite symbols, in condescension to the finite
capacity of man', and 'the legitimate object of a rational criticism of
revealed religion is not to be found in the *contents* of that religion, but
in its *evidences*'.[55] Jowett, on the other hand, conceded the imprecision of language (and '[r]eligion cannot place itself above the
instrument through which alone it speaks to man'),[56] but he
maintains that 'it does not follow, if we acknowledge the limits of
human faculties, that our ideas of spiritual things become wholly
indefinite. There are many symbols and images of them in the world
without and below. There is a communion of thoughts, feelings, and
affections, even on earth, quite sufficient to be an image of the
communion with God and Christ.'[57] For both men, the central
symbol or reality is the incarnation, the *logos* made flesh, and again
the nature of representation (of God in Christ and of Christ in
language) is crucial to the debate.

   The linguistic representation of religious experience stretches the
frontiers of fiction; as examples, we need only think of the conclusion
to Charles Kingsley's *Alton Locke* (1850), *Hypatia* (1853), or to John
Henry Newman's *Loss and Gain* (1848) where attempts to represent
the divine dissolve into the language of myth, hagiography, or the
realm of 'as-if' which is central to the creative act of fictional
invention. On his admission to the Roman Catholic Church, the
protagonist of *Loss and Gain* adopts the Patriarchal affirmation that
he has seen the face of God, but the reader's glimpse of the divine is
mediated by the imaginative role of metaphor: 'It was such as to
throw him back in memory on his earliest years, *as if* he were really
beginning life again . . . He went on kneeling, *as if* he were already
in heaven, with the throne of God before him, and Angels around;
and *as if* to move were to lose his privilege.'[58] As Ricoeur notes, this
is crucial to the construction of fictional narrative – '[a]rtisans who
work with words produce not things but quasi-things; they invent the
as-if'[59] – and hence religious fiction becomes emblematic of the
creative act itself. Both the theologian and the novelist deal with the
representation of things unseen as well as seen, although the former
is constrained by the authority (and truth-telling claims) of the

scriptural texts in a more rigid manner than the literary texts of the past constrain the latter. To represent is, after all, 'to make present that which is absent,'[60] and the hermeneutics of adjudication also involve the representation of things not seen by the bench or the legal representatives; they are what Barbara Shapiro has called 'second-level fact evaluator[s]', dependent upon the presentation of evidence given by others for the construction of a coherent narrative of the events at issue.[61] On many occasions, the lawyers and the court have direct and controlled access to the stories of those contesting the facts in dispute, but in the absence of eye-witness testimony or admissions from the parties, the court may have to base its verdict on inferences drawn from circumstantial or 'indirect' evidence of a subsidiary fact to the existence of the main fact in issue.

INFERENCE AND NARRATIVE

It is Alexander Welsh who has argued most incisively for the critical engagement of legal and literary models of representation. In his recent text *Strong Representations*, he argues that 'strong representations, which make the facts speak for themselves . . . became the single most prominent form of narrative in the later eighteenth and nineteenth centuries'. He asserts that '[i]n this period, narrative consisting of carefully managed circumstantial evidence, highly conclusive in itself and often scornful of direct testimony, flourished nearly everywhere – not only in literature but in criminal jurisprudence, natural science, natural theology and history writing itself' (p. ix). His inspirational research on the role of inference in the elucidation of fact (in cases where eye-witness evidence was not available) has opened up new fields of interdisciplinary enquiry. His interest in what he calls (speaking of Fielding) 'the evidentiary basis of . . . realism' (p. 49) has served as the point of departure for my own study. However, Welsh's analysis poses two problems. Firstly, although there may have been popular enthusiasm in the public imagination for any piece of evidence which tended to ensure the prosecution of criminals, the distinction between testimony and circumstantial evidence is somewhat misleading. If circumstantial evidence is defined as evidence of a subsidiary fact from which the existence of the primary fact may be inferred, then testimony serves as the vehicle by which all such evidence is presented to the court.

Both require inference and interpretation to attest their probative value. Welsh argues that circumstantial evidence was 'free from human deliberation at the point of origin', with ambiguities confined to later interpretation (p. 7). This has some validity, but Welsh seems to ignore the fact that most circumstantial evidence is presented to the court in testimonial form. If 'I saw a crime committed' is direct eye-witness evidence, then telling the jury 'I saw a footprint outside the house' remains an oral assertion, even though it relates only to a subsidiary fact in issue from which the existence of the main fact (the crime) may be inferred. Hence, if testimony as to the main fact can be criticised as incomplete or misleading, then so can the testimonial presentation of circumstantial evidence. One exception may be the presentation of any real evidence which can be tendered to the court, such as a murder weapon or forensic samples found at the scene, but this too would require assertions as to its significance – where it was found, who found it, and how was it preserved in the interim. Thus it is difficult to escape from the essential orality of English courtroom procedure.

I have one further criticism of Welsh's analysis. The late eighteenth-century idea of 'facts speaking for themselves' became increasingly discredited as both lawyers and authors realised that professional representations were required to render 'facts' effective as pieces of evidence. Whilst Welsh acknowledges the rhetorical effort involved in making 'facts speak for themselves', he seems to posit something of a seamless continuity between the eighteenth-century notion that 'circumstances cannot lie' and the complicated construc-tion of inferential argument which both lawyers and authors demon-strated as the nineteenth century began. Patey argues that inferential reasoning from signs appeared in the works of physicians and theologians at an earlier date: hence the distinction between a preference for plain fact and an appreciation that all facts require interpretation may be explained in terms of contrasting lay and professional approaches to induction.[62] The criminal trial before a jury juxtaposes both elements.[63] And despite Patey's chronology of inferential development, there is a sense in which such discourse arrived belatedly in the common law courts. Hence, there is an elision in Welsh's argument which appears to disguise a genuine paradig-matic shift in the representation of fact itself in courts of law in the early decades of the nineteenth century. The idea that a fact could 'speak for itself' was anti-hermeneutic in nature, denying any space for professional representations either by lawyers or authors. To concede that facts were complex rather than self-evident was to open the way for legal and literary feats of analysis and rhetorical power. So, instead of adopting a binary model of testimony in opposition to circumstantial evidence (of rhetoric in opposition to scientific method), it is perhaps more accurate to argue that testimony was co-opted to serve in the proof of facts which were increasingly seen as multi-faceted and open to professional manipulation.

Consequently, I argue that the efforts made throughout the early nineteenth century to expand categories of witness competence and to test a story more effectively by an increasing emphasis on cross-examination kept testimony at the forefront of a court's strategies of proof. The model of the criminal trial remained that of the presentation of the admissible elements of various stories to a judge and jury, who would adjudicate upon the evidence and pronounce a verdict and sanction. Prominent legal historians such as John Langbein and Stephan Landsman see the late eighteenth century as a time when non-political criminal trial procedure depended on what Langbein calls the 'accused speaks' theory of the trial, with the assumption that the prisoner served as the court's 'primary testimonial resource', and I base my argument on this model,[64] exploring fictional cases where testimony to the main facts is available and where the acts of perception and interpretation are themselves at stake.

The analysis of types of proof in fictional narratives is vulnerable to the observation that all fictional representation – of material facts or of testimonial evidence – is a form of hearsay evidence; the 'characters' are not real individuals and we are asked to take the representation of their speech and behaviour 'on the author's word'. In this sense, the narrator's reports of the behaviour of Tom Jones, the rumours which surround the Transome family in *Felix Holt*, and the letters of Clarissa which both record her words and yet attest her physical absence, are all alike and indistinguishable as products of the author's inventiveness. Yet, once we enter the world of the narrative and accept as a valid representation of the 'actual' the action and the characters we encounter there, we see that we are invited to compare the qualities of the evidence brought before us, to test its reliability and to judge the actions of the protagonists accordingly.[65] In this study I argue that the first-person speech of the protagonists is crucial to any assent which we make to the realm of the fictional and its claim to the promotion of an ethical agenda. To study the status of first-person testimonial statements in fictional trials is to analyse what it means to be 'taken at one's word', an engagement or trust which goes to the heart of the act of narrative construction itself.

Welsh seems to invest testimony with value only where it assumes the form of a personal 'story of experience' which does not require verification for its interest to the reader (ch. 5). Welsh has less sympathy for the Newman-like belief in testimony as a reliable vehicle for the transmission of religious truth, and he claims that the third-person realist narratives, which manipulate evidence to accuse and then acquit the hero, are again a product of the rise of the paradigm of circumstantial evidence (p. 48). In contrast, I argue that testimony remains a means of proof – not simply an expression of opinion – and that first-person statements of intention and motive on the part of the protagonists are essential to the representation of justice and judgement in third-person fictional narrative. The opposition is not one between fact and opinion as posited by Welsh, but rather a study of the ways in which testimonial declarations are appropriated to serve in the proof of fact.[66] The central motif of this study is that of the martyr on trial for her life because of her beliefs, a dilemma which pits issues of faith and revelation against the rule-bound methodologies of the courtroom and which, in *Callista* and *Romola*, for example, elicits a witnessing to, or an attestation of, a higher truth. This raises questions about how the absolute can be 'seen' or apprehended by the believer. It also draws attention to that which testimony cannot reach, to the grammatical ellipses or hesitant spaces between words (or beyond knowledge) which may be partly glossed over by the confidence with which testimony to the 'real' or the absolute can be presented. To speak involves an ethical choice. Perhaps silence, rather than false testimony, is the converse of the choice to speak truthfully of one's encounter with the 'real' or the divine.[67]

These, then, are some of the issues that have impacted upon my treatment of testimony in the era under discussion. In the first chapter of this study, I consider the close relationship between law and Anglican orthodoxy in the eighteenth century and I explore the role of the oath as a guarantee of testimonial veracity. I then set the higher critics' rejection of the eye-witness status of the gospel narratives alongside the law's increasing expansion of the categories of competent witnesses, and assess how changing theological ideas of evidence impacted upon certain aspects of the legal process. I also provide an explanation of changes in the format of the legal trial in the eighteenth and early nineteenth centuries which serves as a foundation for the subsequent textual discussion. In the early modern criminal trial, belief in a protagonist's innocence was ideally generated by the delivery of 'artless' and sincere speeches in both courts of law and in works of fiction, but the (actual and perhaps anticipated) appearance of defence lawyers began to alter this, and in Chapter 2 I provide a brief analysis of *Tom Jones, Amelia, Clarissa, Caleb Williams,* and *The Heart of Midlothian* in order to assess more effectively how these paradigms of persuasion and proof were to impact upon the development of the great mid-Victorian realist narratives. Chapter 3 is devoted to the advent of full legal representation for felons and its implications for the construction of narrative in the works of Charles Dickens, George Eliot, and Anthony Trollope. I examine both the effect of criminal lawyers on the court's access to a prisoner's story and the extent to which an advocate could then assume the client's right to speak. I argue that the availability of legal representation (to prisoners who could afford it) posed a substantial threat to the status of the accused as the 'primary testimonial resource' (in Langbein's phrase) and that Dickens and Eliot demonstrated significant ethical reservations about the newer theory of the trial which replaced it. Chapter 4 deals with the representation in fiction of the martyr as witness and examines how the alleged availability of direct inspiration to believers on trial for their lives became a point of conflict for competing hermeneutic paradigms. In Newman's writings, in particular, we see a retreat from the evidence-bound methodologies of the courtroom which enables us to explore the historical contingency of the Victorian commitment to proof-based belief. Finally, the Conclusion asks whether legal standards are the only test of truth and seeks to explain why the criminal trial became such an important fact-finding model for authors. I conclude that the rise of the third-person realist novel is simultaneously in imitation of, and in reaction against, the increasing prominence of the activities of defence counsel. Their competition with authors for the most truthful representation of the 'real' ensured that testimony remained a focal point for the expression and attempted resolution of many of the era's most persistent epistemological anxieties.

CHAPTER I

Eye-witness testimony and the construction of narrative

> You have had a long and a fair trial, and sorry I am that it falls to my lot to acquaint you, that I am now no more at liberty to suppose you innocent, than I was before to presume you guilty.
>
> What views you had, or what was your intention, is best known to yourself: With God and your own conscience be it. At this bar, we can judge only from appearances, and from the evidence produced to us: But do not deceive yourself; remember you are very shortly to appear before a much more awful tribunal, where no subterfuge can avail; no art, no disguise can screen you from the Searcher of all hearts: 'he revealeth the deep and secret things, he knoweth what is in the darkness, and the light dwelleth with him'.
>
> Mr Baron Legge, in *R* v. *Blandy* (1752) 18 *State Trials* 1118, at 1188.

As he condemned Mary Blandy to the gallows for the murder of her father, Baron Legge stressed the inherent limitations of earthly justice. Without direct access to God's unmediated knowledge of 'reality', the jury had to decide her fate on the basis of evidence which enabled the court to construe an 'appearance of fact'. Baron Legge noted the disparity between the 'real' and the seemingly real – in the absence of her confession of intent, inferences could only be drawn from external sources of information, but the latter may nevertheless be sufficient to produce assent and conviction in the minds of the jurors. That the jury chose to disregard her protestations of innocence and condemn her to death on the basis of other evidence ensures that Blandy's trial remains relevant to a study of competing evidentiary paradigms in the eighteenth century.

In his enormously influential account of the origins of the realist novel, Ian Watt compared strategies of fictional representation with the activities of the adjudicators in a trial at common law. This passage is well known, but as it forms a point of departure for my subsequent discussion of testimonial evidence, it is worth citing at length:

The novel's mode of imitating reality may . . . be equally well summarised in terms of the procedures of another group of specialists in epistemology, the jury in a court of law. Their expectations, and those of the novel reader coincide in many ways: both want to know 'all the particulars' of a given case – the time and place of the occurrence; both must be satisfied as to the identities of the parties concerned, and will refuse to accept evidence about anyone called Sir Toby Belch or Mr. Badman – still less about a Chloe who has no surname and is 'common as the air'; and they also expect the witnesses to tell the story 'in his own words'. The jury in fact takes the 'circumstantial view of life', which T. H. Green found to be the characteristic outlook of the novel.[1]

In his article entitled 'An Estimate of the Value and Influence of Works of Fiction in Modern Times', T. H. Green had sought to compare the relative merits of the epic poem, the drama and the novel. He noted:

The novel, [unlike tragedy], starts from the outside. Its main texture is a web of incidents through which the motions of the spirit must be discerned, if discerned at all. These incidents must be probable, must be such as are consistent with the observed sequences of the world . . . Observation shows us man not as self-determined, but as the creature of circumstances, as a phenomenon among other phenomena . . . As circumstances make his life what it is, so the particular combination of circumstances called happiness, constitutes its end.[2]

In Green's analysis, 'the circumstantial view of life' fostered by narrative fiction fails to inspire or to educate; instead, it sentimenta-lises the mundane, the trivial, and recommends a timid and selfish morality of 'prudence' in place of more visionary ideas of duty. Whilst the thrust of this criticism was ethical, later critics such as Alexander Welsh have realised the significance of Green's reading for an appraisal of the inter-relationship of fictional narrative and different types of evidence, such as the testimonial statement (which is privileged for the direct access it is seen to provide to intention and personal belief) and the external appearance of fact which Welsh equates with the nascent doctrine of circumstantial evidence in criminal legal procedure.

Watt's analysis emphasised the act of reading and the role of the jury in the process of judgement, and thus he chose not to pursue a closer reading of evidentiary strategies. But his seminal observations have stimulated a number of subsequent studies which examine other aspects of judicial procedure and fictional construction, such as the conception of the literary character as juridical subject and

the effect of fictional omniscience on ideas of moral development
and the redemptive goals of incarceration.[3] Of more immediate
relevance to this study, however, are Douglas Patey's, Barbara
Shapiro's, and Steven Shapin's influential explorations of early
modern conceptions of evidence, probability, and proof,[4] and
Michael McKeon's comprehensive analysis of the emergence of the
realist genre in *The Origins of the English Novel 1600–1740*. All posit
close associations between empiricist standards of proof and the
generation of assent in the construction of fictional narratives and all
are, in a sense, intrigued by Watt's awareness of the historically
conditioned definition of evidence itself; '[f]ormal realism is, of
course, like the rules of evidence, only a convention; and there is no
reason why the report on human life which is presented by it should
be in fact any truer than those presented through the very different
conventions of other literary genres'.[5] So why were English theology,
science, and law preoccupied with weighing proof, finding facts and
ascertaining the reliability of witnesses? In *Probability and Literary Form*
and in *Probability and Certainty in Seventeenth-Century England*, Patey and
Shapiro suggest that each field owed much to the post-Renaissance
replacement of the philosophical quest for absolute certainty with
the understanding that human knowledge was invariably restricted
to the realm of the 'probable', to a reading of 'appearances' rather
than essential forms, or to the Baconian idea of sensory evidence.[6]
The 'probable' could be used to generate an assent to facts which
amounted to moral certainty sufficient for the exercise of choice or
the formation of Christian belief. To explore the indebtedness of
realist fiction to the rules of evidence is thus to acknowledge the
interdisciplinary reliance on the evidence of the senses characteristic
of early modern English thought.

Intellectual historians such as Shapin and Shapiro place the
activities of the members of the Royal Society at the heart of
seventeenth-century changes in scientific and religious epistemology.
In Shapin's analysis, the Royal Society 'repeatedly insisted upon the
insufficiency of authoritative texts and upon the careful inspection of
testimony' and its motto 'Nullius in verba (on no man's word) . . .
crystallized members' insistence upon the problematic status of
testimony and the epistemic virtues of direct individual experience
and individual reason in the constitution of genuine knowledge'. Yet,
as Shapin emphasises, in actuality this 'individualistic rhetoric . . .
would count as a massive misrepresentation of scientific practice'

and many members 'also displayed keen appreciation that there was a proper, valuable, and ineradicable role for testimony and trust within legitimate empirical practices'.[7] I will discuss the philosophy which tied creditworthiness and truth-telling in testimony to issues of honour and gentility of class in Chapter 2. For the moment it is sufficient to note the common preoccupations of the natural philosophers, the Christian apologists, and the courts, all of whom sought to assess testimony which 'fell somewhere short of absolute plausibility'.[8] As noted in the introduction, testimony was not so much opposed to knowledge of circumstances as co-opted to serve as proof of fact. Shapiro has suggested that the concept of 'fact' which was to preoccupy both natural philosophers and divines in subsequent centuries was in turn derived from jurisprudential insistence on the distinction between matters of fact, which were decided by the jury in a common law trial, and matters of law, which lay within the adjudicatory powers of the judge alone. Hence, questions of 'fact' were placed within the realm of the thoughtful layman, and '[c]onfidence in the jury system thus contributed to the general feeling that the average independent person was capable of determining questions of fact in institutional settings with the appropriate safeguards'.[9]

Despite St Paul's assertion that 'faith is the confidence of things hoped for, the conviction of things not seen',[10] early modern theology also became preoccupied with proof of the visible fact; as Shapiro observes, the need to respond to both Catholic conceptions of infallibility and to the scepticism of the atheists 'led the rational theologians to elaborate a religious epistemology that reinforced and in part shaped the more general epistemology of Locke, Boyle, and the Royal Society'.[11] McKeon notes the interpretative consequences of this approach: '[c]ontemporaries certainly understood that the exegetical commitment to "one sense of Scripture, the literal sense", was informed by a commitment to the evidence of the senses':

The celebrated 'plain speaking' of Puritan 'mechanick preaching' therefore consisted not in any paucity of figures but in a richness of reference to the plain things of this world, whose very proximity seemed to facilitate a spiritual pedagogy . . . Protestant belief became so intertwined with the evidence of the senses that in the end the truth of Scripture itself seemed to require vindication as the truth of 'true history'.[12]

Increasingly religion too was seen as provable by the 'evidence of the

senses' and verifiable by the reliability of the witnesses who attested
to the truthfulness of the events described in the scriptural narratives.

Throughout this study I have used the term 'testimony' to refer
both to oral evidence presented to an immediate adjudicative
audience, and to records of oral evidence preserved for future
assessment. In theological terms, 'testimony' refers both to the
accounts of the resurrection contained in the canonical gospels, and
to narratives of conversion in the lives of individual believers.
Despite the passage of time, the immediacy of eye-witness perception
is retained in the case of the modern religious convert; as Ricoeur
points out, believers in any age are essentially eye-witnesses to the
resurrection through the allegedly ahistorical operations of the Holy
Spirit.[13] In legal terms, 'testimony' may encompass several evidentiary categories; the testimony of an eye-witness to a civil or criminal
matter given in court on oath; and the testimony of a party to a civil
or criminal action presented orally, with or without the sanction of
an oath, and, in a criminal case, amounting to either a confession or
a statement of innocence. A confession is defined as 'an admission of
the very facts in issue . . . by a party on trial for a criminal
offence',[14] and it may be either stated in court, or reduced to writing
by an examining magistrate at the pre-trial stage. In the period
under discussion, an accused could not give evidence on oath, and
parties to a civil action were only rendered competent in 1851. The
common characteristic of each category is the emphasis upon eye-
witness perception and recollection, either of supernatural revelation
in the case of religious evidence, or of the facts in dispute in a
courtroom in the case of a trial at law. In contrast, anxieties about
judgement based on gossip or rumour resulted in the formulation of
one of the earliest exclusionary rules of evidence known to English
law, namely the usual inadmissibility of hearsay material.

The role of personal testimony in the revelation and transmission
of truth had long been of special significance to the English history
of ideas. In the aftermath of the Reformation, with its rejection of
the exclusive and infallible authority of the church in questions of
biblical interpretation, the Protestant reliance on the testimony of
enlightened individuals in direct communion with God flourished.
In criminal cases, there was a general (but not unquestioned)
acceptance of the use of confessions to obtain a conviction; in 1824,
the jurist Thomas Starkie could privilege voluntary confessions as

'one of the strongest proofs of guilt' and assert with confidence that '[a] prisoner may be convicted upon his own confession, without other evidence'.[15] As early as 1778, English courts had ruled that confessions must be voluntary if they were to serve as the basis for criminal convictions.[16] Writing in 1842, Henry Joy noted:

In England it is held that a confession, though extra-judicial, if duly proved, is *of itself*, without the aid of any additional circumstance, sufficient to warrant the conviction of a prisoner. This being the strong and decisive effect which they give to a confession, it is justly held by them that such a confession, to be admissible, must be proved to have been freely and voluntarily made; and that it becomes inadmissible if it is tainted by any promises of pardon or application of threats.[17]

In contrast to apprehensions about the role of torture in the generation of confessions in continental or civilian legal systems, spiritual exhortations to confess one's guilt would not invalidate an accused's statement: Joy argues that '[s]uch spiritual convictions . . . seem, from the nature of religion, the most likely of all motives to produce truth.'[18] In an analysis of the literary value of 'voluntariness', Peter Brooks has defined the paradox which lies at the heart of English thought about the status and reliability of confessional material:

Consider that the law as we know it has elaborated as a most basic right of the accused the protection against involuntary confession, while, on the other hand, western literature, from early in the romantic era onward, has made the confessional mode a crucial kind of self-expression, one that is supposed to bear a special stamp of sincerity and authenticity and to bear special witness to the truth of the individual personality.[19]

Brooks thus calls attention to the association between autobiography and the (Romantic) emphasis on confession and the construction of the self, which was perhaps rendered politically and generically suspect with the publication of Jean-Jacques Rousseau's *Confessions* (1765–1770).[20] In courts of law, however, the presentation of both witness testimony (with veracity guaranteed by the administration of an oath) and confessional statements made without access to the oath were governed by the assumption that spiritual convictions generated truth, thus ensuring the inter-relationship of religious epistemology and legal conceptions of evidentiary reliability. Changing attitudes to the status of testimony and confession therefore remained closely aligned with developments in religious thought during the eighteenth and nineteenth centuries.

This study has proceeded on the premise that contemporary debates about proof and the limits of knowledge are incorporated (whether deliberately or not) into the fiction of an era. This assumption presupposes the mimetic nature of fictional endeavours, with narrative emplotment bearing a representational relationship to the world of action and moral choice. Authors such as Samuel Richardson conceived of their own attempts to represent the 'real' in evidentiary terms:

Attentive Readers have found, and will find, that the Probability of all Stories told, or of Narrations given, depends upon small Circumstances; as may be observed, that in all Tryals for Life and Property, the / / (sic) Merits of the Cause are more determinable by such, than by the greater Facts; which usually are so laid, and taken care of, as to seem to authenticate themselves.[21]

William Hazlitt could only agree that Richardson 'sets about describing every object and transaction, as if the whole had been given in on evidence by an eye-witness'; 'every circumstance is made to tell'. The attention to detail 'gives an appearance of truth . . . and we listen with the same attention as we should to the particulars of a confidential communication'.[22] Walter Wilson, the biographer of Daniel Defoe, cites Charles Lamb's observations to the same effect. The reader's assent to the narrative's 'perfect illusion' is generated by repetitive and detailed eye-witness attestations of fact: '[i]t is like reading evidence in a Court of Justice'.[23] Yet fiction is not strictly imitative and the relationship of fiction and evidence remains one of verisimilitude rather than complete identity. As Ricoeur has noted, mimesis may be defined as creative representation – 'the break that opens the space for fiction'[24] – and McKeon is certainly right to define 'realism' as a genre which bears a shifting relationship to that which it seeks to represent; it 'exists to concede the accountability of art to a prior reality, without seeming to compromise the uniquely modern belief that such reality as it is answerable to already is internalized in art itself as a demystified species of spirituality'.[25] Ricoeur stresses the selective hermeneutics of an author's 'pre-understanding of the world of action, its meaningful structures, its symbolic resources, and its temporal character'.[26] For each of the authors discussed in subsequent chapters, evidentiary apologetics and legal procedure constitute a significant part of this 'pre-understanding' of the 'real', which in turn informs their fiction. With the exception of Samuel Richardson and William

Godwin (who nevertheless explore ideas of proof and evidence in their most famous works), each writer has a biographical connection with the law, either by occupation (in the case of Henry Fielding, Walter Scott, Charles Dickens and Wilkie Collins) or by personal enthusiasm (in the case of George Eliot). This is not to suggest that legal training invariably produces narratives dependent upon eye-witness assertions of fact for their authenticity; for example, William Thackeray (himself briefly a law student)[27] experiments in *The Newcomes* (1853–1855) with a detached editorial style 'written maturely and at ease' when the journey of life is approaching completion; it includes assumptions, conjectures, the partial recovery of recollections, as well as frequent adjurations to the reader to enable her to interpret the scenes of fable and fancy for herself.[28] And the reactions of both Newman and Browning to the insistence that proof be tied to evidence at all will be examined in Chapter 4. But these are exceptions which prove the strength of the initial proposition. For the Victorian authors who form the focus of this study, their connections with the law, together with an understanding of the reading public's enthusiasm for accounts of trials and punishments, ensured that evidence-bound paradigms of probability and proof tied their tales to a sense of competition with stories told in courts of law.

The chronological limits of my study refer to events in the lives of two of the writers whose work is most germane to my argument. In 1740, Fielding was called to the Bar, and his professional career as both a lawyer and magistrate spans a time when the modern adversarial format of the English common law trial was first emerging. In 1870, John Henry Newman published *An Essay in Aid of a Grammar of Assent*, the culmination of decades of thought about the pursuit of certitude in religious belief. Newman considers the reliability of testimony (and the role of inspiration in its generation) in a number of his works, but perhaps even more valuable to my argument is his willingness to test empiricist assumptions about the strict relationship between evidence and belief, and to question the need for demonstrable proof in religious affairs. After a century and a half in which Anglican orthodoxy insisted on the 'Evidences' as the basis of Christian faith, we see in Newman's work a retreat from evidence-bound methodologies. Hence, I have regarded 1870 as representing an approximate end-point to the evidentiary apologetics of previous generations. But in order to trace changes in

Victorian conceptions of testimony and proof, I must begin my
analysis a little earlier in the eighteenth century, when the tenets of
revealed religion were increasingly being tested by the methodologies of the trial format.

EIGHTEENTH-CENTURY EVIDENTIARY APOLOGETICS

In 1727, Thomas Woolston published the first of his six *Discourses on
the Miracles of our Saviour*, a series of tracts which questioned the
miraculous attestation of the ministry and resurrection of Jesus and
asserted the allegorical origin of a number of biblical narratives. The
ensuing controversy resulted in the renewal of his prosecution for
blasphemy,[29] and he was subsequently convicted, fined and imprisoned by the Court of the King's Bench.

In 1729, Thomas Sherlock responded to the issues raised by
Woolston's trial in a small publication entitled *The Tryal of the
Witnesses of the Resurrection of Jesus*, in which a narrator and some of
his peers from the Inns of Court convened to assess the evidence of
the resurrection, with reference to the gospels as their authorities in
lieu of Littleton, Plowden, and Coke. They divided amongst themselves the roles of judge, jurors, and counsel to debate the central
issue, 'Whether the Objections produced by Mr. *Woolston*, are of
weight to overthrow the Evidence of Christ's Resurrection.'[30] The
Apostles were arraigned as false witnesses, and the Counsel for
Woolston questioned their capacity as eye-witnesses to authenticate
the miraculous:

[A]ltho in common Life we act in a thousand Instances upon the Faith and
Credit of human Testimony; yet the Reason for so doing is not the same in
the Case before us. In common Affairs, where nothing is asserted but what
is probable, and possible, and according to the usual Course of Nature, a
reasonable Degree of Evidence ought to Determine every Man. For the
very Probability, or Possibility of the thing, is a Support to the Evidence;
and in such Cases we have no Doubt but a Man's Senses qualify him to be
a Witness. But when the thing testified is contrary to the Order of Nature,
and, at first sight at least, impossible, what Evidence can be sufficient to
over-turn the constant Evidence of Nature, which she gives us in the
uniform and regular Method of her Operations? . . . [The Resurrection]
seems to be a Case exempt from human Evidence. Men have limited
Senses, and a limited Reason; when they act within their Limits, we may
give Credit to them; but when they talk of things removed beyond the

Reach of their Senses and Reason, we must quit our own, if we believe theirs. (pp. 58–59)

In reply, the opposing counsel emphasised the violent nature of the Apostles' deaths as attestation of their veracity – 'what greater Evidence of Sincerity can Man give or require?' (p. 81) – thus anticipating the argument which was to dominate debate as to the strength of the Christian 'Evidences' for the next one hundred years. In summation, the judge endorsed the opposing counsel's argument that evidence of the resurrection could fall within the scope of man's senses:

A Man rising from the Grave is an Object of Sense, and can give the same Evidence of his being alive, as any other Man in the World can give. So that a Resurrection consider'd only as a Fact to be proved by Evidence, is a plain Case; it requires no greater Ability in the Witnesses, than that they be able to distinguish between a Man dead, and a Man alive: A Point, in which I believe every Man living thinks himself a Judge. (p. 62)

In such a case 'there wants nothing to be proved, but only the Sincerity of the Reporter: and since voluntary Suffering for the Truth, is at least a proof of Sincerity; the Suffering of the Apostles for the Truth of the Resurrection, is a full and unexceptionable Proof' (pp. 104–105). Consequently the jury found the Apostles not guilty of providing false testimony in the case of the resurrection, and the narrative closes with the judge considering a retainer to return to the Bar 'to undertake the Cause of *Lazarus*' when his case came on next (p. 110).

The Tryal of the Witnesses is an interesting text for a number of reasons. Even in the mid-nineteenth century it was considered a noteworthy example of the 'partisan' theology of the Hanoverian period; in his contribution to *Essays and Reviews* (1860), entitled 'Tendencies of Religious Thought in England 1688–1750', Mark Pattison tells us that it went through fourteen editions, and that it was '[o]ne of the favourite books of the time'.[31] For Pattison, the appropriation of litigious terminology by theologians was a characteristic feature of the rationalist programme, in which the divines of the eighteenth century assumed that their 'beliefs were determined by an impartial inquiry into the evidence'. This bequeathed an unfortunate legacy to subsequent generations: '[t]his stamp of advocacy which was impressed on English theology at the Reformation – its first work of consideration was an "Apology – it has not to this day shaken off . . . Theological study is still the study of topics of defence' (p. 301). The legal discourse of accusation, defence, and proof has long been understood to provide privileged access to the truth. The fact-finding model of the trial has been central to Christian experience since the judgement of Christ and of subsequent martyrs in the reign of various Roman emperors. And as Ricoeur notes, the trial format 'extends to all situations in which a judgement or a decision can be made only at the end of a debate or confrontation between adverse opinions and conflicting points of view'.[32] But the similarities between religious and legal thought in the eighteenth century were not purely methodological; they were bound together by broader metaphysical and eschatological associations which provided a rich fund of imagery for the usage of theologians and authors of fiction alike.

For Bishop Joseph Butler, writing in his *Analogy of Religion, Natural and Revealed, to the Constitution and Course of Nature* (1736), life was a state of probation, an extended trial of moral integrity before the final apocalyptic judgement, and assize sermons also provided regular opportunities for the equation of divine and legal processes of adjudication.[33] For example, on Thursday 16 March, 1769, Henry Venn, Vicar of Huddersfield, preached at the Assizes in Kingston, Surrey, on the topic of 'Man a Condemned Prisoner, and Christ the Strong Hold to Save Him' in which he argued for post-lapsarian depravity and the essential similarity between the common man and the capital offender:

These [felons] are imprisoned to be brought to trial, and, upon conviction according to law, sentenced to suffer a shameful death. The law, their high and mighty accuser, pays no regard to their persons, or fond pleas to escape, or agonizing cries for mercy. Nothing but blood can pay the forfeit. Nothing but blood deter others, from treading in their steps. Exactly the same is the case with us. What man is he that liveth, whom death will not arrest, as the pursuivant of justice, to place him at the Bar of GOD?[34]

So men and women stand at the Bar before God, condemned without Christ's mediation and atonement, and the motif of the trial assumes a theological as well as a penal significance. The idea of life as a trial of one's faith recalls Butler's emphasis on probation and judgement, but it also implies the rationalist strategy of 'trying' the evidentiary basis of one's faith. Both resonances are refracted in novels as diverse as *Callista*, *Romola* and *Robert Elsmere*, and all raise issues of advocacy, representation, and judgement.

The world-view which supported the epistemology of the law

during the eighteenth century has been labelled 'natural theology', and George Levine, amongst others, has drawn attention to the ways in which this very title 'indicates that English science was intimately connected with its religion'; '[r]eligion and science alike were concerned to describe a cosmos all of whose phenomena made sense, manifested intelligence and design'.[35] According to Jowett, natural religion may be defined as 'a theory . . . which appeals to particular evidences for the being of a God, though resting, perhaps more safely, on the general conviction that "this universal frame cannot want a mind"'.[36] In 'Tendencies of Religious Thought', Pattison notes that the rationalist phase of theological development began with the publication of John Locke's text, *On the Reasonableness of Christianity* (1695), and declined with the reaction against the reform movement, and the commencement of *Tracts for the Times*, in about 1830 (pp. 258–259). During this time:

it was not merely that Rationalism then obtruded itself as a heresy, or obtained a footing of toleration within the Church, but the rationalizing method possessed itself absolutely of the whole field of theology. With some trifling exceptions, the whole of religious literature was drawn in to the endeavour to 'prove the truth' of Christianity. (p. 259)

Pattison neatly divides the rationalist era into two fifty-year periods: in the first half of the century, theologians appeared to be more devoted to the internal proofs of Christianity; in the latter half, Pattison traces the dominance of 'the "Evidences", or the historical proof of the genuineness and authenticity of the Christian records' (p. 260). Butler's *Analogy of Religion* was the foremost product of the earlier school of thought. He argued that without clear evidence of incompetence or interest, 'the *natural* Laws of human Actions require, that Testimony be admitted'[37] and he assumed the stance of the impartial judge rather than the impassioned advocate. In Pattison's judgement, Butler 'kn[ew] the laws of evidence, and carefully ke[pt] his statements within them'; he acknowledged any weaknesses in the historical record, thus demonstrating the 'wariness of the judicial mind' (pp. 305–306). For Butler, as for Mansel over a century later, the very obscurity of some aspects of the Christian 'Evidences' was itself illustrative of man's probationary state; he concluded that the temptation to dwell on 'speculative Difficulties in which the Evidence of Religion is involved, may make even the principal Part of some Persons (sic) trial', as they elicit either a 'virtuous Exercise, or vitious (sic) Neglect of their Understanding, in examining or not examining into That Evidence'.[38]

By contrast, the advocates of the school devoted to 'external Evidences' adopted a more strident approach which Pattison called an 'Old Bailey theology', in which 'the Apostles [were] being tried once a week for the capital crime of forgery' (p. 260). William Paley's text entitled *A View of the Evidences of Christianity* (1794) was an enormously influential example of this evidentiary methodology. Paley could conceive of no revealed truth independent of super-natural attestation; 'there was nothing but the miracles attributed to [Christ] by which his pretensions could be maintained for a moment'.[39] Alluding to David Hume's *Enquiry Concerning Human Understanding*, which posited the inability of testimony to transmit evidence of the supernatural, Paley concurred that any interpret-ation of miraculous narratives involves 'a contest of opposite improb-abilities'; it is 'a question whether it be more improbable that the miracle should be true, or the testimony false' (vol. I, p. 11). But whereas Hume concluded that the inherent improbability of the miraculous 'diminish[es] the force of any argument, derived from human testimony . . . in proportion as the fact is more or less unusual',[40] Paley reposed his greatest confidence in the testimony of eye-witnesses to the ministry and resurrection of Christ and the subsequent behaviour of his Apostles. The authenticity of the New Testament is promoted by 'the undesignedness of the agreements' (vol. II, p. 195) between the epistles and the gospel narratives and any discrepancies can also be interpreted as evidence of their truthfulness:

The usual character of human testimony is substantial truth under circumstantial variety. This is what the daily experience of courts of justice teaches. When accounts of a transaction come from the mouths of different witnesses, it is seldom that it is not possible to pick out apparent or real inconsistencies between them. These inconsistencies are studiously dis-played by an adverse pleader, but oftentimes with little impression upon the mind of the judges. On the contrary, a close and minute agreement induces the suspicion of confederacy and fraud. (vol. II, pp. 289–290)

The authority of the written record of this testimony is established in a number of ways; for example, the Johannine gospel is an indepen-dent source of corroboration for the earlier gospels, the gospels have an 'aggregate' as well as a 'separate' authority, and all were received as canonical by the primitive Christian Church (vol. I, p. 155). Like

Butler, Paley maintains that Providence has ensured the preservation and transmission of scriptural evidence, and hence Christian believers can enjoy 'historical certainty' of the facts narrated by the evangelists (vol. I, pp. 163–164, p. 322). Paley bases much of the force of his arguments on the claim that 'men do not suffer persecution from the love of the marvellous' (vol. I, p. 343), an assertion similar to that which would later feature in Newman's *Grammar of Assent*. The confidence he places in the transmission of testimony enables Paley to trust in the tenets of revelation. Creation remains in the care of a loving and accessible God, and man's privileged position in that scheme is guaranteed.

Contemporary fiction inevitably absorbed this preoccupation with the centrality of man's place in Creation, and the Christian teleology – with its emphasis upon redemption and salvation – gave purpose and the prospect of a meaningful closure to both individual lives and a broader idea of history. In labelling this mode of representation the 'providential aesthetic', Thomas Vargish emphasises its dependence upon the fundamental assumptions of natural theology: '[p]rovidence means foresight, foreknowledge, anticipation, preparation, plan, pattern, design'.[41] Levine, too, suggests that many conventions of narrative teleology and closure 'are consonant with the natural-theological view of things'.[42] The ethical implications of natural theology were similarly reassuring; ready access to revealed truth was available through the witnesses to the existence of God, for example, the authority of the scriptures, the power of the church, the model of personal testimonies of conversion, and the work of the conscience. Inferences as to the existence of a Creator could be drawn from the natural world. Such evidence is consciously canvassed in religious and historical novels throughout the nineteenth century – often for polemical and ideological reasons in the conflict between Catholic and Protestant readings of history – but, as Levine points out, assumptions of order and purpose also permeate less didactic works.

THE IMPACT OF GERMAN HIGHER CRITICISM ON THE AUTHORITY OF THE EYE-WITNESS

Although natural theology was not monolithic, there remained towards the end of the eighteenth century a widespread adherence to orthodox literalism which ensured that the gospels were regarded as historical accounts of external miraculous events. Despite some localised expressions of scepticism, apologists were, on the whole, able to appeal to the doctrine of direct verbal inspiration to confirm a consequent infallibility on the part of the evangelists. But over the next few decades, the confident assumptions of the evidentiary school were dealt a number of devastating blows as voices of disagreement gained a greater public circulation. As early as the 1790s, Samuel Taylor Coleridge and dissenting theorists such as Thomas Beddoes had questioned the supernatural attestation of the Christian dispensation, and in her study of English indebtedness to German research, Elinor Shaffer observes that 'the common experience of the Bible . . . was altered in [this] period':

A movement of this significance and scope cannot be reduced to the mechanics (or the moralities) of transmission. The 'collapse of the ontological foundations of religion' (Lukac's phrase) and the consequent reinterpretation of the major religious text of the West is a communal event. It is, of course, also a private event, and proceeds through the inner struggle of individual conscience.[43]

Coleridge himself experienced this transition of the age. In his 'Six Lectures on Revealed Religion, its Corruptions and Political Views' given in Bristol in 1795, Coleridge privileged the historical position of the earliest eye-witnesses:

At the first Promulgation of a divine Mission Miracles are its best and only Tests. But the full force of such preter-natural Evidence can operate on the Eyewitnesses only. Their influence gradually decreases and becomes more and more faint and then the Accomplishment of predicted Events is substituted and discovers to us the truth of the Revealed Doctrines to us (sic) by a sufficient though not so overpowering a Light.[44]

But Shaffer describes these Lectures as Coleridge's 'last attempt at a defence of an optimistic and necessarian view of revealed religion based on standard Unitarian authorities' and she argues that the following year he abandoned any adherence to literalism, becoming increasingly critical of Paleyian apologetics and seeking instead 'a revision of the entire conception of the meaning of "witness" which would have revolutionary implications also for the conception of "the visionary character" that he was evolving at the same time'.[45] Coleridge was thus enabled to subjugate 'speculative Reason' to 'the *Substance*, the *Hope*, the *Love*, in one word, the *Faith* [which] are Derivatives from the practical, moral, and spiritual Nature and Being of Man'.[46]

But with the advent of German higher criticism, which gathered force throughout the early nineteenth century and which culminated in the publication of influential texts such as David Strauss's *The Life of Jesus Critically Examined* (1835, translated into English in 1846), and Ludwig Feuerbach's *The Essence of Christianity* (1840, translated into English in 1854), the searing torchlight of scepticism exposed the historical inconsistencies of the sacred texts. For both Strauss and Ernest Renan (whose *Life of Jesus* appeared in 1863, translated into English in 1864), the only way to reconcile the miraculous narratives of the Bible with modern scientific knowledge was to discard the idea of the evangelist as eye-witness and to embrace the conception of the gospels as more or less mythical and legendary in origin; therefore, the modern reader could have no unmediated access to any historical kernel of fact which may (or may not) lie embedded within the narrative.

In evidentiary terms, the probative value of the gospel accounts was correspondingly decreased. They now seemed to share some of the characteristics of derivative or hearsay material which was treated so dismissively in the legal treatises of the period. For example, this description of hearsay evidence suggests clear parallels with the higher critical treatment of the gospel narratives: '[i]t is evident that proof weakens in proportion to its distance from its source . . . *a fortiori* proof is extremely weak when we are obliged to follow out a line (parcourir une filière) more or less complicated, before we can arrive at direct testimony'.[47] John's gospel (which had long been treasured as the most authoritative and sophisticated eye-witness account, with a particular appeal for the nineteenth century)[48] was now subject to destructive criticism, thus enabling Strauss and Renan to undermine the idea of inspiration as divine dictation. Like Coleridge, Friedrich Schleiermacher offered an alternative response to the deficiencies of the evidentiary school of thought, and, in his later work, he showed a greater willingness to resign the claim of the Christian record to historical accuracy and to remodel ecclesiastical Christology independently of its grounding in historical facts or 'events'. As Shaffer has noted:

If, by their own critical endeavour, it became clear that none of the Gospels was an eye-witness account, the status of the 'event' therein recounted must, on the old view, be diminished, its credibility undermined; but if there are no such privileged accounts, if all event is interpretation, then the Gospels need not suffer. . . The miracle becomes the paradigm of reported historical event; the historical events reported by eye-witnesses represent instantaneous myth-making.[49]

Shaffer argues that the fundamental ambiguities of the resurrection narratives came to be regarded as a new typological basis for poetic endeavour; if '[a]t the very moment of "ocular witness" the fact is lost . . . [and] moulded by the perceiver' then all perception is equally imaginative in genesis.[50] Schleiermacher, amongst others, was able to construct a theology capable of accommodating this critical scepticism.

Schleiermacher's work, *A Critical Essay on the Gospel of St. Luke*, was translated into English in 1825, and reflects his theological manifesto that 'the most pure, simple faith, and the keenest investigation are one and the same thing, inasmuch as no one who wishes to believe what is of divine origin can wish to believe illusions.'[51] Rejecting Eichhorn's hypothesis of an Aramaic proto-Gospel which summarised apostolic teaching and which pre-dated and informed the work of the canonical evangelists, Schleiermacher instead undertook the linguistic equivalent of an archaeological investigation, sifting through the internal evidence of Luke's textual structure to uncover differing narrative strata, identifying contributions from contrasting sources and seeking traces of an apostolic hand. Schleiermacher dwelt upon the inconsistencies between the synoptic accounts, and explains gaps in the Lucan version by renouncing the automatic equation of evangelist with eye-witness:

Only under one view does the omission of these incidents excite no surprise, but seem natural, that is, if we suppose that the first written accounts originated in the efforts, and at the instance of persons, who, not personally acquainted with Christ, and therefore not in the same sense his contemporaries, sought for circumstantial accounts, and aimed at perpetuating by writing the voice of oral tradition before it died away. (p. 110)

Some passages, such as Chapters 8: 22–56, and 16: 16–18, and the record of the crucifixion, 'betray. . . the eye-witness from beginning to end by [their] unreserved explicitness, and vivid mode of representation' (p. 131); much of the rest is the consolidation of primitive narratives, either oral or written, from a variety of sources. Schleiermacher concludes that Luke 'is from beginning to end no more than the compiler and arranger of documents which he found in existence, and which he allows to pass unaltered through his hands' (pp. 313–314). As editor, Luke's task was to include in his account pre-existing pieces which he adjudged 'genuine and good' and thus his work is acclaimed as 'judicious', the result of careful human judgement, and divine inspiration is reduced to 'the law according to which he arranged [the material which came into his hands]' (pp. 313–314, p. 163).

For Schleiermacher, as for Coleridge, faith was the decisive factor which enabled him to escape unnecessary reliance on the historically bound Christological paradigms of orthodoxy and to repose in a confident apprehension of the divine presence; we see his emphasis on music and emotion as the essence of the religious life in works such as *Christmas Eve* (1826). He presented a series of public lectures on the life of Jesus, beginning in 1819, and although they were not published until 1832, the notes of the lectures profoundly influenced David Friedrich Strauss, who drew on Schleiermacher's work in his seminal text *The Life of Jesus Critically Examined*.[52] The influence of Schleiermacher's *Essay on St. Luke* also informed Charles Hennell's *An Inquiry into the Origins of Christianity* which appeared in 1838.

Hennell's *Inquiry* is notorious as one of the texts which furthered George Eliot's liberation from the tenets of evangelical orthodoxy. He portrayed Jesus as profoundly human, a product of Essene education and the expectations and fervour of a Messianic age.[53] Hennell adopted Schleiermacher's assessment of Luke's role as an evangelist, and he summarily dismissed any claim to immediate eye-witness perception on the part of the authors of Matthew and Mark: the former 'collected the relics of the acts and sayings of Jesus reported by Matthew the Apostle, introducing some traditions which he found elsewhere, and filling up copiously from his own invention' (p. 80); the latter was an honest writer who was frequently led by the 'warmth of narration . . . to exaggerate and to embellish upon the materials before him; but not more than has been done by many historians of good credit, since the minute particulars filled up by him, are, in general, only such as would be suggested by the belief of the main facts' (p. 92). But Hennell reserved his most damaging criticism for the Johannine gospel. Whereas this text had previously been esteemed as the mature, sophisticated production of the favourite disciple of Christ, devoid of the errors and omissions which flawed the synoptic accounts, Hennell saw only a 'species of imposition' deliberately designed to enhance Jesus's Messianic claims (p. 109). Divine inspiration thus became a form of economy with the truth which bordered on 'wilful falsehood' (p. 117). John equated the promptings of his own imagination with the work of the Holy Spirit,

a confusion which Hennell accepts as consonant with the hope of
the early church that the Paraclete would comfort them after Christ's
death (p. 111). Hennell then seeks to define the etymology of the
word 'witness' in purely theological terms:

> In the book of Acts, the Apostles are frequently made to profess themselves
> 'witnesses, μαρτυξες, of the resurrection of Jesus'. But as the word does not
> signify, of necessity, an eye-witness, but rather an assertor or testifier, this
> declaration of the Apostles may mean only that they believed, and were
> ready to assert, that he was risen. That they had actually *seen him alive* since
> his supposed resurrection, is quite a distinct assertion, and not included in
> the former. (p. 114)

Consequently, religious men and women may meditate on 'the
interesting incidents which have for ever consecrated the plains of
Palestine; but . . . for this exercise no single spot of earth, and no
one page of its history, furnishes the exclusive theme' (p. 369).

Many of Hennell's most critical observations were pre-empted by
David Strauss's *The Life of Jesus Critically Examined*, which was
translated into English from the fourth edition by George Eliot and
Rufa Brabant Hennell in 1846. Eliot's translation of Strauss's work
was to be of profound influence on the mid-Victorian age; as Shaffer
has noted, 'the Biblical criticism which in Coleridge's youth might
appear an obscure, difficult, largely foreign scholarly technique
confined to a handful of professors of Oriental languages becomes
by George Eliot's time the medium of secular religious experience'.[54]
Like Hennell, Strauss begins with the assumptions that 'we do not
possess the immediate record of an eye-witness in any one of the four
gospels', that the 'infection' of factual material with the ingredients
of legend occurs at the very earliest stage of church history, and that
the definition of eye-witness perception does not preclude fabrica-
tion: 'Eye-witnesses in the more extended sense, who had only seen
Jesus occasionally and not been his constant companions, must, on
the contrary, have been strongly tempted to fill up their imperfect
knowledge of his history with mythical representations.'[55] John in
particular is 'tax[ed] . . . with free invention' and any reliance on
passages from his narrative – for example the quotation of Chapter
14: 25–26 to prove the assistance of the Paraclete in the construction
of the gospel accounts – is vitiated on the grounds of circularity; it is
both philosophically flawed 'to prove the truthfulness of the discourses in John, by a promise which appears nowhere but in those
discourses' and unscientific to appeal to the operation of a super-

natural agency in the midst of rational enquiry.[56] In his whole-hearted acceptance of the mythological paradigm, Strauss rejects Schleiermacher's premise that the boundary between fact and fiction – and hence the traces of apostolical authorship – can be identified by the expenditure of energy and expertise. Instead, Strauss argues that it is intellectually more consistent to discard any claim of a connection with historical reality: 'we must not . . . seek in the particular supernatural cures which the Gospels narrate, the natural reality; on the contrary, we must admit that this is totally lost to us, and that the supernatural has usurped its place.'[57] He thus seeks to articulate the ideas – Messianic, Judaic, or Platonic – which may have informed an evangelist's representation of a particular incident, and this enables him to strip the notion of 'event' of any relation to the historical record. His treatment of the narratives of Christ's transfiguration is typical; he discounts both the orthodox super-natural explanation, and the rational approach (which postulates a trick of the light visible to the watching disciples), in favour of a mythological interpretation which stresses the Messianic expecta-tions of the Jewish people:

the natural system of interpretation, while it seeks to preserve the historical certainty of the narratives, loses their ideal truth – sacrifices the essence to the form: whereas the mythical interpretation, by renouncing the historical body of such narratives, rescues and preserves the idea which resides in them, and which alone constitutes their vitality and spirit . . . [A]ccording to the mythical interpretation, I do not, it is true, see in the evangelical narrative any real event, – I yet retain a sense, a purpose in the narrative, know to what sentiments and thoughts of the first Christian community it owes its origin, and why the authors of the gospels included so important a passage in their memoirs.[58]

For Strauss, the truth of an 'event' is synonymous with the expecta-tions of the witness, which both generate, and retrospectively shape and collate, the subject under observation. The orthodox apologist Henry Liddon saw this idea of perception as creation epitomised in the work of Ludwig Feuerbach. Feuerbach had argued that '[t]he power of miracle is . . . nothing else than the power of the imagination',[59] and Liddon saw in this theory the suggestion that Jesus was 'divinised' by the enthusiasm of his disciples.[60] But Feuerbach's influential treatise, *The Essence of Christianity* (1841), which was translated into English by George Eliot in 1854, was less concerned with the origins of the gospel narratives as historical

records than with the contradictions inherent in the ideas of revelation and incarnation. It was left to Renan to extend this hermeneutic
regime to the mind of Jesus himself and to argue that both master
and disciples deliberately generated signs of his authority. For
Renan, there was no event without mythical interpretations and
legendary accretions, and John in particular 'transformed his master
in wishing to describe him'.[61] As Liddon was to note in his Bampton
Lectures of 1866, the claims of modern criticism (represented by
Feuerbach) involved a reclassification of the genre of the gospel
narratives; 'we are driven to the theory that the closest friend of
Jesus was believed by apostolical Christendom to be writing a
history, when in truth he was only composing a biographical
novel'.[62]

The impact of the disintegration of the tenets of Christian
orthodoxy was clearly felt in the fictional narratives of the mid-
Victorian period. In his historical novel, *Hypatia*, first published in
serial form in *Fraser's Magazine* in 1852 and 1853, Charles Kingsley
dramatised the moment in which his Christian protagonist confronts
the richness of the competing classical ideas which inform Hypatia's
teaching:

[Philammon] had been listening to the whole lecture, and yet not so much
listening as watching, in bewilderment, the beauty of the speaker, the grace
of her action, the melody of her voice, and last but not least, the maze of
her rhetoric, as it glittered before his mind's eye, like a cobweb diamonded
with dew. A sea of new thoughts and questions, if not of doubts, came
rushing in at every sentence on his acute Greek intellect, all the more
plentifully and irresistibly because his speculative faculty was as yet
altogether waste and empty, undefended by any scientific culture from the
inrushing flood. For the first time in his life he found himself face to face
with the root questions of all thought – 'What am I, and where?' 'What can
I know?'[63]

For Kingsley, the moment of epistemological crisis has a distinctively
Christian dimension. As his protagonist compares the ignorance of
the monks with the aristocratic refinements of the philosopher
Hypatia, Philammon questions the Church's claims to exclusive
truth: 'he shuddered and asked himself involuntarily – were these
the ministers of a Gospel? were these the fruits of Christ's Spirit? . . .
And a whisper thrilled through the inmost depth of his soul – "Is
there a Gospel? Is there a Spirit of Christ? Would not their fruits be
different from these?" '[64]

For many Victorians, it was the publication of Darwin's *On the Origin of Species* in 1859 which most significantly undermined the basis of natural theology, and the controversy generated by Darwin's apparent severance of the natural world and an implied cosmic designer overlapped with the response to *Essays and Reviews* which appeared in March 1860.[65] As Shaffer notes, *Essays and Reviews* enabled the mythological school to present to a wider audience ideas which had previously been confined to 'the serious thinkers of the time'.[66] With their deification of the progressive civilisation of society and their acceptance of the fossil record in preference to the creation narratives of Genesis, the contributors to *Essays and Reviews* sought to emphasise the ethical dimensions of Christianity at the expense of its envelope of superstitious dogmatism. Henry Wilson acknowledged their collective indebtedness to the German biblical critics, but also suggested that the erosion of the authority of the traditional 'proofs' was only one of a number of problems 'probably of genuine English growth' confronting the local ecclesiastical hierarchy.[67] At a fundamental level, the communal conception of God had changed. As Jowett was to note in a later essay:

It is impossible that our own feeling towards nature in the present day can be the same with that of the Psalmist . . . To us, God is not in the whirlwind nor in the storm, nor in the earthquake, but in the still small voice . . . God has removed himself out of our sight, that He may give us a greater idea of the immensity of His power.[68]

Writing at the end of the nineteenth century, the philosopher William James also attributed the decline of the evidentiary school to a shift in the public perception of divinity:

That vast literature of proofs of God's existence drawn from the order of nature, which a century ago seemed so overwhelmingly convincing, to-day does little more than gather dust in libraries, for the simple reason that our generation has ceased to believe in the kind of God it argued for. Whatever sort of a being God may be, we *know* to-day that he is nevermore that mere external inventor of 'contrivances' intended to make manifest his 'glory' in which our great-grandfathers took such satisfaction, though just how we know this we cannot possibly make clear by words either to others or to ourselves.[69]

The evidentiary basis of Paleyian apologetics had thus lost much of its probative value, and it was largely ignored by later Victorian authors and theologians seeking to provide the younger generation with a new basis for moral action.

Amongst the contributors to *Essays and Reviews*, it was Baden
Powell who most savagely attacked the Church's adherence to the
Paleyian assumption that revelation required an external, miraculous attestation. In his contribution to the earlier volume of *Oxford
Essays* (1857) entitled 'The Study of the Evidences of Natural
Theology', Powell had discussed and accepted Immanuel Kant's
criticisms of the so-called *a priori* proofs of the existence of God.
Powell, like Kant, conceded that the 'ontological' and the 'cosmolo-
gical' proofs failed. However, like Coleridge, he confirmed the
(limited) value of the 'physico-theological' argument which, though
it could not prove the existence of an omnipotent Creator, could
generate proofs 'sufficient for moral and practical ends'.[70] In a
subsequent book entitled *The Order of Nature* (1859), Powell argued
that scientific discoveries progressively tended to disclose '*one grand
principle of law pervading nature, or rather constituting the very idea of
nature*'.[71] Hence, supernatural interruptions to the natural order are
(*pace* Hume) antecedently incredible; 'modern science cannot conceive religious truth confirmed by a violation of physical truth'.[72]
Powell allowed scope for the truth of the Christian dispensation by
arguing that 'the belief in miracles, whether in ancient or modern
times, has always been a point, *not* of *evidence* addressed to the *intellect*,
but of *religious faith* impressed on the *spirit*',[73] and he criticised Hume
for failing to acknowledge sufficiently that 'a purely *spiritual* revelation . . . stands on quite distinct grounds from the idea of *physical*
interruption'.[74] But his own contribution to *Essays and Reviews* the
following year was to paint a yet bleaker picture of the role of
testimony in the transmission of religious truth.

In his essay entitled 'On the Study of the Evidences of Christianity', Powell suggested that the 'Old Bailey' approach to the
question of fraudulent apostolic testimony could be discarded.
Discussions of the falsity of the Apostles' testimony need not assume
motives of malice or deception on their part. But 'even in cases
where we were ourselves witnesses', the perception of any event is
mediated by 'our prepossessions previous to the event, and by the
momentary impressions consequent upon it'.[75] Powell's fundamental
assumption that the laws of nature are uniform means that 'the
probability of *some* kind of mistake or deception *somewhere*, though we
know not *where*, is greater than the probability of the event really
happening in *the way* and from the *causes* assigned':

What is alleged is a case of the supernatural; but no testimony can reach to the supernatural; testimony can apply only to apparent sensible facts; testimony can only prove an extraordinary and perhaps inexplicable occurrence or phenomenon: that it is due to supernatural causes is entirely dependent on the previous belief and assumptions of the parties. (pp. 106–107)

Since the order of nature is inviolable, testimony to the performance of miracles must be rejected; '[t]estimony, after all, is but a second-hand assurance; – it is but a blind guide; testimony can avail nothing against reason' (p. 141). Powell shared Pattison's anxieties about the adversarial methodology of evidentiary apologetics; like an impassioned advocate, Paley had sought not the truth but the promotion of his client's case (p. 131). Like Schleiermacher and Hennell before him, Powell could embrace the ethical excellence of Christ's teachings without adhering to physical evidence in support of its divine origins; 'the boundless region of spiritual things' lies beyond 'the domain of physical causation' (p. 127). Hence, faith is a matter of internal conviction and personal judgement, beyond the need for '*external facts as supported by testimony*' (p. 131). As a consequence, current scientific developments could be reconciled with religious faith, but at the expense of a belief in the strict accuracy of the historical record.

Inevitably, the debate about the proper subject and scope of religious testimony found its way into the fiction of the period. In an interesting study of the impact of religious and legal ideas of evidence and confession on the emergence of gothic fiction as a genre in the late eighteenth century, Victor Sage seeks precedents in religious and legal sanctions (such as the idea of Providence, the role of the oath, dying declarations, rules in favour of voluntary confessions, and the idea of exclusion) for the authentic representation of the supernatural in gothic narratives. He reminds us that formal realism is not the only convention which the rules of evidence can generate.[76] He is correct to note that '[t]estimony is a matrix of different contexts, and it reveals "authority" in actuality as a form of mutual borrowing between law and theology'.[77] However, Sage is more interested in largely ahistorical questions of genre and his treatment of realist texts is purely for the purposes of comparison. My emphasis is instead upon changes in the idea of evidence, of literary responses to a movement of ideas; and whilst Sage is surely correct to illustrate the ways in which anti-Catholic prejudice allowed distorted representations of ritual and 'superstition' to feed into the Protestant gothic genre,[78] I am more interested in the ways in which German higher criticism and the 'mythological' school of biblical criticism tried to purge the scriptures of the supernatural, to expunge any suggestions of the miraculous. Instead of authorising the representation of ghosts, the mythological school sought a reading of the Gospel narratives consonant with rationalist ideas of the probable and the 'real'. Yet in fiction, the vocabulary of orthodox theology lingered despite the loss of the Christocentric paradigm. As Gillian Beer has observed, '[t]he loss of omniscience is felt particularly in fiction where the design of the narrative and the activity of narration would seem to imply an organising power . . . The 'Providential' organisation of fiction becomes a conscious issue.'[79] Increasingly, Victorian fiction registered the loss of religious and historical authority which accompanied the dissolution of traditional notions of revelation and a linear understanding of history.[80]

TOWARDS AN ADVERSARIAL CRIMINAL TRIAL

If we pause to consider concurrent developments in legal methodology, we can discern a similar loss of confidence in the tenets of revelation and a gradual adoption of more evidence-based methodologies for the assessment of guilt or innocence. In the public imagination, the majesty of the criminal law and the authority of religious exhortation were combined in the theatrical pageantry of the Assizes,[81] and, whilst not wishing to attribute all similar epistemological developments to the work of a *zeit-geist*, the interdependence of religious and legal ideas ensured that assumptions of order and design also inform the juridical thinking of the eighteenth century. In William Blackstone's famous *Commentaries on the Laws of England* (1765–1769), the term 'law' was defined to include laws of nature impressed upon matter at creation just as a 'workman forms a clock'.[82] Numerous critics have noted the Paleyian imagery. It was left to a later generation of jurists and theologians to untangle the term 'law' from all the metaphorical associations imparted to it by the tenets of natural theology; John Austin, in particular, devoted a series of lectures to the task of proper definition in 1828, and these were published in 1832 as *The Province of Jurisprudence Determined*. Austin painstakingly sought to distinguish between divine laws, human commands issued by a superior authority and enforced by sanction (which form 'the appropriate matter of jurisprudence, general or particular'), morality, and laws 'metaphorical or figurative' (such as the 'laws of nature') which are improperly designated as laws on the basis of 'slender' analogies.[83] A similar clarification was to occur in theology, as Jowett also attacked the imprecision of the term 'law', reminding the reader of his commentaries on *The Epistles of St. Paul to the Thessalonians, Galations, Romans* (1855) that within four verses (Romans 7: 21–24), five different 'modifications' of the word νομοσ are translated as 'law'.[84]

Leaving aside questions of linguistic or analogical precision, the law of revelation had traditionally been regarded, in Jowett's phrase, as 'part of the law of the land', a position which allows for mutual influence; '[w]e are brought up in [Christianity], and unconsciously receive it as the habit of our thoughts and the condition of our life . . . Not only may we say, that it is part and parcel of the law of the land, but part and parcel of the character of each one, which even the worst of men cannot wholly shake off.'[85] The status of Christianity as national religion alters some aspects of religious practice; for example, Jowett notes that consequently modern believers rarely experience conversion in the same terms as their apostolical predecessors;[86] conversely, questions arise as to the evidentiary significance of the Prayer Book in courts of law after the *Act of Uniformity*, and of the Articles and the scriptures themselves in trials for heresy.[87]

It is not surprising, then, that historians have related the emergence of the rules of evidence to the demise of the widespread belief that the truth is revealed. Authors such as Julius Stone and Thomas Green have placed the rise of the jury alongside the disuse of more primitive ideas of trial which presupposed miraculous interposition to establish innocence, such as ordeal by fire or water (in the Anglo-Saxon manner) or by battle (the Norman mode of proof).[88] In 1215, the Church prohibited the use of the ordeal as a type of proof and by 1220 the trial jury had, from embryonic beginnings a decade or two earlier, emerged to determine the guilt or innocence of those named by the presenting jury.[89] It is widely accepted that the medieval jury was a self-informing body chosen from the local area in which an offence occurred and its members were allowed to accumulate information about an offender and the event themselves.[90] Hence, historians claim that early jurors functioned essentially as witnesses; they 'were primarily called, not to consider evidence put before them, but to disclose to the court what they thought of the matter'.[91] As a verdict could then be reached on the basis of their general knowledge, rules governing the admissibility of the evidence tendered to the court were superfluous. The demise of the self-informing jury seems to date from around 1500, although historians agree that the exact date cannot be known and that vestiges of the old practices appeared in occasional cases in Tudor and Stuart times.[92] But once it was established that the jury could act only on the basis of evidence presented to the court by various witnesses, then a new judicial sensitivity to questions of witness reliability appeared, and, over time, means were devised to test the admissibility and relevance of their narratives.

If we turn, then, to the characteristics of a criminal trial in Tudor and Stuart times, we see a largely non-adversarial proceeding in which:

Counsel seldom participated, few, if any, rules of evidence constrained enquiry, judges routinely examined witnesses and defendants in the most vigorous, and at times ruthless, manner, only prosecution witnesses were allowed to swear testimonial oaths and thereby enhance the credibility of their statements, jurors were free to utilize private knowledge gained outside the confines of the courtroom, judges frequently introduced their political views into proceedings, and there was virtually no appellate procedure.[93]

With the exception of jury composition and privileged prosecution access to the sanctity of the oath – which was remedied by parliament in 1702 by an Act which extended the oath to witnesses for the defence (but not the accused person)[94] – this largely was the format which Henry Fielding encountered when he entered legal practice in 1740 and when he was elevated to the bench in 1748. The legal historian John Beattie explains that the criminal trials of the era were heard quickly – the average time was some thirty minutes[95] – and John Langbein adds that the cases were often decided in clusters, with the jury hearing a number of cases before retiring to reach multiple verdicts.[96] Lord Denman, writing in *The Edinburgh Review* in 1824, noted that 'it is not without some alarm we hear of the execution of criminals in England, within a week of the perpetration of their crime'; '[i]n a country where we believe the rights of property are held so sacred, that no civil suitor can recover an undisputed debt of the most inconsiderable amount, without some weeks of preliminary process, ought the life of a man to be so

speedily extinguished in the name of justice?'[97] The cultural context
of the early modern trial has been discussed at length elsewhere, and
I can only provide a brief summary here of the fine work undertaken
by legal historians. As Douglas Hay and V. A. C. Gatrell have both
noted, the brevity of trials for felony in the eighteenth century was a
corollary of the central role played by the scaffold and the spectacle
of punishment in the cultural conception of criminal justice; in Hay's
words, '[t]he death sentence . . . was the climactic emotional point
of the criminal law – the moment of terror around which the system
revolved'.[98] By the middle of the eighteenth century, an increasing
number of offences against property had been created and made
punishable with the sentence of death – the so-called Bloody Code
which Hay has described as evidence that the ideology of the
criminal law in the eighteenth century was in fact a 'ruling-class
conspiracy' for the protection of commercial activity and the
manipulation of the labouring poor.[99] Despite Langbein's effective
critique of this hypothesis,[100] Gatrell and Hay have shown how the
law was enforced at this time as much by its qualities as a theatre of
terror as by its insistence on the detection of crime, or the probative
qualities of evidentiary material.

In the sixteenth- to eighteenth-century context of brief and
confrontational hearings, Langbein argues that '[t]he essential
purpose of the criminal trial was to afford the accused an opportunity to reply in person to the charges against him', and he
describes this old view of the criminal trial format as 'the "accused
speaks" theory'. While this view prevailed:

the defendant's refusal to respond to the incriminating evidence against
him would have been suicidal. Without counsel, the testimonial and
defensive functions were inextricably merged, and refusing to speak would
have amounted to a forfeiture of all defense. The sources show that
criminal defendants did not in fact claim any such self-destructive right.[101]

The assumption 'that the defendant should be routinely available as
a testimonial resource' remained the 'fundamental premise' of the
criminal trial until the late eighteenth century, and 'testimonial' in
this context is defined to mean 'that the defendant spoke to the
merits, even though, until the Criminal Evidence Act, 1898 . . . [he]
was forbidden from speaking on oath'.[102] Langbein adds that the
'aspiration to capture the defendant as a testimonial resource is
perfectly understandable'; '[h]e is, after all, the most efficient
possible witness. Guilty or innocent, he has been close enough to the

events to get prosecuted for the offense.'[103] Access to the accused's
narrative of criminal responsibility places testimony at the heart of
the criminal trial. But as Christopher Allen cautions, attention could
always be drawn to the status of this narrative to diminish the
significance of the accused's account; in Lord Brougham's words, the
prisoner's tale 'being without the sanction of an oath, and not being
liable to cross-examination, went for no more than the speech of his
counsel or his plea of "not guilty" '.[104]

The conduct of an accused's defence – the nature of the testimony
he could give on his own behalf, or his ability to challenge aspects of
the prosecution case – is intimately associated with the availability of
legal representation. In the old view of the felony trial, the accused
spoke for himself because he was not entitled to the benefit of
counsel on questions of fact. According to Langbein, there were
three major reasons why felons remained unrepresented in the
eighteenth century: the role of the trial judge was assumed to include
that of counsel for the prisoner; 'an inchoate notion of the standard
of proof in criminal cases' led to the expectation that a man would
not be convicted unless the evidence of his guilt was plainly manifest;
and it was believed that the 'facts' of the case which emerged from
the accused's admissions would in some way guarantee the discovery
of the truth.[105] The conception of the trial as an 'oral conflict
between two unprepared amateurs'[106] was assumed to reveal the
true facts of the offence. As Sergeant William Hawkins observed in
1721:

[G]enerally every one of Common Understanding may as properly speak
to a Matter of Fact, as if he were the best Lawyer; . . . it requires no
manner of Skill to make a plain and honest Defence, which in Cases of this
Kind is always the best, the Simplicity and Innocence, artless and
ingenuous Behaviour of one whose Conscience acquits him, having something in it more moving and convincing than the highest Eloquence of
Persons speaking in a Cause not their own . . . Whereas on the other Side,
the very Speech, Gesture and Countenance, and Manner of Defence of
those who are guilty, when they speak for themselves, may often help to
disclose the Truth, which probably would not so well be discovered from
the artificial Defence of others speaking for them.[107]

As Langbein notes, '[t]he words *speak*, *speech*, and *speaking* appear four
times in this short passage, epitomizing in contemporary narrative
the image of the "accused speaks" trial'.[108] In Langbein's terms, the
accused speaks 'either to clear himself or to hang himself'.[109] As he

was unrepresented by counsel, 'there was scarcely any possibility of distinguishing the accused's role as defender and as witness',[110] and hence many of the rules of evidence which were dependent upon a division of the accused's role had not yet developed. John Bender has drawn attention to the emergence of the term 'alibi' during the early eighteenth century, and he defines it as 'the inverse image of the indictment, a story brought to court at the Old Bailey in order to counter or cancel a justice of the peace's narrative reduction of evidence to writing', and both Bender and Grossman explore the association between the alibi and realistic fiction.[111] For my purposes, though, what is significant about the alibi is the way in which it required of the defendant a positive assertion of his innocence, a declaration that he could prove his denial of responsibility for a crime rather than simply pick holes in the prosecution case. The alibi is closely related to Langbein's theory that the accused must proffer a genuine defence to secure an acquittal.

Hawkins' description of the ideal defendant places honest, artless narrative (which seemingly maintains a close association between language and the 'reality' it purports to describe) in competition with inventive rhetoric which may serve to sever or distort the relationship between essential truth and its linguistic representation. To insist on plain fact is to seek to tether appearances to reality. In Hawkins' analysis, the defendant must rely on his bare word for his defence, a word without the support of the oath, a statement of 'fact' without subjective interpretation. McKeon suggests ways in which the puritan preference for plain speech is related to the narratives formulated by Royal Society members in the seventeenth-century: '[l]ike that of the Protestant "mechanick preacher", [the] plainness [of the scientific recorder] is at once a rhetorical and cultural attribute'. McKeon, like Shapiro, traces in this 'negative capability' a reaction against the strategies of rhetoric which were historically associated with the formation of opinion rather than scientific knowledge; 'the "plainness" of the plain style connotes the artlessness both of transparency and of untutored roughness and irregularity'.[112] However, the rejection of rhetoric itself becomes a rhetorical stance, and subsequent moves towards the provision of legal representation for those accused of felony involved a recognition that artless, uneducated speech cannot necessarily bridge the gap between language and the events it seeks to describe.

The legal disadvantage that personal defence imposed upon those

accused of felony was something of an historical anomaly. Representation had been permitted in cases of misdemeanour since medieval
times and the defendant could then answer the charges through the
agency of counsel. In 1696, representation was extended by act of
parliament to those charged with treason;[113] after that time, the
accused could still answer the charge in his or her own words (but
not on oath) even if s/he retained counsel to speak on his or her
behalf.[114] Hence, we see the availability of legal representation to
those political activists accused of seditious libel and treason in the
1790s and the concomitant opportunity given to practitioners such as
Thomas Erskine to develop an impressive profile as a defence lawyer
in the decades before what David Cairns calls the abolition of the
'felony counsel restriction'.[115]

As Grossman rightly notes, the treason trials of 1794 entrenched
the adversarial trial format in the public imagination,[116] but at the
same time it must be remembered that defendants charged with
non-political crimes – '[t]he vast mass of felonies, involving death
and exile, lengthened imprisonment, corporal punishment, perpe-
tual infamy, and attainder of blood' – did not routinely enjoy legal
assistance.[117] Langbein notes that '[i]n the later 1710s and 1720s
prosecution counsel is reported appearing [at the Old Bailey] in
cases of felony perhaps once a year'.[118] It was not until 1734 or 1735
that defence counsel seem to have been permitted, by acts of judicial
discretion, to assume some responsibilities of leading evidence for
the prisoner and cross-examining prosecution witnesses, and Langbein suggests tentatively that this may have resulted from a 'greater
use of prosecution counsel' in the years immediately prior to the
relaxation of the prohibition.[119] Landsman details the increasing
refinement of techniques of cross-examination displayed by defence
counsel in the late eighteenth-century courtroom,[120] but even at this
date, criminal lawyers could fulfil only a limited adversarial role;
they were unable to address the jury – and hence to create a
persuasive narrative from the fractured facts of a client's story – until
1836.[121]

Several important consequences flowed from the introduction of
defence counsel in felony trials and the gradual expansion of their
initially limited role. Langbein identifies these as, firstly, a diminution
of the accused's significance as a testimonial resource – '[d]efending
no longer required testifying' – and a clarification of the structure of

the trial: 'In place of the rambling altercation that had persisted into the practice of the early eighteenth century, the criminal trial underwent that articulation of sequence into prosecution and defense "cases" that so characterizes adversary procedure.'[122] Bender has described the profound consequences for narrative organisation which followed the introduction of defence counsel in felony trials in the second half of the eighteenth century. Their expanded role 'subject[ed] the prosecution's evidentiary constructs to articulated standards of reliability', which he defines as a legal manifestation of realism, and rendered the courtroom a forum for the work of 'expert voices'. Adopting Bahktin's definition of ' "polyglossia" as the defining trait of novelistic discourse', Bender thus argues that the 'lawyerization' of the criminal trial could be called a form of 'novelization.'[123] Counsel assuming the duties of cross-examination limited opportunities for the accused to make inculpatory admissions in the course of his or her interrogation of prosecution witnesses,[124] and legal objections to prosecution evidence – for example, on the grounds of admissibility or irrelevance – became increasingly important to the case for the defence. At the same time, the emergence of these 'expert voices' suppressed other stories and less rigorous accounts of an 'event'; thus we see the hardening of rules against the admission of hearsay material and involuntary confessions, and the emergence of a gradual recognition of the accused's right to silence.[125] Langbein describes this new version of the trial as the 'testing the prosecution' format. The 'ascendance of defense counsel' placed the prisoner 'in a position to defend by proxy'.[126] And as counsel 'assumed the defensive function', they 'suppressed the defendant's testimonial role',[127] thus replacing the plain speech of the prisoner with the suspicious rhetoric of the professional practitioner.

At the end of the nineteenth century, the influential jurist James Thayer argued that evidentiary procedure evolved to control the material that a jury could consider as the basis for its decisions.[128] But for Langbein, the advent of legal representation was 'about to cost the judges their commanding role in the procedure, and thereby to make the jury much more dangerous': '[t]he formation of the law of evidence from the middle of the eighteenth century is more or less contemporaneous with the onset of lawyerization of the criminal trial . . . [T]he true historical function of the law of evidence may not have been so much jury control as lawyer control.'[129] According to Bender, '[t]he emergent rules of evidence and proof relocate judicial administration within narrative categories – ways of proceeding – rather than personifying authority in a visible actor' and, with the displacement of the judge, '[c]ontrol is lodged in rules and categories themselves through the very act of subscription to them'; '[t]he reformulation of authority in terms of ostensibly autonomous rules finds its counterpart in the convention of transparency that distinguishes the realist novel'.[130] This likeness was emphasised by the fact that in Victorian England the trial – lengthened and professionalised by the voices of the lawyers – came to represent the culmination of the public quest for criminal justice in place of the scaffold. In both Gatrell's and Michel Foucault's accounts, the late eighteenth and early nineteenth centuries saw a gradual decline in the pan-European spectacle of punishment, as attention increasingly turned from the inscription of punishment upon the body of a malefactor to surveillance, incarceration, and the reformation of the individual offender.[131] After decades of agitation against the unseemly behaviour of the unruly masses at Tyburn and, later, at Newgate, executions were finally removed from the offended middle-class gaze in 1868.[132] In Grossman's analysis, public interest in the administration of justice now moved from the spectacle of the scaffold to the unfolding (but perhaps less salacious) drama of forensic investigation, the eloquence of the trial lawyers, and the anxiety of the verdict. Literature which dealt with transgression and punishment altered accordingly.[133] The expansion of the role of defence counsel in the early nineteenth century coincided with a time of widespread reform of schemes of punishment as well as of the laws of evidence and procedure.[134]

EYE-WITNESS TESTIMONY AND CIRCUMSTANTIAL EVIDENCE

In his *History of the Common Law*, first published posthumously in 1713, Matthew Hale located the peculiar virtue of the English criminal trial in a combination of factors, such as the publicity of the proceedings, the impartiality of the judge, and the 'open course of Evidence'.[135] Once the jurors are sworn, he notes:

[T]he Evidence on either Part is given in upon the Oaths of Witnesses, or other Evidence by Law allowed, (as Records and ancient Deeds, but later Deeds and Copies of Records must be attested by the Oaths of Witnesses) and other Evidence in the open Court, and in the Presence of the Parties, their Attornies, Council, and all By-standers, and before the Judge and Jury, where each party has Liberty of excepting, either to the Competency of the Evidence, or the Competency or Credit of the Witnesses, which Exceptions are publickly stated, and by the Judges openly and publickly allowed or disallowed . . .[136]

He asserts the importance of the opportunity for the judge and jury to watch a witness present his evidence, for 'many times the very Manner of a Witness's delivering his Testimony will give a probable Indication whether he speaks truly or falsly (sic)':

The very Quality, Carriage, Age, Condition, Education, and Place of Commorance of Witnesses, is by this Means plainly and evidently set forth to the Court and the Jury, whereby the Judge and Jurors may have a full Information of them, and the Jurors as they see Cause may give the more or less Credit to their Testimony, for the Jurors are not only Judges of the Fact, but many times of the Truth of Evidence . . .[137]

Hale goes on to compare the English trial with its civilian counterpart, where the weight to be given to pieces of evidence is prescribed in advance; the jury, in contrast, is flexible and pragmatic in its assessment of the probative value of evidence. Yet, influenced by Locke and continental traditions, the author of the most influential early treatise on evidence moved away from Hale's assumption that the appraisal of oral testimony lay at the heart of the jury trial. In *The Law of Evidence* (first published in 1756, but probably completed prior to 1726),[138] Gilbert formulated what became known as the 'best evidence rule' – namely, '[t]hat a Man must have the utmost Evidence, the Nature of the Fact is capable of':

Now this in the first Place, is very plain, that when we can't see or hear any Thing ourselves, and yet are obliged to make a Judgment of it, we must see and hear by Report from others; which is one step farther from Demonstration, which is founded upon the View of our own Senses; and yet there is that Faith and Credit to be given to the Honesty and Integrity of credible and disinterested Witnesses, attesting any Fact under the Solemnities and Obligation of Religion, and the Dangers and Penalties of Perjury, that the Mind equally acquiesces therein as on a Knowledge by Demonstration, for it cannot have any more Reason to be doubted than if we ourselves had heard and seen it; and this is the Original of Trials, and all Manner of Evidence.

Gilbert was aware of 'the Imperfections of Memory' and he formulated rules to govern the reception of proof in the event of

inconsistencies arising in the statements of witnesses.[139] Yet despite
this discussion, the bulk of the treatise is devoted to the treatment of
documentary material and Landsman sees Gilbert as assuming
implicitly the superiority of written evidence to oral testimony; he
argues that Gilbert was hampered by 'hierarchical analysis and
mathematical thinking' which were non-adversarial in their
approach and 'strikingly like the mathematical methods developed
in the Roman-canon system'. Landsman asserts that the increasing
importance of lawyers in the trial format of the late eighteenth
century enhanced the role of oral evidence in court; although he sees
the oath as gradually diminishing in significance, the refinement of
techniques of cross-examination produced a 'shift . . . to a decidedly
more adversarial approach based on litigant presentation and
interrogation'.[140]

The somewhat tenuous distinction between testimony and circumstantial evidence was discussed in the Introduction, but the popular
history of circumstantial evidence requires some mention here. Patey
notes that circumstances played a role in Augustan physico-
theological discourse and its 'hierarchy of signs',[141] but Shapiro
argues that the indirect evidence of inferences to be drawn from
facts in courts of law was initially treated with suspicion because of
its roots in presumption. Except in cases where testimonial evidence
was not available, Shapiro notes that early modern jurists regarded
'[p]resumptive evidence . . . [as] a less valid, or less certain mode of
proof'.[142] But both Welsh and Shapiro argue that the dominance of
testimonial evidence was eroded in the course of the eighteenth
century as the fear of undetected perjury resulted in an elevation of
the status of circumstantial evidence. The reliability of 'fact' was
asserted in cases such as *R* v. *Blandy* (1752), *R* v. *Barbot* (1753)[143] and *R*
v. *Donellan* (1781)[144] as courts attempted to find ways of identifying
motives for action in the absence of confessional material: 'where
that presumption [of guilt] necessarily arises from circumstances,
they are more convincing and satisfactory, than any other kind of
evidence, because facts cannot lie.'[145] As one of the prosecution
counsel explained to the court in Mary Blandy's trial for the
poisoning of her father:

Experience has taught us, that in many cases a single fact may be supported
by false testimony; but where it is attended with a train of circumstances
that cannot be invented (had they never happened), such a fact will always
be made out to the satisfaction of the jury, by the concurring assistance of

circumstantial evidence. Because circumstances that tally one with another are above human contrivance.[146]

Despite suggestions that the accused was ignorant of the nature of the powder she gave her father and despite her own repeated protestations of innocence, Mary Blandy was convicted of murder and executed in Oxford on the 6 April, 1752. However, suspicion of circumstantial evidence clearly remained; in 1785 Paley could still criticise the maxim that 'circumstantial evidence falls short of positive proof' as an unwarranted prejudice tending to produce 'injudicious acquittals'. Juries, he argued, should acknowledge that '[a] concurrence of well-authenticated circumstances composes a stronger ground of assurance, than positive testimony, unconfirmed by circumstances usually affords. Circumstances cannot lie'.[147] Yet the idea that circumstances cannot lie was not so much a sophisticated rhetorical tool as a naive epistemological confidence in the reality of appearances, and as such it bears little resemblance to the more complicated doctrines of inference and oratory which were to appear in the following decades.

A more sophisticated assessment of the role of inference and circumstantial evidence was provided by Jeremy Bentham in *A Rationale of Judicial Evidence*, a collection of papers written between 1802 and 1812 and published by J. S. Mill in 1827. Although Bentham upheld the usual reliability of eye-witness narrative,[148] he used the doctrine of circumstantial evidence to attribute evidentiary significance to the disposition of the witness in the box and to assess false testimony, where that testimony was known to be false.[149] However, it is arguable whether Bentham's formulation of the doctrine is an unproblematic extension of the older and more epistemologically naive belief that the circumstances of any case can 'speak so strongly' as they seemed to in Blandy's case.[150] The attraction of the old faith in the 'speech of facts' was the seamless connection it seemed to imply between the circumstances which, under novelistic or panoptical conditions of surveillance, were seen to circumscribe an individual life, and legal ideas of evidence; if 'facts' could 'speak for themselves' or if 'circumstances could not lie' then this seemed to promise a closer correspondence between the 'reality' of guilt or innocence and the findings of the court based on the forensic appearances or traces of the crime. Professional representations would not then be required. If all circumstances of an individual life amount to evidence (a model particularly appropriate for the omniscient authors of fiction), then the judgement of the court is infallible and hence more like its divine counterpart. The idea that facts cannot mislead seemed to circumvent the limitations of testimonial evidence, and both Welsh and Shapiro provide accounts of the value and significance of decisions based on such readings of fact.[151] Welsh explores the 'shift in terminology' from Romano-canonical ideas of weak and strong presumptions of guilt to the language of 'circumstantial evidence' in the eighteenth century (p. 19), but it may be that he compresses too readily the distinction between the popular, mythic hope expressed by the likes of Paley that 'circumstances cannot lie' and the more complicated theories of inference which constituted the doctrine of circumstantial evidence as it became known to nineteenth-century jurists such as Bentham and James Fitzjames Stephen.

The distinguishing feature is the resistance to the role of interpretation in the pursuit of truth. It is arguable that the lay-person's belief in the trustworthiness of 'plain fact' is simply not the same as the court's cautious assessment of subsidiary facts from which the existence of the fact in issue can be inferred;[152] such evidence requires skilful (professional) interpretation.[153] Yet, as Welsh notes, there is no doubt that some jurists and many public commentators in the early nineteenth century felt they were responding to a competition between the modes of proof. For example, in a popular biography of the notorious poisoner William Palmer, published in 1856, we see the familiar assertion that 'no proofs can possibly be so satisfactory as those derived from circumstantial evidence, where the chain of that evidence is really complete' and the familiar assumption that eye-witness testimony is comparatively fallible.[154] But Fitzjames Stephen was a staunch critic of this popular trend to compare and contrast the efficacy of the two types of evidence. In his 'Introduction' to the *Indian Evidence Act* (1872), he identified what he saw as the cause of the confusion:

The use of the one name 'evidence' for the fact to be proved, and the means by which it is to be proved, has given a double meaning to every phrase in which the word occurs. Thus, for instance, the phrase 'primary evidence' sometimes means a relevant fact, and sometimes the original of a document as opposed to a copy. 'Circumstantial evidence' is opposed to 'direct evidence'. But 'circumstantial evidence' usually means a fact, from which some other fact is inferred, whereas 'direct evidence' means testimony given by a man as to what he has himself perceived by his senses.

It would thus be correct to say that circumstantial evidence must be proved by direct evidence – a clumsy mode of expression, which is in itself a mark of confusion of thought. The evil, however, goes beyond mere clumsiness of expression. People have naturally enough supposed that circumstantial and direct evidence admit of being contrasted in respect of their cogency, and that different canons can be laid down, as to the conditions which they ought to satisfy before the court is convinced by them. This, I think, confuses the theory of proof, and is an error, due entirely to the ambiguity of the word 'evidence'.[155]

I will return to Stephen's critique in subsequent chapters of this study. Clearly, as Stephen notes, most evidence is 'mixed' in nature;[156] for example, even the evangelists' narratives privileged by the church as eye-witness accounts of the resurrection of Jesus encompass inferences to be drawn from the facts (such as the emptiness of the tomb), just as most facts – either subsidiary or at issue – have to be narrated to the court in the vehicle of eye-witness testimony (such as vestiges of a crime left at a scene). Following Langbein and Landsman, I place the oral presentation of narrative in the courtroom at the heart of the criminal trial; the mid-eighteenth century confidence in the stubbornness of empirical fact was soon challenged by the advent of professional orators, and even the more sophisticated doctrine of circumstantial evidence was used primarily where testimonial evidence was not available, or to test its strength, rather than to supplant it altogether.[157] Welsh dates the loss of confidence in facts and circumstantial evidence to the mid-Victorian years (p. 17). In Chapter 3, I argue that belief in the solidity of empirical fact ended earlier, with the movement towards the extension of full representation to those accused of felony.[158] The expansion of the rules of testimonial competence and the debate regarding the extension of full legal representation to accused felons which gathered pace in the 1820s were both associated with the loss of faith in the infallibility of 'fact' and a recognition that inference – like the presentation of testimony itself – may be influenced by bias or predetermined by an individual's beliefs. Increasingly, jurists came to recognise that the interpretation and the arrangement of facts were not completely impartial or objective – that circumstances in fact can 'lie'.

It is somewhat ironic that theologians were becoming increasingly suspicious of eye-witness claims to reliability at the same time that the law was relaxing its attitude to receiving sworn evidence provided by a wider range of witnesses. Clearly, a distinction can be drawn between testimony to the existence of the miraculous (in its seen or unseen forms) and testimony to a dispute within the realms of rational enquiry. But the evidentiary rules most altered by the reforms of the nineteenth century related to the competence and compellability of witnesses. As noted previously, at common law in the eighteenth century the parties to either a civil suit or a criminal proceeding were unable to give evidence on oath in court as a consequence of the law's deep fear of biased testimony arising from self-interest. In criminal proceedings, this gave rise to two problems. Firstly, unsworn evidence was perceived to be of less weight than its sworn counterpart and this may have prejudiced the presentation of the accused's narrative to the jury. The inequity of this comparison between sworn and unsworn testimony was noted in the nineteenth century with respect to the position of the witnesses for the accused:

> Another difficulty with which a prisoner formerly had to contend was, that his witnesses were not examined on oath; and an excellent reason was assigned for it. It was said, that they would thus have a greater latitude in which to speak on behalf of the prisoner; but when a conflict arose between their statements and the evidence for the prosecution, the judges always told the jury, that one party was sworn, and that the other was not.[159]

Historically, the provision of evidence on oath elevated it to a position of privilege, and according to Shapiro, the 'medieval practice [was to grant] equal weight to all evidence given under oath';[160] to exclude a potential witness from access to the oath was to exclude him or her from a divine pledge of veracity, and this had grave consequences for the assessment of narrative authenticity and verisimilitude. In semantic terms, the oaths – in the case of a juror, a promise to deliver a true verdict, and in the case of a witness, a promise to tell the truth – seek to tie speech to identity; in Ricoeur's analysis, they function as the quintessential performative statements which are 'remarkable in that the simple fact of uttering them amounts to accomplishing the very thing that is stated'. Drawing upon John Austin's analysis of promises in *How to do Things with Words*, Ricoeur argues that 'performatives have the feature of "doing by saying" only when expressed by verbs in the first person singular of the present indicative'; and then '[i]f saying is doing, it is indeed in terms of acts that we must speak of saying . . . [L]anguage is included on the very plane of action'.[161] For Ricoeur, 'attestation' – the belief in the speech of the one giving testimony – 'defines the sort of certainty that hermeneutics may claim' and it remains vulnerable to suspicion: '[b]ut there is no recourse against false testimony than another that is more credible; and there is no recourse against suspicion but a more reliable attestation'.[162] Attestation and testimony are then closely aligned with ideas of the persistence of selfhood and a 'sameness' of moral identity over time. The anxiety that a person could evade responsibility for his or her actions by renouncing a continuous, metaphysical conception of self had been expressed in Butler's *Analogy of Religion*; testimony, in Ricoeur's terms, becomes an insistence on identity (and on the continuing truth-value of confessions of that identity) to the point of death, thus deproblematising some of the issues of responsibility. Perjury became a crime in 1536,[163] and thereafter, legal and religious sanctions combined in an attempt to ensure the court's access to truth in testimony.

Secondly, the fact that the accused could only give unsworn evidence resulted in a further disadvantage; it weakened the court's analysis of intent or motive by devaluing the status of the accused's narrative. In the case of *R* v. *Hardy* (1794) 24 *State Trials* 199, Lord Chief Justice Eyre discussed the admissibility of exculpatory declarations made by the accused prior to his trial on a charge of high treason. Aside from any evidentiary difficulties arising from issues such as where those declarations were made and who heard them, he concluded that such statements by the prisoner as 'I did not intend to commit a felonious murder when I did the act' were inadmissible on the basis of a presumption of inherent unreliability:

Nothing is so clear as that all declarations which apply to facts, and even apply to the particular case that is charged, though the intent should make a part of that charge, are evidence against a prisoner and are not evidence for him, because the presumption upon which declarations are evidence is, that no man would declare any thing against himself, unless it were true; but that every man, if he was in a difficulty, or in the view to any difficulty, would make declarations for himself. Those declarations, if offered as evidence, would be offered, therefore, upon no ground which entitled them to credit. That is the general rule. (pp. 1093–1094)

Thus, even the importance of identifying a person's intent at the time of the alleged offence is subordinate to a rule which would act to preclude evidence of innocence. For if intent is only to be inferred from the commission of the act, as Mr Bower (for the prosecution) argued in *R* v. *Hardy* and as George Eliot was to portray so clearly in the trial of Felix Holt, then the accused is deprived of one valuable argument as to his or her absence of moral liability for what would otherwise amount to a crime.

The list of people unable to give sworn evidence in legal proceedings at the beginning of the nineteenth century was a lengthy one. In his recent study entitled *The Law of Evidence in Victorian England*, Christopher Allen agrees with the observation of the Common Law Commissioners in their Report of 1852–1853 that the outstanding feature of the Victorian law of evidence as practised in the superior courts of common law was 'the extent to which it prevented potential witnesses from giving testimony'.[164] The parties to a civil case and the accused in a criminal trial were the most notorious examples (on the grounds that their interest in the outcome of the proceedings rendered their evidence unreliable),[165] but many other potential witnesses were prevented from testifying on oath, by reason of their past histories or their religious beliefs. Non-Christians were regarded as incompetent to give evidence as they were unable to be bound by the solemn oath of truthfulness, and, prior to 1744, there was some doubt whether Jews or Hindus were able to testify. These issues were raised in the case of *Omychund* v. *Barker* (1744) 1 Atk. 22 when, in the interest of expanding international trade and commerce, the Solicitor-General asserted that the substance of the oath is universally recognised:

The oldest books of all countries mention the solemnity of an oath, as a security for a person's speaking the truth; they can do no more than lay him under the most sacred and binding obligations; they call it appealing to God for the truth, and deprecating his vengeance as they speak truth . . . No country can subsist a twelvemonth where an oath is not thought binding, for the want of it must necessarily dissolve society. (pp. 33–34)

As the potential witnesses in the case before the court shared a belief in a supernatural being and in divine punishment for perjury, a variation in the form of the oath they had taken was deemed irrelevant. The Lord Chief Baron agreed, claiming on the authority of Tillotson's teachings that '*[t]he form of an oath is voluntarily taken up and instituted by men*', and consequently their evidence was accepted (p. 42).

Whilst this ruling demonstrated some cross-cultural sensitivity and religious relativism, it did not seem to lead to a relaxation of the rules in respect of English witnesses. The evidence of children was not to be accepted unless they understood the obligations of the oath and the affirmation of Quakers was not yet regarded as sufficient to ensure the reliability of their testimony. In *A Rationale of Judicial Evidence*, Bentham criticised the continuing usage of this exclusionary scheme as a 'mendacity licence' issued by the courts to facilitate the perpetration of crime:

Consult your lawyer, or your law books: note the description of witnesses (and a most multifarious and extensive list of them you will find), by which, were it not for the exclusionary system, your transgression would be capable of being made apparent, but under which, be your transgression what it may, you are safe.

According to Bentham, '[e]vidence is the basis of justice: to exclude evidence is to exclude justice', and hence the application of the exclusionary rules can be seen to encourage criminal activity. For example, '[e]xclusion put upon all persons of this or that particular description, includes a licence to commit, in the presence of any number of persons of that description, all imaginable crimes'.[166] Instead, he argued for a more inclusionary approach: 'The rule will be, – Let in the light of evidence. The exception will be, – Except where the letting in of such light is attended with preponderant collateral inconvenience, in the shape of vexation, expense, and delay'. With respect to the competence of witnesses, he concluded, 'in principle there is but one mode of searching out the truth . . . – see everything that is to be seen; hear every body who is likely to know anything about the matter: hear every body, but most attentively of all, and first of all, those who are likely to know most about it, the parties'.[167]

The reformers of the nineteenth century became increasingly aware of the difficulties these restrictions created for the administration of justice: '[i]t was . . . clear that the more witnesses were categorically excluded, the greater was the chance that the main purpose of rational inquiry, namely the ascertainment of the true facts, might be frustrated'.[168] Legislative reforms in 1828 and 1833 permitted Quakers, Moravians, and Separatists to give evidence in criminal matters after making a solemn affirmation in lieu of an oath,[169] and Allen details the subsequent enactments which also enabled witnesses with more general religious objections to give evidence on affirmation.[170] The Evidence Act of 1843 provided that no person was to be excluded from giving evidence by virtue of any prior convictions, and past criminal activity on the part of a witness was now regarded as a question of credibility rather than competence.

More importantly, the Evidence Act of 1843 enabled people with a pecuniary or proprietary interest in the outcome of civil proceedings to give evidence, and again the extent to which interest may influence the reliability of testimony became a question of weight not admissibility. The Preamble to this Act expressed parliament's confidence in the impartiality and discernment of the judicial mind and in the immutable meaning of truth which can be discovered by rational application:

[T]he Inquiry after Truth in Courts of Justice is often obstructed by Incapacities created by the present Law, and it is desirable that full Information as to the Facts in Issue, both in Criminal and in Civil Cases, should be laid before the Persons who are appointed to decide upon them, and that such Persons should exercise their Judgment on the Credit of the Witnesses adduced and on the Truth of their testimony. . . .[171]

However, the biggest change to date was ushered in by the Law of Evidence Amendment Act of 1851 which rendered the parties to most civil proceedings competent to testify on their own behalf, except as provided in section 4 with respect to proceedings for adultery and for breach of promise of marriage (these exceptions were repealed in 1869). After 1851, both plaintiff and defendant were competent and compellable witnesses in a civil suit, and the plaintiff could compel a defendant to testify if necessary.[172] Lord Brougham observed in 1858 that despite widespread anxiety at the time of the Bill's enactment, there had been no consequent increase in perjury,[173] and Allen details the efforts that were made in subsequent decades to extend competency to the accused in criminal proceedings.[174] Finally, in 1898, the Criminal Evidence Act[175] came into force and the accused was at last empowered to give sworn testimony in his or her own defence if he or she chose to do so. According to Stone, the 'nineteenth century reforms chose rather to risk the consequences of the human weakness, than to retain the crippling restraint of so drastic an exclusion of relevant testimony'.[176]

In the following chapters, I examine the implications for narrative fiction of these changing ideas of witness reliability. Authors, too, experimented with the inclusion or exclusion of different voices and different types of evidence whilst both criticising and imitating the law's methods of representing reality. As with legal discourse, the history of the realist genre is also the history of the construction of credible testimonies.

CHAPTER 2

The origins of the novel and the genesis of the law of evidence

> [V]ery many Men among us were bred up from their Youth in the Art of proving by Words multiplied for the Purpose, that *White* is *Black*, and *Black* is *White*, according as they are paid. . . My Neighbour, said I, I will suppose has a mind to my *Cow*, he hires one of these Advocates to prove that he ought to have my *Cow* from me. I must then hire another of them to defend my Right, it being against all Rules of *Law* that any Man should be allowed to speak for himself. Now in this Case, I who am the Right Owner lie under two great Disadvantages . . . [M]y Advocate being . . . practiced from almost his Cradle in defending Falsehood; is quite out of his Element when he would argue for Right, which as an Office unnatural, he attempts with great Awkwardness, if not with Ill-will . . .
>
> Jonathan Swift, *Travels into Several Remote Nations of the World by Captain Lemuel Gulliver*, 2 vols. (London: Motte, 1726), vol. ii, pp. 71–73.

Henry Fielding and Samuel Richardson stand at the very threshold of the era which ushered in significant changes in criminal trial procedure. Within fifty years of their deaths, the criminal trial would be revolutionised by the advent of defence counsel and the evolution of rules of evidence which extended more rigid control over what a witness could say in the courtroom. In this brief period then, between the 'rise' of the novel and the more widespread appearances of defence lawyers later in the eighteenth century, we can see how authors undertook the defence of their characters without specific reference to the work of the Bar. In Richardson's texts we see an attempt to tell a story in the characters' own words, captured with all the immediacy of a pre-trial interrogation and frozen for the benefit of the readership; in Fielding's work we see a more conscious effort to manipulate evidence that has already been assessed for its probative value by its counsellor-like author. The advent of the criminal lawyer is thus clearly foreshadowed; in Welsh's terms, '[t]he novel . . . may be seen to come to the aid of its subjects a couple of generations before the criminal law afforded much of a defense' (p. 11). As we explore ways in which their fiction is indebted to contemporary ideas about the reliability of various types of oral proof, we uncover anxieties about the status of evidence which can be traced, through the work of Godwin and Scott, into the mid-Victorian narratives of Dickens and Eliot.

For the purposes of the two questions which shape this study – 'who can speak in a court of law?' and 'what are the limits of their licence to speak?' – the most relevant aspects of eighteenth-century evidentiary procedure are the great reliance on character evidence and the emergence of the related issue of creditworthiness or credibility in narrative. The influential studies undertaken by McKeon, Shapin and Shapiro all concur in suggesting the importance of truth-telling as a quality of the gentle classes in medieval and early modern England. Traditional social distinctions in England were based on the idea of honour, defined by McKeon as 'a unity of outward circumstance and inward essence [which] is the most fundamental justification for the hierarchical stratification of society by status, and [which] . . . is so fundamental as to be largely tacit'; '[w]hat it asserts is that the social order is not circumstantial and arbitrary, but corresponds to and expresses an analogous, intrinsic moral order'.[1] The 'imputed constancy, steadfastness, and reliability' of gentlemen had been a 'master-figure of the traditional honor culture of medieval Europe' and hence a justification of the maintenance of feudal hierarchies. Shapin observes that 'while conceptions of gentility changed, and while the honor culture underwent substantial alterations in early modern Europe, . . . the outcome was recognizably the same: the distribution of imputed credit and reliability followed the contours of authority and power'.[2] In evidentiary terms, Shapin argues that gentlemen were considered more likely to provide reliable testimony because they were of independent means. Hence, the presentation of truth becomes a class issue, with freedom from interest defined by economic criteria. Unlike a yeoman or a labourer, who were constrained to obey the orders of their employers or their landlord, a man of quality could be taken at his word. In Shapin's analysis, this is the basis of the social order: 'Trust is, quite literally, the great civility' (p. 36). Nascent empirical and philosophical enquiries were also shaped by 'what was morally expected of participants in gentlemanly civil conversation: the exercise of decorum, the prudential adaptation of means to ends, displaying due regard to the continuance of that conversation as a good in itself':

> The power of the 'credible person' as a resource to end 'wrangling' and to close the interpretative circle resided in local understandings and local practices. Cultural silence about the identification of the credible person was not a sign of ignorance but of immense knowledgeability. Participants 'just knew' who a credible person was. (pp. 240–242)

Conversely, mendacity was associated with servility; the constrained circumstances of women, servants, the mercantile classes, Roman Catholics, foreigners, and some members of court, were seen to produce falsity (p. 84). Amongst gentlemen, however, there evolved a complex code for dealing with expressions of dissent. Shapin notes that although open allegations of untruthfulness could end in the deadly violence of the duel, '[i]n general, the practice of opposition was recognized as a serious threat to the good order of civil conversation. Means had to be found to account for and repair faulty utterances and acts without impugning credit, sincerity, or competence' (pp. 107–114, p. 116).

Shapin identifies some signs of erosion in these cultural practices by the eighteenth century, for example in Hume's failure to discuss social distinctions as a criterion of the reliability of testimony to the performance of miracles; '[i]t is the very absence of a crucial discrimination between sorts of men – in their different conditions and with their different virtues – which marks a considerable shift from early modern ethical theory' (p. 411).[3] It is arguable that the rapid progress towards market capitalism generated anxieties that honour was no longer automatically associated with fine clothing and coats of arms, that exterior signs of wealth no longer provided a reliable index to the internally virtuous. Although the urge to assess the creditworthiness of testimony emerged during the previous century in the works of Hale and Locke, there is a sense in which the need for such analysis increased as older methods of constructing identity were challenged and questions of character could no longer be read according to the older interpretative codes: to extend Patey's analysis, confidence in the 'well-marked character', with its transparency of signification, was being eroded.[4] Reputation remained important to social status, but it was increasingly construed according to a different formula. In Christopher Hill's terms, '[t]he supernatural sanction backing the oath of loyalty and the judicial oath – God the supreme overlord – was succeeded in capitalist society by the discovery that it paid a man to make his word his bond because of the rise in social importance of credit, reputation, respectability'.[5] As McKeon concludes, credit was seen to be replacing apparel as a sign of honour.[6] In the new mercantile order, the term 'credit' carried significant cultural freight:

Credit stood for the new authority of the autonomous reporter and experimenter, and, at the same time, for the new social relations between the stockholder and the merchant . . . In its sense of trust, authority or honour it gained currency at the start of the seventeenth century. In its sense of commercial worth or solvency it began to be used from the end of the century.[7]

But creditworthiness remained tethered to the idea of social eminence, and '[t]he grounds of an authoritative story were connected with the grounds of trust in the social and moral order'.[8]

Evidence of character and reputation were also of probative evidentiary significance in eighteenth-century trial proceedings. 'Credit' resonates with a variety of meanings, tying that which is worthy of belief or assent to characteristics of social respectability and economic solidity, as Lovelace observes in *Clarissa*:

I have not found that my generosity to Rosebud ever did me due credit with this pair of friends. Very hard, Belford, that credits cannot be set against debits, and a balance struck in a rake's favour, as well as in that of every common man! . . .

I ought to have been a little more attentive to character than I have been. For, notwithstanding that the measures of right and wrong are said to be so manifest, let me tell thee that character biases and runs away with all mankind. Let a man or a woman once establish themselves in the world's opinion, and all that either of them do will be sanctified. Nay, in the very courts of justice, does not character acquit or condemn as often as facts, and sometimes even in spite of facts? (L252.1, p. 862)

In turn, Clarissa does not 'credit' Lovelace's protestations of innocence accompanied by duplicitous oaths (L263, pp. 902–903); when his hollow perversions of aristocratic sincerity are 'tried' according to Clarissa's own hermeneutic practices, he stands condemned (L266, p. 910). In his fiction, Fielding develops the idea of 'credit' as both an index of fiscal reliability and as a correlative of reputation and respectability; merchants rely on credit to carry out their trade, and thieves are granted credit on account of their reputation as gentlemen of honour. So too, the concomitant idea of 'creditworthiness' is particularly important in the history of the acceptance of testimony in a court of law. In the late seventeenth century, with the demise of medieval assumptions as to the automatic efficacy of the oath, juries increasingly examined the credibility of witnesses and assessed the 'credit' of their testimony.[9] In the *Law of Evidence*, which, as noted previously, was published in 1756 but written as early as 1726, and which may thus reflect ideas of 'creditworthiness' familiar to Fielding, Gilbert attempted to formulate rules for the assessment of the creditworthiness of witnesses. For example:

If there be two Witnesses against two, and no Preponderating as to their Number, they are to be weighed as to their Credit . . .

The Credit of a Witness is to be judged from his State and Dignity in the World, for Men of easy Circumstances are supposed more hardly induced to commit a manifest Perjury.

Their Credit is to be taken from their Principles, for Men atheistical and loose to Oaths are not of the same Credit as Men of good Manners and clear Conversation.

Their Credit is to be taken from their perfect Indifference to the Point in Question; for we rather suppose that the Favour and Regard to a Relation may draw a Man into Perjury, than that it should lie upon a Man wholly indifferent and unconcerned.[10]

In 1786, Lord Mansfield, then Chief Justice, observed that in recent years 'the Courts have endeavoured, as far as possible, consistent with [old] authorities, to let the objection go to the credit, rather than to the competency, of a witness'.[11] By 1788, the idea of credit had been the subject of authoritative judicial definition:

The distinction between the competency and the credit of a witness has long been settled. If a question be made respecting his competency, the decision of that question is the exclusive province of the Judge; but if the ground of the objection go to his credit only, his testimony must be received and left with the Jury, under such directions and observations from the Court as the circumstances of the case may require, to say whether they think it sufficiently credible to guide their decision on the case.[12]

And whilst the credit of a witness's testimony could be undermined by a bad reputation, so too the case against the accused could be weakened or bolstered by the extensive use of character evidence. Langbein explores the extensive and often decisive use of past conviction evidence in criminal trials of the period and he cites a number of cases where the case against an accused was slight and the charge was denied, but convictions were obtained on the basis that the prisoner was a notorious 'cheat' or recidivist.[13] Fielding

raises some of the difficulties associated with the assessment of
character evidence in *An Enquiry into the Causes of the Late Increase of
Robbers* (1751); on the one hand, the prosecution cannot impeach an
accused's character unless the accused calls witnesses to support it,
for '[t]he greatest and most known Villain in England, standing at
the Bar equally *rectus in curia* with the Man of the highest Estimation,
if they should be both accused of the same Crime.'[14] On the other
hand, he allows character evidence to have 'great Weight' but only
when 'it comes from the Mouths of Persons, who have themselves
some Reputation and Credit'.[15] In his fiction, however, Fielding
often chose to explore the plight of those whose stories were less
valued by the legal system. In this Chapter, I use Fielding's work to
examine the institutional treatment of testimony and I then go on to
provide a brief survey of some of the works which became the most
important inheritance for their Victorian successors. In *Clarissa*,
Caleb Williams and *The Heart of Midlothian* the representation of first-
person testimonial speech serves to illuminate anxieties about the
manipulation of evidence and the contingencies of the hermeneutic
act. Both Fielding's awareness of the social and professional forces
which shape the reception of testimony, and Godwin's and Richardson's insistence on the role of rhetoric and interpretation in the
assessment of evidence, were to inform the works of the great mid-
Victorian authors who are the focus of this study.

'THE CHAPTER OF EVIDENCE IS THE MAIN BUSINESS':
FIELDING AND THE SUPERIORITY OF SWORN TESTIMONY

Fielding occupies a unique position in this study as a consequence of
his dual roles as Bow Street magistrate and novelist. Fielding came
to the law rather late in his life after his stage career was prematurely
terminated by the enactment of the Theatrical Licensing Act on 21
June, 1737. After admission to the Middle Temple, he was called to
the Bar on 20 June 1740, and by early 1749 he was both a Justice of
the Peace in the City of Westminster and a magistrate for Middlesex.[16] Many aspects of the contemporary criminal trial inform
Fielding's narrative technique. Amongst the most important are the
access to the narrative of the accused, the role of the examining
magistrate, and the widespread usage of character evidence in the
assessment of guilt. Each of these features contributes to our
understanding of what Welsh describes as Fielding's 'management of

the evidence' in his fictional narratives as well as in his courtroom. As Welsh accurately notes, a sensitivity to eighteenth-century trial procedure 'uncover[s] the evidentiary basis of Fielding's realism' (p. 49).

Langbein notes that '[a]t least from the 16th century the JP [Justice of the Peace] was the principal pretrial officer who investigated cases of serious crime on citizen complaint for trial',[17] and Fielding's writings document the whole-hearted efforts he made on a daily basis to interrogate suspects and witnesses. Bender suggests that Fielding 'apprehended the contention between organized crime and civil power as a trial of jurisdiction over evidentiary and narrative resources', and Fielding's intensive examinations, often conducted in public in his Bow Street chambers, served a dual purpose; to gather inculpatory material and to sift out cases which might not succeed at the Old Bailey.[18] Thus he had to both generate evidence and weigh its probity; that is, to distinguish between what was evidence for the purposes of a trial and what was merely gossip, innuendo, or rumour, which may be the subject of speculation, but rarely the subject of proof.

The standard of proof necessary to establish legal guilt rather than merely moral culpability seems to have concerned Fielding throughout his lifetime. In both his fictional and his non-fictional texts, he asks continuously 'how much proof is necessary to establish guilt'? This emphasis upon a careful assessment of the evidence by both adjudicator and implied audience has led some critics to insist on a close alignment between Fielding's role as a magistrate and the manipulative authority of his narrative voice. Similarly, theorists such as Welsh and Patrick Reilly have suggested that Fielding expected his readers to participate in the act of judging the probity of the evidence with as much discernment as a juror, thus, in Patey's terms, educating the reader on the inferences to be drawn from the 'hierarchy of possible signs'.[19] But there is a sense in which the standards of proof employed in the courtroom distinguish the hermeneutics of the law from the hermeneutics of reading, and Fielding revels in this distinction. The implied reader of Fielding's fiction is both enjoined to judge correctly and yet simultaneously freed from the responsibility of imposing state-enforced sanctions on the prisoner in the dock.

Fielding's attitude to the truth-value of testimony – and indeed of all evidence – is inseparable from the purpose which the material must serve and the tests which will be applied to its probity in its institutional setting. Hence, the tension between Fielding's role as benevolent author and his office as powerful participant in a punitive hierarchy generates some inconsistency in his attitudes to testimony (and indeed, to guilt and innocence) in his fictional and non-fictional work. If *Tom Jones* and aspects of Booth's story in *Amelia* reflect an authorial belief that every man is innocent until proven guilty (an anachronistic motif if we accept that this presumption may not have been regularly articulated in the courts at the time)[20] then as a magistrate Fielding was equally troubled by the prospect of allowing the guilty to escape prosecution and conviction. In his *Journal of a Voyage to Lisbon*, published posthumously in 1754, Fielding expressed his awareness of the ways in which the role of the magistrate is constrained by the need to extract evidence of a certain standard from the interrogation of suspects:

> . . . I have often spent whole days, nay sometimes whole nights, especially when there was any difficulty in procuring sufficient evidence to convict them; which is a very common case in street-robberies, even when the guilt of the party is sufficiently apparent to satisfy the most tender conscience. But courts of justice know nothing of a cause more than what is told them on oath by a witness; and the most flagitious villain upon earth is tried in the same manner as a man of the best character, who is accused of the same crime.[21]

Two standards of proof relevant to Fielding's work were evolving at this time. Although Anthony Morano has shown that the 'beyond reasonable doubt' formulation used in criminal trials first appeared in the *Boston Massacre Trials* of 1770,[22] Shapiro notes that the appearance of this expression caused little controversy as it closely approximated the language employed in Gilbert's text, *The Law of Evidence*.[23] In addition, Fielding often had to consider how much evidence was necessary to commit someone for trial at the Old Bailey; as he notes in his address to the Grand Jury given at the Westminster Sessions on 29 June 1749, this involved testing the evidence for the King to assess whether or not 'there shall appear a probable Cause for the Accusation'.[24] In each case, the standard of evidence necessary to commit the prisoner for trial or to satisfy the bench as to the accused's guilt is privileged by Fielding as a specifically legal criterion, which stresses the legitimacy of courtroom hermeneutics.

In Bender's analysis of Fielding's work, reliability in narration is the site of struggle between state power and criminality: '[r]ealism can be fruitfully regarded as a network of technical innovations that, by increasing the representational power of narrative, brought about the necessity to control its means.' Fielding's attitude to sworn testimony in his capacity as magistrate refracts this prosecutional urge. For example, in *An Enquiry into the Causes of the Late Increase of Robbers*, Fielding notes that the most effective way to proceed against a gang of street robbers is to take up one of the group as a 'crown witness' who then testifies against his accomplices in exchange for a promise of non-prosecution – a considerable temptation to perjury.[25] In his *Enquiry*, Fielding demonstrates an awareness of the potentially unreliable status of accomplice testimony but he affirms the need to use such a source to guarantee the conviction of hardened offenders. He chafes at the law's apparent requirement that the testimony of accomplices be corroborated – 'though the Evidence of the Accomplice be ever so positive and explicite, nay ever so connected and probable, still, unless it be corroborated by some other Evidence, it is not sufficient'[26] – and Langbein suggests that this may be a formulation of one of the earliest rules of evidence.[27] Such corroboration was almost impossible in the case of gang robberies where the perpetrators were disguised and used violent means to silence their victims. Fielding wrestles with Hale's defence of the rule and argues that the reception of accomplice testimony should be a question of credibility for the jury rather than of the competence of the witness to testify. To exclude it from the jury's consideration is to confuse the distinction between the competence of witnesses and the credibility of their testimony:

[I]f the Evidence of an Accomplice be not sufficient to put the Prisoner on his Defence, but the Jury are directed to acquit him, though he can produce no Evidence on his Behalf, either to prove an *Alibi*, or to his Character, the Credibility of such Testimony cannot well be said to be left to a Jury. This is virtually to reject the Competency of the Witness: For to say the law allows him to be sworn, and yet gives no Weight to his Evidence is, I apprehend, a mere Play of Words, and conveys no Idea.[28]

In this passage Fielding canvasses two types of evidence for the defence which may secure acquittal, namely, the provision of an *alibi* (which as mentioned in Chapter 1, is an assertion of substantive innocence) and the production of character evidence. Both feed into the origins of realist narrative, as for example, a protagonist may have both a good story to tell in his or her own defence and some reliable friends to vouch for his or her character. Alternatively, a popular fictional narrative can be generated from a disjunction of the two, as, for example, when the character of the accused is such that public opinion will not accept a court's finding of his or her guilt or innocence which does not tally with his or her reputation.

To the charge that a man 'swears to save his own life' – testimony in exchange for life and liberty[29] – Fielding asserts that the law of perjury provides protection against deliberate falsehood, and if this fails, the fear of spiritual damnation should act as a deterrent: 'But [the Accomplice] must not only run the Risk of his Life but of his Soul too . . . even these persons can scarce be thought so very void of Understanding as to lose their Souls for nothing.' The providential paradigm thus operates to protect the integrity of testimony; the oath demanding the statement of truth retains the force of a religious sanction. Combined with the rigour of contemporary interrogation, Fielding believed that the teleology of judgement could ensure the reliability of testimony: '[alibi] witnesses should always be examined with the utmost Care and Strictness, by which Means the Truth (especially if there be more witnesses than one to the pretended Fact) will generally be found out.'[30] In his judicial capacity, then, Fielding seems to have assumed that the trial format and the force of religious sanctions will disclose truth in testimony.

If we turn, then, to Fielding's fictional works, we see in *Tom Jones* a surprising ambivalence as to testimonial veracity which pervades both method and mode of narration. As Welsh argues:

> The main thrust . . . is against testimony of one form or another. The novel itself stands over against narratives that supposedly flow from the pen of one or more participants in the action – against memoir and confession and analogous forms of direct testimony – while scene after scene described in the novel devolves into erroneous or partial testimony . . . [T]he evidence that holds up in *Tom Jones* is nearly all indirect, and the evidence that misleads is mostly direct. (p. 57)

Welsh presents a persuasive reading of *Tom Jones* as an exercise in mitigation, a lengthy submission for the defence which anticipated widespread representation of felons in criminal trials and which converted the usual manipulation of facts by a skilful prosecutor to the redemption of an accused 'born to be hanged'. For Welsh, *Tom Jones* is essentially an assertion of the primacy of circumstantial evidence (as both subject and mode of narration) above its allegedly more unreliable testimonial counterpart. He equates Fielding's technique with the approach of the courts in trials such as that of Mary Blandy which proclaimed that circumstances (or more appropriately, a chain of circumstances) cannot lie; 'since circumstantial evidence gained preeminence in criminal prosecution, novels conceivably aspired to a true representation of fact by opposing the prosecutorial use of the evidence' (p. 76). The novelist is then seen to be appropriating the dominant hermeneutic paradigm of the courtroom in the defence of his hero, an approach which both acknowledges the author's indebtedness to contemporary epistemology and yet emphasises his inventiveness in turning such paradigms to the service of fictional convention and the role of the protagonist.

Tom Jones contains many passages in which testimony proves to be unreliable – including perhaps the most sceptical episode in which even Tom's narrative of innocence to Partridge is exposed to the implied reader as self-serving and incomplete.[31] But it is perhaps more accurate to see Fielding's criticisms directed against the prevalence of damaging gossip in the novel; as Welsh notes, 'a slightly different reading of the novel would present the narrative's counter-theme as slander perhaps' (p. 58). Certainly the narrator is at pains to point out that 'Scandal . . . never found any Access to [Allworthy's] Table' (vol. I, Book II, ch. vi, p. 98), or that the Squire 'was a Stranger to the public Voice, which seldom reaches to a Brother or a Husband, tho' it rings in all the Ears of the Neighbourhood' (vol. I, Book III, ch. vi, p. 140). In a sense, this is the rule against the admission of hearsay material in operation, as information which is based only on gossip and rumour is excluded from consideration in the magistrate's dispensation of criminal justice.[32] Allworthy's efforts to consider only material which is relevant and admissible in his decision-making process does not of course preserve him from error – for example, he wrongly punishes Partridge despite exclusion of the gossip – but ultimately the narrator discloses all, and, dismissing rumour as an inappropriate basis for judgement, adjudicates justly on the basis of narratives of innocence, confessions, and on evidence of good character. And in so far as circumstances are themselves in need of interpretation, they too 'lie' time and time again; for example, the fact of Molly's pregnancy (which seems to undermine the integrity of Tom's provision for her family) is later explained away as the likely result of her simultaneous affair with one Will Barnes; Tom's dalliance with Molly at the time of Allworthy's illness, initially suggestive of cold-heartedness, is ultimately adjudged

an inappropriate display of deep feeling. That each of these circumstances can be imbued by the omniscient narrator with the quality of
innocence rather than guilt at the conclusion of the novel suggests in
a sense the instability of fact as a basis of judgement; the facts do not
'speak for themselves' and, depending on their purposeful arrangement, may condemn or acquit.

Conversely, the providential teleology of the resolution presupposes the acceptance of the truth value of testimony; the eye-witness
testimony or confession of several characters serves to confirm Tom's
goodness, and Partridge's consistent narrative of innocence is finally
accepted by Allworthy. And testimony is also implicated in the
genesis of Fielding's work; he regularly stresses that he describes
'Characters taken from Life' ('I believe I might aver, that I have writ
little more than I have seen')[33] and that he has 'good Authority for
all [his] Characters, no less indeed than the vast authentic
Doomsday-Book of Nature' (vol. 1, Book IX, ch. i, p. 489). In
appealing, like a reliable historian, theologian or lawyer, to an
authoritative source to guarantee his veracity (a commitment to the
probable rather than the marvellous),[34] Fielding privileges mimesis
as one aspect of his fictional representation, even if he resists the
pose of eye-witness.

Fielding's recognition that facts, or indeed chains of facts, can
generate misleading inferences anticipates the debates of the 1820s
and 1830s on the possible extension of legal representation to felons
on trial for their lives. The complexity of the deductions which can
be drawn from 'facts' was persistently mooted as one of the reasons
the accused would most need the assistance of counsel (see discussion
below, pp. 105–109). If we accept for a moment Welsh's model of
circumstantial evidence as the dominant legal paradigm of Fielding's
time, then in fact Fielding – like Richardson – seems to undermine it
by demonstrating clearly that circumstances cannot speak for themselves, that they 'lie' and mislead according to their construction and
interpretation. If *R v. Tom Jones* is the perfect trial, or more
appropriately, the perfect acquittal, then Fielding's strategy of
narration itself demonstrates the falsifiability of a chain of circumstantial evidence. As Welsh observes, Fielding's aesthetics overturn
'the judicial thesis of the time': '[t]hat thesis celebrated as inimitable
any series of closely connected evidentiary facts; Fielding demonstrated that a long and very carefully arranged fiction can do the
trick' (p. 67). Despite the fact that eighteenth-century jurists spoke in

terms of locating 'truth' in courtroom narratives (and its unproblematic accessibility was assumed well into the nineteenth century, albeit increasingly to be elicited by the skill of competent practitioners and the safeguards of adversarial praxis), Welsh's hypothesis, then, serves to emphasise the fallibility of courtroom proceedings decided on potentially incomplete or misrepresented evidence. That the 'good magistrates' in Fielding's fiction (in *Jonathan Wild*, Allworthy in *Tom Jones* and Dr Harrison in *Amelia*) are prepared to seek out extra-judicial evidence to acquit a worthy character of an unjust charge perhaps reflects some anxiety on Fielding's part about the limited possibilities of appeal or review in eighteenth-century criminal procedure.[35] As an author, Fielding was aware that a benevolent writer could correct judicial mistakes in accordance with comic and providential conventions; as a lawyer, he knew the gallows awaited the innocent as well as the guilty.

In *Tom Jones*, the fate of the hero contrasts starkly with that of the alleged horse-thief who features in Partridge's narrative to the Man of the Hill. The thief was found riding the missing horse at a fair – a fact or circumstance which clearly told against him – and he was committed for trial before one Lord Justice Page at the Assizes. Partridge relates:

'[The judge] began to thunder at the [prisoner]; and when he asked him, if he had any Thing to say for himself, the Fellow said he had found the Horse. "Ay!" answered the Judge, "thou art a lucky Fellow; I have travelled the Circuit these forty Years, and never found a Horse in my Life; but I'll tell thee what, Friend, thou wast more lucky than thou didst know of: For thou didst not only find a Horse; but a Halter too, I promise thee." To be sure I shall never forget the Word. Upon which every Body fell a laughing, as how could they help it. Nay, and twenty other Jests he made which I can't remember now. There was something about his Skill in Horse-Flesh, which made all the Folks laugh. To be certain the Judge must have been a very brave Man, as well as a Man of much Learning. It is indeed charming Sport to hear Trials upon Life and Death. One Thing I own I thought a little hard, that the Prisoner's Counsel was not suffered to speak for him, though he desired only to be heard one very short Word; but my Lord would not hearken to him, though he suffered a Counsellor to talk against him for above half an Hour. I thought it hard, I own, that there should be so many of them; my Lord, and the Court, and the Jury, and the Counsellors, and the Witnesses all upon one poor Man, and he too in Chains. Well, the Fellow was hanged, as to be sure it could be no otherwise . . .' (vol. I, Book VIII, ch. xi, pp. 459–460)

The poignancy of this account is increased by the naivety of the reporter, who interprets the judge's caustic comments as bravery and learning, and by its almost incidental placement in a comic narrative about ghosts. But the tragic fate of the thief displaces and disrupts the comic focus of the tale; like the institutional injustices in *Amelia* it fissures through the providential scheme, disturbing us even as we expect and await the redemption of the protagonists. In this brief passage, Fielding summarises many features of contemporary trial process which have been uncovered by legal historians such as Langbein and Landsman; the sarcasm of the domineering judge, the inequality of the defendant before the evolution of adversarial praxis which ceded control of litigation from the bench to the parties,[36] the gradual appearance of counsel (initially for the prosecution) in the early to middle decades of the eighteenth century, and the prejudice to those accused of felony from the prohibition on defence counsel (which, as previously noted, was slowly being eroded in practice but not yet in law). The thief's explanation was dismissed by the oppressive structures of '[his] Lord[ship], and the Court, and the Jury, and the Counsellors, and the Witnesses all upon one poor Man, and he too in Chains'. Despite a suggestion of his innocence, he is convicted on the basis of an inference drawn from fact and the narrator's irony emphasises the injustice of his execution.

Fielding's final novel reveals an equally pessimistic view of the law's treatment of the artless and innocent accused. In *Amelia* (1748), the discourse of morality is confused deliberately with the language of commercial expediency; the 'credit' of the characters refers to both reputation and solvency as Fielding explores 'debts of friend-ship' and the methods by which such debts may be paid or discharged. Zomchick has provided a powerful reading of *Amelia* as a representation of the process by which Booth is transformed from an incontinent adulterer to a stable and committed husband by contact with the law in the capacity of criminal subject; he moves via a 'juridically instigated epiphany' from the position of offender to the role of prosecutor, becoming at last 'a juridical agent who uses the law to protect his family' from the predations of their 'larcenous maidservant'.[37] As Booth moves from defendant to potential prose-cutor, Fielding explores the social factors which determine the probative weight to be given to a subject's story.

The novel opens with the portrait of an unjust magistrate in action, and the narrator emphasises the ways in which evidence may be manipulated to operate against the impoverished and the oppressed. Justice Thrasher finds evidence of guilt in the testimony of an Irish accent and the assumption that an offender cannot be both honest and poor. Booth's imprisonment arises as a consequence of that assumption:

Tho' the Bare Word of an Offender can never be taken against the Oath of his Accuser; yet the Matter of this Defence was so pertinent, and delivered with such an Air of Truth and Sincerity, that had the Magistrate been endued with much Sagacity, or had he been very moderately gifted with another Quality very necessary to all who are to administer Justice, he would have employed some Labour in cross-examining the Watchmen; at least he would have given the Defendant the Time he desired to send for the other Persons who were present at the Affray; neither of which he did. In short, the Magistrate had too great an Honour for Truth to suspect that she ever appeared in sordid Apparel; nor did he ever sully his sublime Notions of that Virtue, by uniting them with the mean Ideas of Poverty and Distress.[38]

Booth's narrative is quashed by the weight of the sworn testimony offered against him; his bare word – an unsworn statement – is insufficient to establish his innocence, especially given the unfavourable evidence of his impoverished appearance. This diminution of the value to be ascribed to the accused's story goes to the heart of Fielding's narrative form in *Amelia*. Unlike Justice Thrasher, Fielding recognises the importance of a right reading of narratives of innocence. Amelia hears Mrs Bennet's confession with compassion and acquits her of 'crimes in the blackest Degree' (Book VII, ch. i, p. 267), and Dr Harrison eventually accepts Amelia's assertions of Booth's innocence to charges of financial profligacy (Book IX, ch. i, p. 359) despite the fact that 'ocular Demonstration appeared to be the Evidence against them' (Book IX, ch. i, p. 358). As the unscrupulous Murphy points out in *Amelia*, 'The Chapter of Evidence is the main Business; that is the Sheet-Anchor: that is the Rudder, which brings the Vessel safe in Portum. Evidence is indeed the Whole, the *Summa totidis*, for *de non apparentibis et non insistentibus eandem est ratio*' (Book I, ch. x, p. 61). Fielding's application of this legal maxim emphasises the power of the definition of 'evidence' to manipulate judgements and secure verdicts, for 'that which is not seen must be treated as if it did not exist';[39] that which is not classified as evidence is not admissible as a basis of judgement, either in the enforcement of law or in the construction of fiction. Both lawyers and authors must be adept in manipulating such evidence to either condemn or acquit their subjects and Fielding's fiction seems to display a defensive drive quite foreign to his non-fictional works.

Critics have long been troubled by this contrast, and Ian Bell attempts to reconcile the paradoxical positions of Fielding as advocate for the poor and oppressed and Fielding as magistrate seeking the more effective enforcement of the criminal law. He notes the apparent inconsistency of Fielding's move from the theatre to the bench, but he manages something of a reconciliation by stressing the ability of the comic genre to express and yet contain both conservative and critical values:

> The comic novel becomes . . . a kind of moot, a hypothetical working out of test cases, or a forensic tribunal without the immediate pressure of individual judgement or the painful responsibility of sentencing, to which all the relevant evidence might be presented. The author offers the controlled and disciplined comic novel as a fantastic replacement for the existing tribunals of justice, and, in so doing, finds room for a sustained, slyly insinuated critique of those present institutions.[40]

Paternalism, omniscient narration, and a continuing commitment to the comic genre thus allow Fielding to condemn the legal system as oppressive and simultaneously to celebrate the Liberties which it so strongly upholds. Fielding is free to present the narrative of the executed horse-thief in *Tom Jones* as it both grounds the danger to which the hero is exposed (i.e. people are sent to the gallows and Tom could be one of them) and emphasises the author's benevolence in redeeming him from such a fate. So too, he can criticise the law's harsh treatment of poor men like Booth in the knowledge that he can redeem him from Justice Thrasher, then elevate him to a position of wealth and respectability – which procures individual salvation but brings no demand for more widespread reform. Bell reminds us that some of Fielding's representations of legal fallibility may in fact be 'conventional comic devices – a way of making things go wrong so that they may eventually be put right – and they do not amount to a highly-charged satiric onslaught on the flawed institutions of legality'. Bell sees the discipline of comic fiction as providing 'an ideological space in which the author can both accommodate himself to the defects he identifies, and feel free to criticise them'.[41] It is thus possible to reconcile his prosecutorial and defensive stances, while each effectively comments on (and destabilises) the other.

'AN HONEST ARTLESSNESS IN THY STORY': *CLARISSA* AND
THE GENDERED COMPETITION FOR CREDIBILITY

The contrasting narrative techniques employed by Richardson and Fielding have long been the subject of discussion. In an inchoate Preface to *Clarissa*, Richardson dismissed the 'dry narrative' style of other authors as 'the dead Tolling of a single Bell' whilst likening his own compilation of testimonies to the 'wonderful Variety of Sounds which constitute the Harmony of a Handel:'[42] on the other hand, in *Shamela* Fielding lampooned the artificial immediacy of the epistolary style which depended for its authenticity on the instantaneous documentation of all actions and intentions. *Clarissa* appeared in 1747–1748, immediately prior to the completion of Fielding's own masterpiece, *Tom Jones*. As historians of the origins of the novel have frequently commented, the two texts differ radically in their treatment and analysis of textual evidence; Richardson purports to present the stories of his characters in their 'own words' for the reader to judge, without excessive artificial interruption on the part of the editorial voice; Fielding, at least in *Tom Jones*, 'present[s the reader] instead with a sifted and clarified report of the findings'.[43] Richardson provides us with a text which lays claim to a more immediate representation of the real; the edited texts of Clarissa's letters are purportedly made available to the reader with certain conventional devices which seek to guarantee their authenticity – all the protagonists describe events in a 'lively present-tense manner',[44] and writing is praised as a permanent memorial; 'the pen is a witness on record' (L183, 588).

Richardson's narrative technique is essentially that of his villain; just as his creator sought to 'preserve and maintain that air of probability, which is necessary to be maintained in a story designed to represent real life' with the detailed presentation of 'circumstantial and minute' narratives (p. 1499) so too Lovelace explains 'I never forget the minutiae in my contrivances. In all doubtable matters the minutiae closely attended to and provided for are of more service than a thousand oaths, vows and protestations made to supply the neglect of them . . .' (L131, p. 473). Similarly, for Clarissa, the first-person narration of particulars carries ethical weight; in a world of imposture and simulation, she seeks to be 'circumstantial, that you may not think me capable of reserve or palliation' (L311, p. 997). Yet although we are given much greater access to Clarissa's story as told

in her 'own words', Richardson's carefully orchestrated persecution
and ultimate defence of his innocent, artless heroine is in many
ways similar to Fielding's equally legalistic prosecution and ultimate
acquittal of his good-hearted and artless hero, Tom. Both texts are
indebted to Butler's conception of life as a state of probation
(which, as Welsh notes with respect to *Tom Jones*, legitimises the
extension of legal terminology to the many trivial quandaries of life
as well as to its major conflicts), both explore the correspondence
between the nascent rules of evidence and what Welsh labels 'the
conventions governing characters who tell their stories in a novel'
(p. 63), and both use the hermeneutics of the courtroom to probe
the methodology of narrative construction and to explore the act of
reading.

As Lovelace plots the final entrapment of Clarissa, he asks Belford
'is it not taking pains to come at the finest creature in the world, not
for a *transitory moment* only, but for one of our lives? – The struggle,
whether I am to have her in *my own way*, or in *hers*?' (L239, p. 809).
The competition, between gendered readings of character and
action, and, as Zomchick has argued, between bourgeois and
aristocratic attitudes towards the acquisition and accumulation of
property, is enacted at the point at which language becomes
evidence. The weapons are the claims of misrepresentation by which
each party seeks to wrest control of the narrative from the other and
present an account which corresponds most closely to 'reality'. As
Satan tested Job, so Lovelace claims to be trying Clarissa's virtue:
'An innocent person, if doubted, must wish to be brought to a fair
and candid trial . . . What must that virtue be which will not stand a
trial? – what that woman, who would wish to shun it?' (L110, p. 430).
In a radical misappropriation of the private realm of passion and
virtue by the public realm of demonstration, he will then 'love . . .
her upon proof' (L110, p. 431). In order to persuade each other, and
the reader, of the validity of their respective positions, Clarissa and
Lovelace enlist the authority of the nascent rules of evidence,
bolstering their claims to credibility by reference to court procedure
and conventions for the assessment of oral testimony. As the
protagonists, their friends and various members of their families
arrange and interpret their letters, they adopt the stance of magistrates and tribunals, sifting and weighing evidence, resolving issues
of admissibility and apportioning weight to oral evidence on the
basis of its credibility. They also assume the roles of prosecution and

defence counsel, constructing allegations of accusation and reply from the evidence. In this way, although they are committed to radically different ethical and economic schemes, the main characters are all equally indebted to what Zomchick describes as the juridical imagination of their day.[45] At stake is the relationship between the signification of language and the 'real', between the right to tell one's own story and the activity of just judgement. *Clarissa* explores the correspondence between artlessness and truth, between plain fact which 'speaks for itself' and the need for interpretation and arrangement of evidentiary material which can only be read rightly by those with the requisite interpretative experience. As Terry Castle has noted, *Clarissa* is a study of 'the *license* at the heart of the hermeneutic act' and thus, above all, a tragedy of interpretation.[46]

Richardson uses theological and legal tropes of judgement and surveillance to locate truth in the epistolary exchanges between Clarissa and her friend Anna Howe. Both share a commitment to sincerity, to the closure of the gap between language and the 'real', which in turn guarantees testimonial probity. As Anna states: 'You know I am incapable of flattery; and that I always speak and write the sincere dictates of my heart' (L57, p. 240). Language is thus, in Castle's analysis, 'the heart's dictation',[47] and this theory shares some of the characteristics of the idea that 'plain speech' is most closely related to the accurate description of fact which we considered in Chapter 1. Language should provide unmediated access to meaning: 'for what are *words* but the *body* and *dress* of *thought*? And is not the mind indicated strongly by its outward dress?' (L161, p. 543). Similarly Clarissa insists on plain honest speech in others; she criticises Lovelace for his volubility, his oft-repeated but meaningless vows and protestations. The struggle for power, and indeed the competition for testimonial creditworthiness, between the sexes and between the adherents to different economic codes, is thus situated in the space between appearances and 'reality'; true virtue resides in a moral consistency of 'being' and 'seeming'. For example, in the breakfast scene at Mrs Sinclair's brothel, the hostess is seen to wipe her eyes with her handkerchief, and Clarissa poignantly notes that 'I hope for the sake of her sincerity she wetted it, because she would be thought to have done so', thus drawing attention to the space in which such evidentiary manipulation can occur (L157, p. 531). A hypocrite is the worst of all men because his speech cannot be trusted (L68, p. 278) and dissimulation is one of 'the most odious of all vices' (L116, p. 445).

The cultural preference for facts spoken in plain words – for the artless self-defence of true innocence idealised by Hawkins – is both upheld and undermined as Clarissa's story unfolds. To describe a narrative as 'artful' is to seek to displace it from any relationship with truth; 'artfulness' is a term of abuse bandied about by all the characters as they struggle to present an authoritative reading of the real. For example, despite Clarissa's own protestations of disinterestedness and sincerity, her family fear her capacity to 'paint her distresses so as to pierce a stone' (L60.1, p. 253) and her sister accuses her of being 'one of the artfullest creatures' she knew, persuading others to do her bidding with her 'silver tongue' and her '*best manner*, so full of art and design' (L42, pp. 194–195). Lovelace too accuses Clarissa of being 'a watchful and open-eyed charmer' and 'a false little rogue' who 'make[s] an honest fellow look like an hypocrite' (L99, pp. 400–401). He regularly ascribes her proclamations of innocence to the artfulness of the female sex; 'I HAVE heard her story! – art, damned, confounded, wicked, unpardonable art, in a woman of her character – But show me a woman, and I'll show thee a plotter! – This plaguy sex is *art* itself: every individual of it is a plotter by nature' (L228, p. 737). Lovelace imagines his activities in terms of that of the lawyer; he admires, and in fact shares, their ability to 'make white black and black white' (L233, p. 770). Unlike Clarissa, whose virtue is such that her opponent's letters can be appropriated to serve in her own narrative of exculpation, Lovelace prefers 'to tell [his] own story when it must be known, than to have an adversary tell it for [him]' (L325, p. 1038). Like a lawyer, he seeks to manipulate the evidence; he must control that which should be suppressed and exaggerate that which can be revealed:

'So thou seest, Belford, that it is but glossing over *one* part of a story, and omitting *another*, that will make a bad cause a good one at any time. What an admirable lawyer should I have made! And what a poor hand would this charming creature, with all her innocence, have made of it in a court of justice against a man who had so much to *say*, and to *show* for himself'. (L443, p. 1287)

Ultimately his own 'arts' extend to the use of drugs and the impersonation of relations to effect Clarissa's rape (L260, p. 887, L255, p. 876). As Castle notes, there is an elision of rhetorical 'arts' and physical control; his earlier hermeneutic violations of Clarissa's reading of the world becomes an equally non-consensual bodily penetration.[48] Paradoxically, Lovelace simultaneously recognises the 'glorious power of [Clarissa's] innocence' (L281, p. 949), that 'virtue itself spoke when she spoke', thus confirming a correlation of language and actuality when he finds it convenient to do so (L167, p. 552).

According to Judy Cornett, *Clarissa* 'exposes the fundamental assumptions underlying the Lockean framework of eighteenth-century evidence law'.[49] Cornett extends Castle's analysis of Clarissa as 'naive exegete'[50] into a reading of Clarissa as 'naive juror'. Cornett notes the paradox of the jurors' position in eighteenth-century legal proceedings; on the one hand, they were 'Lockean *tabula rasas* . . . prepared to have the truth inscribed upon them by the evidence presented in court'; on the other hand, they were not utterly passive, but were expected to judge the creditworthiness of the evidence before them on the basis of their own 'store of knowledge derived from observation and experience'.[51] As '[v]irtuous eighteenth-century women had no legitimate source of experience on which to draw in interpreting the evidence of the senses', Clarissa's story is a study of the ways in which 'power relations define the interpretation of evidence':[52]

Because the type of experience assumed by Gilbertian evidentiary principles was not neutral and universally available to all knowers, it inscribed culturally determined power relations within the eighteenth-century law of evidence. Thus Clarissa's story exposes what Gilbert's scheme obscures: the inadequacy of the Lockean model of cognitive self-sufficiency for knowers who are innocent and powerless.[53]

Throughout the novel, Clarissa is knowledgeable about Lockean and Gilbertian theories for testing the creditworthiness of testimony; she is aware, for example, that Solmes' aspersions upon the character of Lovelace lack credibility as they are not disinterested (L78, p. 315), she is aware that Lovelace is a man '[a]theistical and loose [as] to oaths' (in Gilbert's words) and hence his 'solemn vows and protestations' have 'the less weight with [her]' (L57, p. 242), and she proposes a formal hearing of the issues in dispute with her family, with 'the facts to be stated and agreed upon by both; and the decision to be given according to the force of the arguments each shall produce in support of their side of the question' before an impartial judge (L53.1, pp. 227–228). She is aware of the strategies that should be used to test proof (just as she is aware of the power of her siblings'

misrepresentations to determine her parents' verdict), but because of
what Castle labels as her naive hermeneuticism – her assumption
that a signature on a letter guarantees its authenticity, that a person's
apparel indicates their social standing – she fails to detect Lovelace's
continual frauds, impostures and forgeries.[54] Her lack of standing in
a patriarchal society (without any one to 'plead' on her behalf), her
lack of social experience, prevent her from being able to see that
evidence can be manufactured, that circumstances can mislead.

But if legal strategies of proof and persuasion are imitated
throughout the novel, it is an explicit rejection of the publicity of the
law and its patriarchal biases which generate the very production of
Clarissa in its epistolary form; indeed, it is the one of the few texts
discussed in this study which does not feature the fictional representation of a formal hearing. Clarissa's story opens with her refusal to
proceed against her father for the control of her own estate, and
although Anna, Mrs Howe, and Dr Lewen later argue in favour of
the presentation of 'public evidence' against Lovelace in an 'open
court' on the assumption that there is 'little difference . . . between a
suppressed evidence and a false one' (L427, pp. 1251–1252), this urge
towards public exposure and judgement is displaced onto the writing
of her story (L372, p. 1152) and the editing of her letters by Belford
(L379, p. 1163). As Clarissa argues, only a private audience could
properly understand 'the grievous methods to which he had recourse' (L428, p. 1253); this format offers greater scope for admitting
more general evidence of Clarissa's purity of intentions and her
subsequent grief before the court of the readership. Instead of the
need for her to appear as a witness for the prosecution, she can now
seek to forgive Lovelace and acquit him of malicious intentions; he
in turn is co-opted to serve as her witness in Richardson's carefully
orchestrated demonstration of her innocence of character.

Yet if litigation is problematic, Clarissa is nevertheless aware of
the difficulties inherent in the attempt to tell one's own story; her
narrative of self-defence may cast aspersions on members of her own
family – '[w]hat an unhappy situation is that which obliges her, in
her *own defence* as it were, to expose *their* failings?' (L13, p. 82) – and
she may be unable to maintain a tenor of impartiality; 'I fancy, my
dear, however, that there would hardly be a guilty person in the
world, were each *suspected* or *accused* person to tell his or her own
story, and be allowed any degree of credit' (L36, p. 172). She
acknowledges that testimony is invariably self-serving; without it,

however, '[her] crime will be known without the provocations, and without the artifices of the betrayer too' (L94, p. 382). After rigorous self-examination, Clarissa 'cannot charge [her]self with one criminal or faulty inclination' (L173, p. 565); in legal terms again, her account reveals no 'accomplice-inclination' (L279, p. 943). She sees the moral of her story as the disjunction of appearances and essential reality – that circumstances can lie, that speech can be misleading, 'that the eye is a traitor, and ought ever to be mistrusted; that form is deceitful'. (L187, p. 601). Yet it remains significant that she tells her tale in her own words, that the reader has access to her own statements of the purity of her intentions. If Richardson is seen as preempting the role of defence counsel in cases of felony, then he is also allowing the reader to assess the evidence (sifted and organised by the editor, yet at the same time with urgent narrative immediacy) of her worthiness to receive the providential rewards conferred by narrative closure. Belford is a culturally empowered juror, an 'adept in the pretended science of reading men' (L370, p. 1145), and he studies the evidence 'with the significant air of a Middlesex Justice' (L292, p. 963) before conferring approval on her character and course of conduct. He constrains the desires of Lovelace, the skilled rhetorician, to appropriate her story, her body, her last testament and finally her embalmed heart. Her innocence is thus endorsed by careful editorial practice which simultaneously depends upon the sincerity of her own 'heart's speech' and the purity of her intentions as evidenced in her letters.

'TRUSTING YOUR VINDICATION TO THE PLAUSIBILITY OF YOUR TALE': *CALEB WILLIAMS* AND FICTIONS OF SELF-DEFENCE

William Godwin's disturbing masterpiece was written in 1794 at a time when the prosecution of the twelve members of the London Corresponding Society for treason ensured that verbal evidence of intention was regarded as politically suspect. Although the novel was completed immediately prior to the first of the trials, Pamela Clemit has noted that Godwin dated his Preface so as to inscribe within the text the date of Thomas Hardy's arrest,[55] thus providing evidence of his sympathy with the accused and his concern that in such a political climate, 'even the humble novelist might be shown to be constructively a traitor'.[56] Hardy, Horne Tooke and other members

of the London Corresponding Society were in fact charged with a
form of constructive treason as their alleged activities were not
specifically proscribed by the terms of the Treason Act (25 Edward
III, st. 5, cap. 2). In Godwin's *Cursory Strictures on the Charge Delivered by
Lord Chief Justice Eyre to the Grand Jury* (1794), we see the locus of his
anxiety to be the contest between plain, clear, and unambiguous
statute law which judges should interpret in a strictly literal way, and
creative, subjective interpretations which seek to extend the ambit of
the criminal law without recourse to parliament. Godwin insisted
that creative interpretation played no part in the establishment of
the law; '[t]he meaning [the judges] found in the statute yesterday,
that meaning, and no other, they are to find today'.[57] Thomas
Erskine made similar points in his defence of the accused. The Act
must always be interpreted literally, which, in John Barrell's profound analysis, means that 'it must not be interpreted at all, must be
treated as if – as Coke . . . had put it – it has no "IMPLICATIONS
OR INFERENCES WHATSOEVER"'.[58] Barrell notes that
Erskine is here indulging 'the Benthamite fantasy that the language
of legislation is, or could be, a perfectly unambiguous and transparent language'.[59] In his *Enquiry Concerning Political Justice, and its
Influence on General Virtue and Happiness* (1793), Godwin criticised the
tendency of the courts to 'wrest the law to include a case which was
never in the contemplation of the author', for which travesty the
'quibbles of lawyers and the arts by which they refine and distort the
sense of the law, are proverbial'.[60] *Caleb Williams* shares points of
contact with the subsequent defence of Hardy and Horne Tooke.
Randa Helfield has presented a provocative reading of *Caleb Williams*
as a treasonous text; Caleb 'set[s him]self as a spy upon [his master's]
actions' (p. 10), he seeks to appropriate his story, and he ultimately
imagines, encompasses and brings about the death of his monarch-
like adversary. His boundless thirst for knowledge becomes a
'treason against the sovereignty of truth' and suggests that, as in the
cases of Hardy and Horne Tooke, imagination is the *mens rea* of
Caleb's crime. Yet as Helfield notes, the novel portrays a radical
instability of innocence and interpretative activities, thus suggesting
that 'legal truth is a matter of linguistic construction'.[61]

Critical opinion is divided as to whether the conclusion of *Caleb
Williams* represents a triumph for his 'plain unvarnished tale of
innocence' artlessly told in response to the wrongful charge of theft,
or whether it in fact embodies a victory for rhetoric as Caleb learns

to speak the language of false honour and servility demonstrated by Falkland himself.[62] Caleb and Falkland face parallel accusations in the first part of the novel and the contrasting weight assigned to their narratives of exculpation by public opinion clearly reveals the social forces which predetermine the admissibility and creditworthiness of such stories as evidence. Both assert their innocence, but Falkland, mortified by the need to call witnesses in support of his character, can appeal to the qualities of gentility and honour which he shares with his auditors as a guarantee of his veracity. His peers discharge him 'with every circumstance of credit', and with regret that 'a mere concurrence of circumstances made it necessary that the best of men should be publicly put on his defence, as if really under suspicion of an atrocious crime' (p. 106).

Caleb, on the other hand, must confront many obstacles in the construction of his narrative of innocence which engender public suspicion of his narrative reliability. Although he is aware of anecdotes in which circumstantial evidence had proven to be untrustworthy, he believes that '[i]nnocence and guilt were, in [his] apprehension, the things in the whole world the most opposite to each other' and that '[v]irtue [would rise] superior to every calamity, defeating by a plain unvarnished tale all the stratagems of vice' (p. 167). But his idealism is undermined when, as custodian of Falkland's confession, he is subject to increasingly repressive surveillance lest he breach his oath of non-disclosure.

His plea for help to Mr Forester – disjointed so as to protect Falkland's admission of guilt – is seen as concealing 'a mystery', 'something at bottom that will not bear the telling' (p. 155). Caleb cannot tell the whole story without appropriating a plot which is not his to recount, but this is interpreted as a lack of openness by those who will assess the authenticity of his tale. Caleb 'felt [his] own innocence, and was determined to assert it' in open confrontation (p. 166), but like later radical heroes such as Felix Holt, his confidence proves unfounded. Falkland describes his innocence as 'art' (p. 168) and alleges a charge of theft against him.

Falkland's brother Forester begins the process of categorising and constraining Caleb as criminal subject. He insists that Caleb is heard in his own defence in an appropriate forum and he advises Caleb to '[m]ake the best story you can for yourself – true, if truth, as I hope, will serve your purpose; but, if not, the most plausible and ingenious you can invent' (p. 169). Although circumstances appear to tell

against him – the missing property has been planted in his boxes –
Caleb follows the example of Sergeant Hawkins' ideal defendant in
asserting the consistency of his demeanour with his substantive
innocence: 'I am innocent. It is in vain that circumstances are
accumulated against me; there is not a person upon earth less
capable than I of the things of which I am accused. I appeal to my
heart – I appeal to my looks – I appeal to every sentiment my tongue
ever uttered' (p. 175). Caleb's strategy is vulnerable to a simple
denial and it is perhaps no surprise that Hawkins is executed for
Falkland's crime on the basis of circumstantial evidence despite his
protestations of innocence; the assumption promulgated by his
namesake that it requires 'no manner of Skill to make a plain and
honest Defence' is itself seen as indefensible. As Forester indicates, if
Caleb 'trust[s his] vindication to the plausibility of [his] tale, [he]
must take care to render it consistent and complete' (p. 177). Artless
innocence, it seems, requires careful rhetorical construction; as in
Clarissa, it is a fine line between an *ingenious* defence which bears no
real relation to criminal responsibility and an *ingenuous* explanation
which reveals 'plain fact'. The opposition between artless and artful
characters (especially in women) has proven to be particularly
popular with subsequent Victorian authors; think, for example, of
the opposition between Blanche and Laura in Thackeray's *The
History of Pendennis*, between Rachel and Beatrix in *The History of
Henry Esmond*, and even between Stephen Blackpool and Thomas
Gradgrind in Dickens's *Hard Times*. But Caleb, like Clarissa (and
Laura, Rachel, and Stephen after him), sees speech as the 'heart's
dictation'; '[w]hy have we the power of speech, but to communicate
our thoughts?' (p. 178). However, this fails to satisfy his auditor, who
is tethered to the same equation of creditworthiness and gentility as
his accuser:

'[T]he charge against you is heavy; the direct evidence strong; the
corroborating circumstances numerous and striking. I grant that you have
shown considerable dexterity in your answers; but you will learn, young
man, to your cost, that dexterity, however powerful it may be in certain
cases, will avail little against the stubbornness of truth . . . Take my word
for it, that the true merits of the case against you will be too strong for
sophistry to overturn; that justice will prevail, and impotent malice be
defeated . . .' (p. 179)

As if 'retained as a defence counsel to assist [him]' Forester advises
Caleb not to criticise his master in his self-defence; such subversion

would ensure his conviction 'even if the proper evidence against [him] were glaringly defective' (p. 179).

The same reluctance to sever the connection between gentility and its correlatives, honour and credibility, is demonstrated by the examining magistrates towards the end of the novel, when Caleb, driven to despair by Falkland's tireless pursuit, seeks legal redress for his oppression. His bare assertion that 'this man is a murderer, that I detected his criminality, and that, for that reason, he is determined to deprive me of life' (p. 285) is rejected on the grounds that he did not aid or abet the offence, and more importantly that a man of six thousand per annum was regarded in law as automatically credit-worthy (p. 286). Hence, the court refuses to hear his story and he despairs that '[s]ix thousand a year shall protect a man from accusation; and the validity of an impeachment shall be superseded, because the author of it is a servant!' (p. 287). Very much like Clarissa, Caleb is learning the preconditions for the acceptance of evidence in courts of law.

As he seeks to begin his life anew Caleb clings to his belief in the simple, direct communication of facts. But even the honest Laura refuses to credit his assertions and clings to a naive exegetical assumption that an action in need of defence is inherently unworthy: 'True virtue shines by its own light, and needs no art to set it off' (pp. 309–310). To concede the necessity of defence is to acknowledge the existence of grounds of suspicion. Caleb is finally driven to use speech as a weapon of offence: 'I will unfold a tale! – I will show thee to the world for what thou art; and all the men that live, shall confess my truth!' He explicitly asserts his testimonial competence: 'I was in every respect a competent witness. I was of age to understand the nature of an oath; I was in my perfect senses; I was untarnished by the verdict of any jury, or the sentence of any judge' (p. 328). It is arguable that, in this act of self-defence, he has learnt to replace his imperfect, mutilated tale with a speech which meets certain rheto-rical conditions, such as the expression of reverential deference to one's social superiors (p. 331). But he maintains that he has delivered 'a plain and unadulterated tale' and Falkland concedes that 'the artless and manly story' Caleb has told 'has carried conviction to every hearer' (pp. 334–335). Falkland ultimately loses this competi-tion for creditworthiness and dies; but with his death Caleb assumes an ambiguous burden of guilt and acknowledges that he too is now a murderer. In Zomchick's analysis, Booth is both chastened and rewarded for his reformation by the law; Caleb, on the other hand, is a juridical subject both created and ultimately destroyed by the constraints of the criminal law.[63]

My placement of *Caleb Williams* in the tradition which contrasted the preference for plain speech and an honest defence with the artful rhetoric of the law courts draws attention to the forces which generate testimonial veracity. In his *Enquiry*, Godwin defined sincerity as a 'strict adherence to truth' and hence one of the highest human virtues. He argues that 'real sincerity deposes [the speaker] from all authority over the statement of facts': 'Did every man impose this law upon himself, he would be obliged to consider before he decided upon the commission of an equivocal action, whether he chose to be his own historian, to be the future narrator of the scene in which he was engaging' (vol. I, pp. 239–240). Like Clarissa, he emphasises the transparency of language; 'the face, the voice, the gesture are so many indexes to the mind' (vol. I, p. 242) and truth should never need to 'seek . . . alliance with concealment' (vol. I, p. 251): ' "An upright man," it has sometimes been said, "ought to carry his heart in his hand". He ought to have an ingenuousness which shrinks from no examination. The commerce between his heart and his tongue is uniform. Whatever he speaks you can depend upon to be the truth and the whole truth' (vol. I, p. 275). This is consistent with his belief in the transparency of the language of statute, noted earlier, and it is for this reason that Godwin dislikes the oaths which purport to verify the accuracy of evidence given in courts of law; although less 'atrocious' than oaths of office, oaths of evidence imply 'that no man, at least no man of plebeian rank, is to be credited upon his bare affirmation; and what it takes for granted it has an irresistible tendency to produce' (vol. II, pp. 634–635). An honest man, he argues, 'knows that a plain story, every word of which is marked with the emphasis of sincerity, will carry conviction to every hearer' (vol. II, pp. 650–651). Despite the repetition of almost these same words in *Caleb Williams*, Godwin has not produced a simple fictional illustration of his theories of language or his idea of pure legal interpretation; instead the *Enquiry* and the *Cursory Strictures* form something of an ironic commentary on a fictional work whose conflation of guilt and innocence is so troubling. Despite Godwin's theoretical confidence in the power of 'naked innocence' and the plain fact of statute law, Caleb's story emphasises that the quest to escape hermeneutics is essentially doomed to failure.

SINCERITY AND THE ROLE OF THE OATH IN *THE HEART OF MIDLOTHIAN*

In his description of sincerity in the *Enquiry*, Godwin spends some time deliberating whether 'painful truths' should be disclosed 'to those already in the most pitiable circumstances'; for example, whether the death of a spouse should be disclosed to a woman dying of a fever, or whether a Jacobin sympathiser who falls into the hands of loyalists should lie to save his life. He concedes that a lie in the latter circumstances would be acceptable, but it is not the most admirable course: instead the Jacobin should refuse to 'violate the majesty of truth' and he could 'offer himself up a victim at the shrine of veracity' (vol. 1, p. 243). Walter Scott provides the most dramatic fictional illustration of this dilemma with his portrait of the plight of Jeanie Deans in *The Heart of Midlothian*. As Welsh notes, speaking of Rachel Verinder's position in *The Moonstone*, '[s]ince such heroines are committed both to truth telling and to being true, a double bind can easily be tied by putting the two commitments at odds' and he argues that this is 'a favorite English plot, a test of the heroine's truth' (p. 228). For the purposes of this study, however, Scott's interest lies in his emphasis on the power of the oath to guarantee truth-telling in matters of both religion and law.

Like Fielding, Scott combined a legal career with the demands of the authorship of fiction. He was admitted to the Bar of Scotland in 1792; in 1799 he was elevated to the position of Sheriff-deputy of Selkirkshire, and in 1806 he became a clerk to the Scottish Court of Session in Edinburgh.[64] As Welsh observes, Scott's conception of the role of providence is considerably more secularised than Fielding's (p. 91), but *The Heart of Midlothian* is perhaps something of an exception in that, as David Brown has noted, authorial organisation is increasingly absorbed into his heroine's expectations of divine intervention as the novel progresses.[65] In *The Heart of Midlothian* (1818), Scott dramatises the efficacy of those legal and religious sanctions which operate to guarantee the veracity of oral testimony given in a court of law; within the providential framework of the novel, access to the truth (in both litigation and religion) is ensured. Scott's representation of the pivotal significance of the oath – that moment at which the hierarchy of the spiritual world is called upon to ensure accurate recollection of earthly events – dominates the structure of the narrative. In contrast to Fielding's fiction, where false testimony generates injustice (only to be corrected at the point of narrative closure), the unfolding of Scott's narrative sequence depends on Jeanie's adherence to the strict terms of the oath as binding her to speak the truth.

After engaging in a secret liaison which results in the birth of an illegitimate child, Effie is indicted upon a charge of infanticide, in which a presumption of guilt is to be inferred from 'certain *indicia* or grounds of suspicion' which are independent of any proof that the child has suffered harm.[66] Effie's lover, Robertson, confirms that Effie is guiltless of infanticide and he advises that she will be acquitted if she had disclosed the fact of her pregnancy to her sister. Thus, Robertson seeks to rehearse with, and to enforce upon, Jeanie the narrative formulation that would save her sister's life; ' "You asked her questions on the subject?" he said eagerly. "You *must* remember her answer was, a confession that she had been ruined by a villain . . . You will remember all this? – That is all that is necessary to be said" ' (ch. xv, p. 155). But he over-estimates the extent to which Jeanie may be persuaded by his impassioned plea. Brought up to revere the truth by a father who 'consider[ed] his life as dedicated to bear testimony in behalf of what he deemed the suffering and deserted cause of true religion' (ch. xii, p. 124), Jeanie refuses to 'be man-sworn in the very thing in which [her] testimony is wanted' or to 'do evil, even that good may come out of it' (ch. xv, pp. 155–156). She shares her father's assumption that legal and religious truths are essentially indistinguishable. To be a faithful Christian witness is to be a trustworthy deponent in a court of law.

The quest for consistency between private religious conviction and public participation in legal procedure affects David Deans's choice of a lawyer for Effie. The greater liberality of Scottish law at the time of the novel's action permits her to retain both solicitor and counsel (and indeed for the non-conforming Jeanie to be sworn in as a witness) and evidence can thus be generated and marshalled on her behalf. When Jeanie is called to the stand, Scott emphasises the momentous nature of the promise the Judge asks her to make to God and to the court:

The solemn oath – 'the truth to tell, and no truth to conceal, as far as she knew or should be asked,' was then administered by the Judge 'in the name of God, and as the witness should answer to God at the great day of judgement;' an awful adjuration, which seldom fails to make impression even on the most hardened characters, and to strike with fear even the most upright. Jeanie, educated in deep and devout reverence for the name and attributes of the Deity was, by the solemnity of a direct appeal to his person and justice, awed, but at the same time elevated above all considerations, save those which she could, with a clear conscience, call HIM to witness. She repeated the form in a low and reverent, but distinct tone of voice, after the Judge, to whom, and not to any inferior officer of the court, the task is assigned in Scotland of directing the witness in that solemn appeal, which is the sanction of his testimony. (ch. xxiii, p. 229)

The Judge warns her that ' "the truth is what [she] owe[s] to [her] country and to that God whose word is truth, and whose name [she has] now invoked" '; ' "remember, that what you may be tempted to say beyond what is the actual truth, you must answer both here and hereafter" ' (ch. xxiii, p. 229). As he both creates and enters into the teleological paradigm of Jeanie's religion, Scott generates in the reader an expectation that the statements of the witness will in fact be guaranteed by divine sanction.

Effie's counsel assumes that Jeanie ' "came to bear false witness in her sister's cause" ', but as agent of Effie's best interests, he treats it as his professional duty ' "to see that she has plenty of time to regain composure, and to deliver her evidence, be it true, or be it false – *valeat quantum*" ' (ch. xxiii, p. 230). The lawyer is completely unprepared for Jeanie's assertion that she has no relevant, exculpatory evidence to offer. Her anguished cry ' "Alack! alack! she never breathed word to me about it" ' corroborates the prosecution's case of concealment and duplicity (ch. xxiii, p. 231). There is a nascent scepticism here about the role lawyers play in the pursuit of truth (and this will be explored more fully in the following chapter), but the providential aesthetic which governs *The Heart of Midlothian* ensures that Jeanie's subscription to the oath elicits nothing but the truth, however damning that truth is for Effie. In Butler's sense again, it is Jeanie who is on trial (as a test of her faith)[67] and she secures her own acquittal by resisting the temptation to commit an act of perjury which would undermine her religious as well as her legal credibility.

In the absence of any proof to the contrary provided by Jeanie's narrative, Effie is convicted on the basis of a number of factors: her child cannot be found, and this is presumptive of its death under the statute; there is no onus on the prosecution to establish that the child was ever born alive; and her own extra-judicial confessions are taken into evidence against her. The status of these declarations is clearly a matter of interest to Scott, and he debates briefly their admissibility and relevance. In summation, the Judge binds the jurors' standards of judgement to the rule of law; the oath invokes the deity, but it also ties the citizen to more earthly allegiances:

> He and the jury were sworn to judge according to the laws as they stood, not to criticise, or to evade, or even to justify them . . . [W]hen [the present law] was found too severe for its purpose, it would doubtless be altered by the wisdom of the legislature; at present it was the law of the land, the rule of the court, and, according to the oath which they had taken, it must be that of the jury. (ch. xxiii, p. 234)

Consequently, Queen Caroline's initial insistence on the lawfulness of Effie's conviction is legally correct (ch. xxxvii, p. 366). Without amendment or repeal of the statute, Effie's release must be secured by a pardon rather than an acquittal; as with Fielding, Scott's representation of the amelioration of injustice is restricted to individual cases and as the narrative moves towards its just resolution, he abandons calls for more widespread reform. Jeanie is able to present her plea to the proper forum, and, demonstrating authentic eloquence in her direct and heart-felt appeal to the Queen's compassion, mercy and greatness, she secures Effie's pardon.[68] In dramatising Jeanie's successful quest to preserve her integrity and save her sister's life, Scott testifies to his own desire for unmediated access to the truth of an 'event'. The accuracy of evidence given on oath is the organising principle on which the drama and the providential teleology of *The Heart of Midlothian* rests.

It is arguable that *Clarissa*, *Tom Jones*, *Amelia* and *Caleb Williams* reveal the problematic evidentiary naivety of the idea that 'plain facts' speak for themselves long before this criticism was widely accepted by the legal profession and used as an argument for allowing the extension of representation to those accused of felony. In a sense, authors are experimenting with narrative techniques that respond to and anticipate the activities of their counterparts, counsel in courts of law. As Welsh observes, it is the imagined presence of the defence counsel which shapes the strategies of acquittal employed by Fielding long before lawyers could become fully active on behalf of the prisoner in the criminal courts;[69] the shadowy figure of the defence lawyer on the horizon can also be traced throughout the other English texts discussed in this chapter. There are perhaps several reasons why this is so. The comparatively late arrival on the scene of criminal defence lawyers provided authors with an imaginative space to occupy; in *Tom Jones*, for example, Welsh suggests that Fielding appropriated prosecution strategies of proof for the service of the author-as-defence-lawyer. Although the idea of full legal representation of suspected felons was anachronistic in Fielding's and Richardson's days, there may have been some interest on the part of the authors to correct state prejudice in favour of successful prosecutions by seeking to show that some accusations and/or convictions could be unjust. Such a reading relies upon an assumption that authors wished to experiment with strategies of acquittal in response to the perceived lack of such adequate defence services in the criminal courts, and also that they wished to work within what was increasingly perceived as the great common law tradition in defence of the innocent. Again, literature's relation to the law is one of both imitation and the imaginative exploration of its deficiencies, although whether or not *Caleb Williams* quite fits this analysis depends upon whether the legal sub-text is read as constructive treason (in which case the paradigm is one of the imitation of the activities of defence counsel, as lawyers had been allowed to represent those accused of treason since 1696) or the felony of theft (in which case the creative paradigm is one of the absence of a formal legal model, as full representation for felony was not available until 1836). Yet the representation undertaken by these authors is such that, perhaps *Tom Jones* aside, at the climactic points of the narrative, where the reader is asked to judge the actions of the protagonists, we rely upon their statements of intention in their 'own words'. We have access to Clarissa's accounts of her own motives, to Caleb's account of his own intentions, to Amelia's or Mrs Bennet's or Booth's own stories in first-person accounts which invite the reader's sympathy as well as their judgement. In a sense this is a replication of the criminal trial in transition; authors as lawyers can ask questions but cannot assume the right to tell the client's story to the jury. But at best this is a delicate balance. 'Facts' may not speak for themselves (thus creating a space for acts of legal and fictional representation) but, as in contemporary criminal trials where legal assistance was limited, the characters must 'speak for themselves' instead. Fictional testimony may depend on the skills of the author-as-advocate for its effective arrangement, but, again perhaps *Tom Jones* aside, first-person accounts are invariably necessary to a true judgement of a character's actions. This resistance to the professional appropriation of personal statements is to be found regu-

larly in Victorian narratives. When first-person accounts are excluded, there is no substantial link between judgement and internal
merit, and this concern was to come to the fore with the extension of
full legal representation to those accused of felony in the early
nineteenth century. For there is another, perhaps more sinister,
reason why advocacy was seen to be intimately associated with the
work of authors, namely the inherent association of fiction, defending and lying. This nexus of interests will be explored in the
following chapter.

CHAPTER 3

Criminal advocacy and Victorian realism

'"No counsel (said Lord Coke) is allowed in cases of felony, because the evidence ought to be so clear that it cannot be contradicted." And this passage of Lord Coke's was adopted by Lord Nottingham, on the trial of Lord Cornwallis for the murder of Robert Carr. He said, when acting as Lord High Steward on that trial, "No other good reason can be given why the law refuseth to allow the prisoner at the Bar counsel on matters of fact, in the result of which his life may be concerned, but only this, because the evidence by which he is condemned ought to be so very evident, and so plain, that all the counsel in the world should not be able to answer it."'

Lord Lyndhurst's speech to the House of Lords on the
second reading of the Prisoners' Counsel Bill as reported in
The Morning Chronicle on Friday, 24 June 1836.

The conception of evidence as 'evident', and of facts as 'speaking for themselves', underpinned the theory of the criminal trial current in the early eighteenth century. It supported Hawkins's belief, cited earlier, that 'every one of Common Understanding may as properly speak to a Matter of Fact, as if he were the best Lawyer; . . . it requires no manner of Skill to make a plain and honest Defence'. Prisoners charged with felony were unable to secure full representation to deal with the merits of their case and the defence they made to the charges against them had to be personally constructed and presented. As discussed in Chapter 1, what Langbein describes as the 'old "accused speaks" theory' of the criminal trial ensured that 'the testimonial and defensive functions [of the prisoner's role] were inextricably merged'. This was challenged by the gradual appearance of defence counsel throughout the eighteenth century, although their numbers were not 'quantitatively significant' until the 1780s and restrictions were to remain upon the extent to which counsel could fully represent a prisoner for a further fifty years.[1]

During this time, a lawyer could assist an accused felon in the preparation of his statement outside the courtroom; in court, he could cross-examine a witness on the client's behalf, but he could not assume the right to tell the client's story and he could not address the jury in an opening or closing speech, which was clearly a disadvantage. The move towards the widespread provision of legal representation for felons involved discussion of two inter-related issues; should the role of defending oneself against a criminal charge be fragmented and divided between the accused (in Langbein's phrase, the 'primary testimonial resource') and a professional agent or advocate, and if so, what is the status of the accused's own narrative of events? This in turn raised questions about the extent to which the interests of the client and his agent are identical and whether the truth is more likely to be disclosed or obfuscated by the mediation of an advocate who will stand between the prisoner's narrative and the power of the sentencing judge. After an impassioned debate lasting more than a decade, the old prohibitions against the full representation of felons were finally removed, with the enactment of 6 & 7 Will. iv, c. 114, more familiarly known as the Prisoners' Counsel Act.

The legal historian Wilfrid Prest notes that 'until about the eve of the Civil war, barristers were not generally recognized as constituting a distinct order of legal practitioners in the same way as attorneys or serjeants',[2] and their advocacy work was initially restricted to civil disputes and the trial of misdemeanours in the common law courts. The right to represent those accused of treason was conferred by statute in 1696 and the Prisoners' Counsel Act of 1836 represented a further extension of the barristers' potential caseload. As an ancient institution for the education and employment of gentlemen,[3] the legal profession had long been satirised for sophistry and the exploitation of personal narratives for profit,[4] but the expansion of the role of defence counsel gave the issues a sharper focus. The advent of lawyers as representatives of felons had significant ethical implications for the construction of narrative. It was seen to taint legal discourse with vicarious guilt (just as Lovelace attributes guilt to his 'advocate' Belford for his failure to intervene on Clarissa's behalf)[5] and the years immediately after the enactment of the Prisoners' Counsel Act saw a vigorous debate about the ethical limitations of an advocate's brief, especially the extent to which he could manipulate evidence in defence of a client whom he knew to be guilty. Anxieties about the nature of professional agency found their way into a number of fictional narratives as writers explored the morality of criminal representation and the dangerous divorce it seemed to encourage between truth and rhetoric. The legislatively-sanctioned presence of lawyers in the criminal courts impacted upon both the presentation and suppression of eye-witness testimony given by witnesses for either side as well as by the accused, and thus the work of the Bar was to affect the interpretation of 'plain facts' and the discovery of truth by forensic analysis in the courtroom.

In this Chapter, I continue my exploration of the qualifications of a witness and the limits of his or her testimony by addressing the state of exclusionary rules of evidence at the time of the enactment and subsequent implementation of the Prisoners' Counsel Act. As noted in Chapter 1, categories of witness competence were expanding throughout the early nineteenth century, to the extent that James Fitzjames Stephen, writing in 1863, could comment on the dismantling of the old rules of exclusion with satisfaction:

In former times, rules as to the competency of witnesses formed the most important branch of the law of evidence; some of them, especially the rule as to incompetency from interest, being highly complicated. Within the last few years all objections as to the competency of witnesses, with a few exceptions, have been abolished; and in civil cases this has been carried so far, that the parties to an action are now competent witnesses. This great change in the law is due principally to the influence of Bentham. One leading maxim of his work on judicial evidence is, that 'in the character of objections to the competency of a witness, no objection ought to be allowed to prevail'. This is founded on the principle that, though it may be expected that particular classes of witnesses will not always tell the truth, yet their testimony will have some sort of relation to it, from which it may be inferred what the truth really is . . . [E]vidence, whether true or false, is almost always instructive, and ought therefore to be given in all cases for what it is worth.

Stephen noted that at the time of writing, only three rules of exclusion on the grounds of incompetence remained in criminal matters. The accused (and his/her spouse), the insane, and those suffering from 'want of religious belief' (notably atheists and children) were unable to give evidence on oath.[6] Stephen's contemporaries, Charles Dickens and George Eliot, chose to explore in fiction the position of these excluded and marginalised figures; the plight of the accused received attention in *Bleak House* and *Felix Holt*, the mentally incapacitated in *Barnaby Rudge*, and the position of children in *Bleak House*. And Dickens is especially sensitive to the ways in which the removal of 'the felony counsel restriction' (in David Cairns's phrase)[7] changed both the value of the accused's story and his strategies of defence.

With the exception of the *Pickwick Papers*, which contains a commentary on the morality of advocacy contemporaneous with debate generated by the Prisoners' Counsel Act, Dickens's and Eliot's later works were written after significant legal reforms had occurred. Like Stephen, they can explore the inequities of legal procedure in the late 1820s (*Bleak House*) or early 1830s (*Felix Holt*) in the knowledge that significant amelioration of injustice has occurred in the interim, notably the reform of Chancery proceedings in the early 1850s and the advent of full representation for felons in 1836. For example, William Holdsworth has argued that the action of *Bleak House* may occur in or about 1827, at the conclusion of Lord Eldon's chancellorship, and he notes that all of Dickens's assertions of injustice in the novel 'could be verified by the statements of the witnesses who gave evidence before the Chancery Commission, which reported in 1826'.[8] But in his dismissive reading of *Little Dorrit* in the *Edinburgh Review* in 1857, Stephen asserted that '[i]n every new novel [Dickens] selects one or two of the popular cries of the day, to serve as seasoning to the dish which he sets before his readers', including 'the Poor Laws, or Imprisonment for Debt, or the Court of Chancery'.[9] Probably both eras informed Dickens's representation of court procedure, just as Eliot's awareness of the imminent enactment of the Second Reform Bill directed her attention to the time of the First Bill and the injustices (of land ownership or political or legal representation) which were under scrutiny in the period of time 'framed' by the two acts.[10] In this way, the status of a witness's or a prisoner's testimony in the 1830s becomes the topic both of immediate fictional engagement (in *Pickwick Papers*) and subsequent analysis in relation to the events of the mid-Victorian years (in *Bleak House* or *Felix Holt*). Other novels such as *Silas Marner* or *Adam Bede* also touch on aspects of the same debate about the reliability of plain 'fact' and the status of an accused's story which ultimately secured full representation for felons. In the works of Dickens and Eliot, we see some of the subsequent benefits and disadvantages of the Act's implementation.

THE ENACTMENT OF THE PRISONERS' COUNSEL ACT

In his study of the developments in advocacy which led to the introduction of the Prisoners' Counsel Act, Cairns has noted that there were two stages to the parliamentary debate about representation, in the years from 1821 until 1828 and then again between 1833 and 1837.[11] There is not space to describe fully the legislative history of the bill in this study, but I will summarise some pertinent points made by members about the nature of fact and the role of inference in judgement before turning to a discussion of Dickens's and Eliot's fiction. Central to the debate was the extent to which facts required interpretation and arrangement by a trained mind in order to serve as effective pieces of evidence. In his article for the *Edinburgh Review*, cited earlier, which coincided with the earliest efforts at legislative reform, Denman illustrated the weaknesses of Hawkins' insistence on personal defence in imaginative terms which suggested the mutual interest of law and literature in the interpretation of character and circumstance:

Perhaps the accused is the victim of an artful conspiracy, arranged by the real offender; or the appearances that accuse him may admit of no elucidation, which will not either betray secrets important to be kept on other grounds, or compromise the safety of other persons justly entitled to protection from the accused. A smuggler or a poacher, detected in combining his own clandestine measures, is naturally implicated in a horrible crime committed near the same time and place; an anatomist is discovered (in one of Holcroft's novels according to our memory), with a bloody knife in his hand, leaning over a body newly torn from the grave, and the purpose of dissection is one that he is by no means anxious to avow; a love intrigue has perhaps thrown him in the way of suspicion, and the party can hardly be expected to purchase his liberation by an instant avowal of the truth.[12]

As we see in *Clarissa*, *Caleb Williams*, *Mary Barton*, and *The Trial*, the ability to defend oneself may be hampered by the ethical urge to avoid the accusation of another, and authors clearly found this complication a fertile field for their own narrative advocacy. Before parliament, Henry Brougham, later Lord Chancellor, suggested that, far from being conclusive evidence of guilt, an untangled morass of facts could suggest culpability where in fact there was none:

Suppose the counsel [for the prosecution] did confine himself to a dry statement of facts, no case could be harder than for the whole web to be, as it were, united together by the juxtaposition of all the circumstances, so as to make up such a picture of the prisoner's guilt as that a man could not rid his mind of it, and fancied he saw the prisoner committing the fact. To unravel all this, would require the acutest observations of a prisoner's counsel; for in such a case nothing could tell more strongly against a prisoner than a simple detail of circumstances.[13]

The involvement of a skilled advocate was necessary to ensure that conviction did not result from the erroneous assumption that facts, especially when arranged in a 'chain' or 'web', could not lie.

But the arguments which stressed the vulnerability of facts to manipulation and insidious arrangement were not yet persuasive with the House. In 1826, the Attorney-General, John Copley (later Lord Lyndhurst), put the case for the prevailing epistemology of self-evident fact forcibly in his lucid rejection of any proposed reform. The contemporary trial should generally consist of 'dry statements' that 'ought to have no influence upon the verdict of a jury' and in which the evidence was

heard dispassionately and calmly, unaccompanied by any excitement or appeal to the feelings. The evidence for the prosecution having been gone through, the prisoner was called on for his defence, which was conducted precisely in the same way; with this exception, that the evidence which he had to produce, was not prefaced by a speech from his counsel. This, however, was unnecessary; as the speech of the counsel for the prosecution, addressed itself merely to facts, that for the defence would be a mere repetition of that which was already known. The evidence on both sides having been heard, the judge, not as counsel, as was erroneously supposed, for either the prisoner or the Crown, but placed where he was, impartially to administer justice, summed up, and taking a calm, dispassionate, and collected view of the case, and going regularly through the evidence, submitted it to the jury, who were bound to return an unbiassed verdict. Now, he would ask, whether it was likely, that a system like this . . . would derive any benefit by the change proposed by his hon. and learned friend . . . Instead of the calm and deliberate justice with which criminal prosecutions were at present carried on, the effect of allowing counsel to speak for the defence would be to convert the court into an arena, where opposing advocates might meet in professional conflict, and where, instead of endeavouring to elicit the truth by a reference to plain facts, or the real merits of the case, the time of the public would be wasted by contests between the counsel on either side, animated, as they would be, by all the excitement, zeal, and pertinacity, which such contests usually inspired.[14]

Lord Lyndhurst evinced a complete distrust of the law's increasing adversarialism, and his fear that meaningless rhetoric may obfuscate the trial's quest for truth prevailed. Reform was rejected in 1826 but interest in the issue was by no means extinguished.

The theory that conviction or acquittal was dependent upon the assessment of self-evident facts was finally laid to rest with the Second Report of His Majesty's Commissioners on Criminal Law, tendered on 9 June 1836. The Commissioners (Thomas Starkie, Henry Bellenden Ker, William Wightman, Andrew Amos, and John Austin) discarded the old notion that the judge is in any way counsel for the prisoner and emphasised the power of competent advocacy to uncover truth:

The advocate possesses more certain means than the Judge, of distinguishing between true and false testimony, between that which is substantial and that which is merely colourable. When the charge is false, he possesses, through his intimate knowledge of the real facts, an almost infallible key to the truth; he can show that all the evidence truly given is consistent with the innocence of the accused, and is prepared to examine into and comment upon those discrepancies upon which innocence must frequently depend for its manifestation.[15]

Access to the 'real facts' in the event of innocence is guaranteed by the advocate's access to the prisoner's story; the web of circumstances may be as indicative of innocence as of the concealment of guilt. The Commissioners also rejected the assumption, implicit in Hawkins's conception of the trial, that guilt is inevitably (or providentially) manifest in physical terms; they conceded that 'shame, disgrace and fear', 'bodily infirmity or mental incapacity' may render a prisoner unable to speak coherently in his own defence and they acknowledged that '[i]t frequently happens that hardened villains may possess more coolness and composure than the innocent'.[16] Ultimately, the Commissioners concluded that, even in a speech which purports to be solely an exposition of the relevant evidence, the presentation of every fact is subject to some arrangement by the mind which seeks to adduce it:

The giving order and connexion to a mass of facts tends to impress the Jury with their materiality and to impart greater force to the evidence than it would otherwise possess . . . It is, we apprehend, not merely difficult, but impossible, to distinguish between the effect of a skilful arrangement of facts and of a commentary upon them; an impression is often made upon the minds of the Jury by an able address, before the evidence is given, which is not the less dangerous for the professions of fairness and candour with which it may be accompanied.[17]

Consequently, they recommended that 'the power of being heard by Counsel is essential to the attainment of truth'.[18]

When the Prisoners' Counsel Bill appeared before parliament in 1836, the members of the House of Lords accepted that the adoption of an overtly adversarial format need not result in a 'verbal circus'; even Lord Lyndhurst had altered his stance and moved for the second reading of the Bill. In the years between the early debates and the Bill's enactment in 1836, we see what Cairns has identified as a transition from a conception of fact as 'plain' to 'complex'.[19] Confidence in the unadorned reality of empirical fact had increasingly been replaced by a widespread acknowledgement that perception is arranged by the mediating mind of the witness, whether (in Welsh's dichotomy) the evidence be circumstantial or testimonial. The vulnerability of circumstantial evidence to manipulation (whether deliberate or otherwise) and the consequent weakness of convictions based upon such evidence is a feature of the parliamentary debates, and it is perhaps this recognition which ended any possible threat by the tenets of circumstantial evidence to the supremacy of confessional or eye-witness testimony. Stephen, writing on circumstantial evidence in his *General View of the Criminal Law* (1863), was scathing in his criticisms of the supposed superiority of circumstantial evidence and he attacked the basis of any distinction between the two types of probative material; he concedes that '[t]o be circumstantial in [the sense of relating details in narrative] is one element of strength in evidence, but this is not the sense in which the phrase is generally used': 'It has been made the basis of an elaborate theory intended to set up in particular cases a standard of strength in the evidence itself, irrespective of the circumstances under which it is given and of the persons to whom it is addressed' (p. 265). This theory, Stephen argues, disguises the extent to which inferences are required in order to make sense of any piece of evidence; it undervalues the role of inference in the interpretation of direct evidence and it simultaneously conceals the need for the jury to rely on conjecture to interpret circumstantial evidence. Stephen notes that the phrase 'circumstantial evidence . . . proposes a sham canon of proof, and leads jurymen to believe that they are deciding on a particular kind, and a highly scientific and ingenious kind, of evidence when, in fact, they are making a conjecture' (p. 271). As noted in Chapter 1, Stephen thus rejects the traditional distinction between testimonial and circumstantial evidence (p. 273). He concludes by observing that, with the increasing appearance of criminal lawyers, the idea of circumstantial evidence is now a tool for the defence rather than the prosecution:

The only real purpose which the phrase ever serves is that of supplying prisoner's counsel with a convenient sophism. Instead of saying, this evidence is incomplete, because such a fact is not proved; or it is inconclusive, because such an explanation of it may be suggested; they say it is circumstantial, and all circumstantial evidence as such is inconclusive or incomplete . . . It is, in short, a word useful only for the sake of puzzling juries, and providing them with a loophole for avoiding a painful, but most important, duty. (p. 274)

The self-evident narrative of guilt suggested by the prosecutor's arrangement of a chain of facts has been appropriated, in Stephen's view, by the accused. Insofar as circumstantial evidence was associated with the epistemology of 'plain' fact, then its demise should be placed some thirty or forty years earlier than the mid-Victorian date claimed by Welsh, in the debates about the extension of full representation to felons. I will discuss other consequences of the development of criminal advocacy as they are raised by Dickens's and Eliot's novels.

DICKENS AND THE BAR

Critics are divided in their assessment of the quality of Dickens's legal knowledge. In the 'License of Modern Novelists' Stephen spoke of his learning in rather dismissive terms; unlike the accomplishments of Scott, who was both 'a lawyer and an antiquarian', Dickens's superficial knowledge was simply that 'of an attorney's clerk'.[20] Dickens did begin his career as a clerk in the office of Ellis and Blackmore where he served from approximately May 1827 until November 1828, before moving briefly to the firm of Charles Molloy in Lincoln's Inn. He was elevated to the staff of the *Mirror of Parliament* in 1831, which afforded access to some of the first Reform Bill debates; the following year, he began freelance work in the Court of Doctors' Commons and in August 1834, he became a reporter for *The Morning Chronicle*.[21] Holdsworth, on the other hand, has been more generous in his appraisal of Dicken's legal knowledge; 'we get in his books that account of the human side of the rules of law and their working, which is essential to the legal historian'.[22] In the most authoritative study of Dickens and the administration of the criminal law, Phillip Collins has followed Holdsworth, adopting a broader definition of 'law' to include the activities of men like Dickens who worked on the margins of the legal profession.[23]

Dickens's earliest sketches, chronologically commensurate with the final stages of the Prisoners' Counsel Act debates, reveal some of the elements that were to appear regularly in his later fiction. His interests in transgression and the psychology of the criminal mind were inevitably going to bring him into conflict with the barristers who were soon to address the jury on behalf of prisoners.[24] In the short piece entitled 'Criminal Courts',[25] we see the professionalisation of the discourse of guilt – the 'calm indifference with which the proceedings are conducted' – and the dispassionate presentation of human tragedy: 'every trial seems a mere matter of business. There is a great deal of form, but no compassion; considerable interest, but no sympathy'. A spectator attuned to the prisoner's plight faints and '[t]he clerk directs one of the officers of the Court to "take the woman out", and fresh business is proceeded with, as if nothing had occurred'.[26] Dickens conceives of the law as institutionally blind to individual suffering, thus creating an imaginative space for literature's claim to the representation of more compassionate and comprehensive ideas of truth. After the publication of *Oliver Twist* in 1837, his apparent fascination with the brutality of capital punishment earned him a temporary place amongst the co-called 'Newgate Novelists' (notably William Harrison Ainsworth and Edward Bulwer-Lytton, who were criticised for glamourising crime and romanticising the escapades of Eugene Aram and Jack Sheppard).[27] Such texts raised important questions about the identification of authors with their criminal protagonists and this is clearly seen in the works of Thackeray who, in *Vanity Fair*, for example, seeks to distance himself from the moral depravity of Becky Sharpe. The representation of the criminal in fiction was a test of the limits of realism – should evil be presented in narrative, and if so, how should an author avoid the stigma of vicarious guilt? In 1842, *Punch* satirised the 'Literary Gentleman' and the gallows literature whose heroes quoted moral truths before cutting a throat or two;[28] authors, it seemed, could not easily distance themselves from their protagonists. Nor could lawyers avoid the perceived contagion of their criminal clients. The most incisive comment on the identification of lawyers with their clients comes at the ending of *Vanity Fair*, when Becky uses her solicitors Burke, Thurtell, and Hayes (all notorious murderers

whose infamy would have been well known to the Victorian readership) to obtain her insurance monies following the suspicious death
of Joseph Sedley.[29] Although these lawyers were solicitors rather
than barristers, Thackeray's audience would have appreciated the
complete equation of author/lawyer and criminal which this relationship implied. It is an ethically charged joke.

But, despite the allegations of sensationalism, Dickens's interests
were as much evidentiary in nature and his fear that the professional
rhetoric of the law displaces personal narrative was most pronounced
when he dwelt upon the plight of the prisoner condemned to death.
His creativity was activated by a profound interest in the ways in
which punishment excluded men from the wider community of
stories; he was interested in the ultimate obliteration of evidence. For
example, in 'A Visit to Newgate' which appeared in the first series of
Sketches by Boz in 1836,[30] he dwells upon the horror of the prisoners'
final days; forced to occupy the condemned pew in the prison chapel
and to 'hear prayers for their own souls, to join in the responses of
their own burial service', they must witness their own social dissolution by the state before their life is even extinguished. Their coerced
participation in the service imparts legitimacy to the penalty which
the law will exact, and Dickens expresses to perfection the authorial
fascination with their plight: 'Imagine what have been the feelings of
the men whom that fearful pew has enclosed, and of whom, between
the gallows and the knife, no mortal remnant may now remain!'[31]
This is the quintessential point of impact between the need to record
individual narratives and the desire to obliterate completely any
evidence of guilt. Even the body – with its fatal injuries recording its
due condemnation and punishment – is dissected and fragmented.[32]
Fagin exclaims in *Oliver Twist*, that 'dead men never bring awkward
stories to light';[33] as Collins notes, this is a source of comfort to 'prigs'
such as Jonathan Wild and Fagin who manipulate evidence to dispose
of unreliable associates,[34] but Fagin greets his own condemnation
with a feeble silence which anticipates the ultimate extinction of his
voice. Dickens dramatises his 'Last Night Alive' with relish; only the
author can re-animate the obliterated consciousness.

Dickens's earliest narratives acknowledge the imperative nature of
judicial power, whether it is exercised to silence a witness by the
application of the rules of evidence, or to silence an accused by the
penalty of incarceration or death. Thus, even in the *Pickwick Papers* –
where the free transmission of stories is seen to add to a man's 'stock

of experience' (ch. xiv, p. 177) – we have the injustice of the hearing
of the breach of promise of marriage in the case of *Bardell* v. *Pickwick*.
The law of the time prevented either of the parties themselves from
testifying on their own behalf; the Evidence Act of 1851, which
extended the categories of competent witnesses to include parties to
a civil action, was still over a decade away and thus the court had no
direct access to the testimony of either Pickwick or Mrs Bardell.
Their stories must be mediated by the narratives of their friends
(who know very little about the matter) and more importantly, by
their agents, the 'professional men' who feature so prominently in
the novel. A number of critics have suggested that *Bardell* v. *Pickwick*
was based on the notorious adultery trial, *Norton* v. *Melbourne*, which
was heard before a Middlesex special jury in the Court of Common
Pleas on 22 June 1836.[35] The Attorney-General, John Campbell, and
Sergeant Thomas Noon Talfourd (later to become a good friend of
Dickens) acted as counsel for the defendant Prime Minister, Lord
Melbourne; Dickens reported the case for *The Morning Chronicle*. His
lengthy report occupied over twenty-six columns of the paper on 23
June and it is interesting to read the judge's summation to the jury as
mediated by Dickens the reporter:

> The question turned upon the evidence, and upon the evidence alone,
> whether the jury were satisfied of the guilt of the defendant. It was perfectly
> clear that there was no direct evidence of the fact of adultery; it was also
> perfectly clear that the law did not require direct evidence of the fact, but
> that it merely required evidence of such circumstances as would lead by
> fair and just inference to it.

Melbourne was found not guilty without the necessity of calling
evidence, and the triumphant anti-Tory editorial of *The Morning
Chronicle* on 24 June serves as a counter-foil for *Bardell* v. *Pickwick*
where a similar trust in an English jury produces an unjust result.
Lord Lyndhurst's speech in favour of the second reading of the
Prisoners' Counsel Bill made the front page of *The Morning Chronicle*
on the same day. The possibility that Dickens may have reported this
parliamentary debate is undermined by his letter to John Macrone
on 23 June (i.e. the day after the trial and the day of the House of
Lords debate): 'I am tired to death to-night, though I have been in
bed all day. Melbourne v Norton has played the devil with me'.[36]
However, after reporting a lengthy trial in which the verdict
depended upon the inferences to be drawn from circumstances by
skilled counsel, Dickens may well have been interested by Lord

Lyndhurst's arguments that felons on trial for their lives also required counsel to assist with the arrangement and interpretation of difficult evidentiary material.

The avaricious partnership of Dodson and Fogg made its first appearance in Part 7 of the *Pickwick Papers* which appeared on 30 September 1836. Although they are attorneys rather than counsel, their obsession with their duty to their client rather than to any higher idea of truth was particularly topical. As they explain to Pickwick,

'We, sir, we, are guided entirely by the statement of our client. That statement, sir, may be true, or it may be false; it may be credible, or it may be incredible; but, if it be true, and if it be credible, I do not hesitate to say, sir, that our grounds of action, sir, are strong, and not to be shaken.[37]

It is interesting to place this episode within the framework of contemporaneous legal developments; within the space of approximately a week in October 1836, *The Morning Chronicle* featured a favourable review of this part of the *Pickwick Papers* (Wednesday, 5 October), Dickens's sketch entitled 'Doctors' Commons' (Tuesday, 11 October), and the report of *R* v. *M'Pherson*, the first case to be heard in London after the implementation of the Prisoners' Counsel Act (Friday, 14 October). In this trial, the reporter paid little attention to the plight of the accused and the emphasis instead was on the speech of the senior barrister:

Mr. ADOLPHUS observed, that this was the first jury who, in the metropolis, had tried a person for felony since a recent statute had come into operation, which allowed the counsel for prisoners to address them. It was a most important alteration in the practice of the criminal law, and he hoped it would prove as great a blessing to the community as the benevolent persons who framed and supported it could expect. Much of the benefit to be derived from it would depend on the conduct of those to whom the administration of justice was confided . . . It might occur that topics of compassion, or arguments founded on speculation, would be addressed to juries; but he trusted they would always recollect that their decisions must be formed on the evidence.

But despite this note of pompous caution, there was a taste of the controversies to come when *The Morning Chronicle* reported an assault case (*Fay* v. *Wardroper*, Saturday, 8 October) with emphasis on the cross-examination of the alleged victim by Charles Phillips, an Irish barrister practising at the English Bar since 1821 and a prominent figure at the Old Bailey. Madeline House and Graham Storey suggest that Phillips was one of the models for Sergeant Buzfuz in the *Pickwick Papers*.[38] His rhetorical excesses were renowned, and Dickens's representations of Buzfuz's activities were again particularly apt. Dodson and Fogg instruct Buzfuz as counsel for the plaintiff, and he converts their moral relativism into rhetoric which in turn determines the jury's decision:

Serjeant Buzfuz began by saying, that never, in the whole course of his professional experience – never, from the very first moment of his applying himself to the study and practice of the law – had he approached a case with feelings of such deep emotion, or with such a heavy sense of the responsibility imposed upon him – a responsibility, he would say, which he could never have supported, were he not buoyed up and sustained by a conviction so strong, that it amounted to positive certainty that the cause of truth and justice, or, in other words, the cause of his much-injured and most oppressed client, must prevail with the high-minded and intelligent dozen of men whom he now saw in that box before him.

Counsel usually begin in this way, because it puts the jury on the very best terms with themselves, and makes them think what sharp fellows they must be. A visible effect was produced immediately; several jurymen beginning to take voluminous notes with the utmost eagerness. (ch. xxxiv, pp. 469–470)

Dickens here draws on traditional fears of rhetoric as a force for the production of impassioned opinion rather than carefully appraised fact. The oration of distress is largely conventional.[39] But it is nevertheless a discourse of power; it imports malicious meaning into harmless domestic exchanges between the parties and confuses the witnesses on cross-examination – 'each was driven to the verge of desperation by excessive badgering' (ch. xxxiv, p. 482). In defence of his manipulative rhetorical strategies, Buzfuz can claim a moral mandate – the duty of counsel to the client; 'let me tell the defendant Pickwick . . . gentlemen, that a counsel, in the discharge of his duty to his client, is neither to be intimidated, nor bullied, nor put down; and that any attempt to do either the one or the other, or the first or the last, will recoil on the head of the attempter' (ch. xxxiv, p. 472). Pickwick's possibilities of defence are completely excluded as Buzfuz converts even the right of spectatorship into an aggressive attack on the other party and her representative. There is no linguistic space left for the innocent defendant to occupy.

Pickwick himself was initially keen to 'confide . . . this matter to a professional man' (ch. xx, p. 274), but he was sceptical of any claim the lawyers could make for the morality of advocacy. He stresses that his innocence is substantial rather than solely rhetorical and he instructs his counsel 'that unless you sincerely believe this, I would rather be deprived of the aid of your talents than have the advantage of them' (ch. xxxi, pp. 430–431). This acts in place of courtroom testimony to assure the reader of Pickwick's innocence; the trial format precludes any other access to his state of mind, and the interference of counsel must not be allowed to raise the possibility of the hero's guilt.[40] But it also discloses Dickens's fear of inaccurate verdicts generated only by the oratory of counsel, and as such it proved to be remarkably prescient of the scandals that were to afflict the legal profession, and Phillips in particular, just a few years later.

When François Benjamin Courvoisier was charged with the murder of Lord William Russell in June 1840, Phillips was retained as defence counsel. Initially, he believed his client's protestations of innocence. While the trial was still part heard, however, Courvoisier made significant admissions of his guilt and the hearing became a *cause célèbre* when Phillips continued to employ all the strategies of defence which he would have used had his client been innocent; he tried to implicate other servants in the crime, he accused the police of planting evidence of guilt in Courvoisier's rooms, he attacked the credibility of an important female witness for the prosecution and he employed improper religious rhetoric in his address to the jury. The indignation of Albany Fonblanque's influential *Examiner* knew no bounds. In large editorial articles which appeared regularly for several weeks after the trial, they called Phillips' line of defence the 'lie' of defence and argued that he had greatly exceeded the bounds of adversarial licence in the service of his client:

Whether all this accords or not with professional morality, it is not for us to decide; but if it does, the public will probably be disposed to think that the profession should change its name from the profession of the law to the profession of the Lie.

We should like to know the breadth of the distinction between an accomplice after the fact and an advocate who makes the most unscrupulous endeavours to procure the acquittal of a man whom he knows to be an assassin. (28 June 1840)

Dickens followed this trial with enormous interest and was outraged by this seemingly shameless attempt to secure the acquittal of a guilty man. Immediately after the trial (at which Courvoisier was convicted and sentenced to death), two letters signed by 'Manlius' appeared in *The Morning Chronicle* under the heading 'The License of

Counsel' which House and Storey attribute, on strong evidence, to Dickens.[41] The first letter (?21 June 1840) accused Phillips of impugning the morality of advocacy and it concluded:

For myself, sir, I am a plain man, and perhaps unable to balance the advantages of continuing that license which is extended to counsel, against the disadvantage of restricting and confining it within more limited bounds. But the impression made upon me (and if it be made upon me, I have a right to assume it is made on many other practical men also), by the perusal of these proceedings, is – firstly, that I would never stretch out my hand to arrest a murderer, with these pains and penalties before me; and, secondly, that no earthly consideration should induce me to permit my wife or daughter to give evidence at the Old Bailey, if any effort of mine could shield her from such a trial.[42]

This letter elicited a prompt response (23 June 1840) from a lawyer of the Middle Temple (which Cairns suggests may have been Phillips himself) who stressed counsel's obligation to 'exert, to the utmost of his power, all his talents and abilities to procure his [client's] acquittal'.[43] He should use 'every means in his power' to do so, but if he cannot do that he must at least ensure that his client is 'legally convicted':

It is therefore his bounden duty to point out to the jury any contradictions, inaccuracies, or omissions that may appear to him in the evidence produced by the prosecutors; and if, through any maudlin sentimentality, or through any fear of inculpating others, he should neglect to do so, he would be guilty of a gross violation of duty, and would deserve to have his gown stripped off his back.[44]

Dickens's response was both prompt and angry. In his second letter dated 26 June, he conceded the importance of an independent Bar and he 'recognise[d] the right of any counsel to take a brief from any man, however great his crime, and, keeping within due bounds, to do his best to save him'; what he denied was the 'right to defeat the ends of truth and justice by wantonly scattering aspersions upon innocent people'.[45] Dickens was present at the execution of Courvoisier on 6 July, and as he later wrote in a letter to the *Daily News*, he had 'a particular detestation of that murderer; not only for the cruel deed he had done, but for his slow and subtle treachery, and for his wicked defence'.[46]

On 12 July, *The Examiner* engaged in more reflective analysis of Phillips' conduct. Acknowledging the contention 'that it is the counsel's duty to act for the prisoner as the prisoner would act for himself if he had his advocate's skill', the editor continued, '[a]dmitting this position, it does not thence follow that it is the duty of the advocate to have recourse to falsehood in defence of his client; for the principle stated would only clothe the advocate with the rights and duties of the prisoner, and it cannot be the duty of the prisoner to lie for his own defence'.[47] In the subsequent discussion about the licence of counsel which took place over a number of years, two positions emerged; one, modelled on Lord Langdale's speech in *Hutchinson* v. *Stephens* (1837)1 Keen 659, stressed that an advocate's zeal should be qualified by 'considerations affecting the general interests of justice'; the other, modelled on Lord Brougham's defence of Queen Caroline in 1820, argued that an advocate must use 'all expedient means . . . to protect [his] client at all hazards and costs to all others'.[48] Eighteen forty-five was a particularly bad year for the beleaguered Bar as it suffered misrepresentation during the 'War between the Bar and the Press' which began as a small dispute between *The Times* and Sergeant Talfourd but escalated into a major skirmish between the two professions. *The Examiner* again resorted with witty abandon to the image of the lawyer as 'liar' and *Punch* also enjoyed many a joke at the Bar's expense.[49] So, too, Sir Fitzroy Kelly's sentimental defence of the notorious murderer John Tawell (which included tears shed in the courtroom) also attracted criticism.[50]

But towards the end of the decade, opinion had settled in favour of some limits to the exercise of adversarial licence; Talfourd entered the fray with an article in the *Law Magazine* which stressed that the zeal of counsel must cease 'when his cause conflicts with the higher requisites of religion, of morality, or of patriotism',[51] and, as a man of letters himself, Talfourd was able to emphasise the features which should unite rather than divide the literary and legal professions. He stressed human sympathy and a natural sense of partisanship as the ingredients of effective legal representation; as a barrister conducts a brief, 'the client's little chapter of life, with all its living interest is opened around him, [and] his client's case becomes part of his own being.'[52] Such careful appropriation of another's thoughts for a brief time echoes Thackeray's poignant farewell to his characters as they fade away into Fable-land; 'they were alive, and I heard their voices; but five minutes since was touched by their grief'.[53] By the end of the 1840s much of the skirmish was over and Lord Langdale's approach was approved by William Forsyth in his book on the history and duties of an advocate, entitled *Hortensius: An Historical Essay on the Office and Duties of an Advocate* (1849).[54] In his Preface to the cheap edition of *Pickwick Papers* in 1847, Dickens was able to observe '[t]he license of Counsel, and the degree to which Juries are ingeniously bewildered, are yet susceptible of moderation . . . But legal reforms have pared the claws of Messrs. Dodson and Fogg; a spirit of self-respect, mutual forbearance, education, and co-operation, for such good ends, has diffused itself among their clerks' (p. xiii). His satisfaction was shortlived, however, as a fresh scandal of advocacy was shortly to attract his attention and contribute to the genesis of *Bleak House*.

On 13 November 1849, Frederick and Maria Manning were executed at Horsemonger Lane Gaol for the murder of their lodger, Patrick O'Connor. Their trial was reported extensively;[55] Collins documents Dickens's intense interest in proceedings and he made a last minute decision to attend their execution. Their trial, on 27 and 28 October, attracted great attention as a consequence of both the barbarity of their crime and the audacity of their defensive strategies in the courtroom. Each tried to exonerate their own behaviour by blaming the other. Debate about the licence of counsel was re-activated, and the conduct of Courvoisier's defence was again subject to scrutiny; although Phillips was not involved in this case, the execution of the Mannings coincided with Phillips's first public explanation of his proceedings in the earlier trial. Two links tie this case to *Bleak House*; Collins records the traditional belief that Maria Manning provided Dickens with the model for the representation of Hortense,[56] the Frenchwoman who murders Tulkinghorn, but it is less well known that the debate in *The Examiner* on 24 November commences with a quote condemning the excesses of counsel from *Hortensius*, thus perhaps suggesting the choice of the murderess's name.[57] More specifically, Dickens's fear of the immorality of advocacy generates his representation of George Rouncewell's plight when he is wrongfully accused of murder.

Rejecting the assistance of lawyers as unethical, George elects to conduct his own defence based upon the 'truth' and his own eye-witness knowledge of his innocence. As he recalls telling the examining magistrates: '"Gentlemen, I am as innocent of this charge as yourselves; what has been stated against me in the way of facts, is perfectly true; I know no more about it". I intend to continue stating that, sir. What more can I do? It's the truth'.[58] Expressing

Dickens's own anxieties about the morality of advocacy, he sees the representation of his interests by another as inherently dishonest and liable to distortion, enabling innocence to be established only upon a technicality:

'I should have got a lawyer, and he would have said (as I have often read in the newspapers), "my client says nothing, my client reserves his defence – my client this, that, and t'other". Well, 'tis not the custom of that breed to go straight, according to my opinion, or to think that other men do. Say, I am innocent, and I get a lawyer. He would be as likely to believe me guilty as not; perhaps more. What would he do, whether or not? Act as if I was; – shut my mouth up, tell me not to commit myself, keep circumstances back, chop the evidence small, quibble, and get me off perhaps!' (ch. lii, p. 706)

Instead, George wants his innocence established on substantive grounds – 'I must come off clear and full or not at all' (ch. lii, p. 706) – and he is content to acknowledge the veracity of facts which may appear unfavourable to his case. True innocence should be established despite the manipulation of evidence by the prosecution:

'[W]hen I hear stated against me what is true, I say it's true; and when they tell me, "whatever you say will be used," I tell them I don't mind that; I mean it to be used. If they can't make me innocent out of the whole truth, they are not likely to do it out of anything less, or anything else. And if they are, it's worth nothing to me'. (ch. lii, pp. 706–707)

These exchanges illuminate the procedural dilemma which confronted practitioners with the implementation of the Prisoners' Counsel Act. Once the choice was made to enjoy the benefit of legal representation, an accused felon was routinely unable to speak for himself. The advent of the lawyers silenced the prisoner; in cases where he could afford legal assistance, he was denied the opportunity to speak. There was some uncertainty as the bench came to terms with the consequences of the Act – and by the end of the century the position was again changing[59] – but, subject to some discretionary judicial variation, the basic rule in mid-Victorian times was that 'if the prisoner's counsel has addressed the jury, the prisoner himself will not be allowed to address the jury also'; as Justice Coleridge told the accused in *R* v. *Boucher* (1837) 8 Car. & P. 141, 'Prisoner, your counsel has spoken for you. I cannot hear you both'. In procedural terms, there was a further complication; as Justice Coleridge explained in *R* v. *Beard* (1837) 8 Car. & P. 142, 'the counsel for a prisoner cannot be allowed to state the prisoner's story, unless he is able to confirm it by evidence':

I cannot permit a prisoner's counsel to tell the jury anything which he is not in a position to prove. If the prisoner does not employ counsel, he is at liberty to make a statement for himself and tell his own story; which is to have such weight with the jury, as all circumstances considered it is entitled to, but if he employs counsel, he must submit to the rules which have been established with respect to the conducting of cases by counsel.

As Cairns has noted, this could lead to severe injustice and the exclusion of the only relevant exculpatory material in a prisoner's defence; as he was not allowed to give evidence on oath, he was not in a position to 'prove' facts of innocence which lay within his knowledge only.[60] For example, in the case of *R* v. *Malings* (1838) 8 Car. & P. 242, the accused's reply to a charge of assault was that he had acted in self-defence; no one else was present at the time, the prisoner was not able to give his version of events on oath and thus counsel's defence could not be founded upon his client's instructions as to innocence. In these exceptional circumstances, the presiding judge, Baron Alderson, allowed the accused to state the material facts for his counsel to comment upon:

It is true that the prisoner's statement may often defeat the defence intended by his counsel; but if so, the ends of justice will be furthered. Besides, it is often the genuine defence of the party, and not a mere imaginary case invented by the ingenuity of counsel. (p. 243)

However, this ruling was not allowed to create a precedent, as Baron Gurney observed in *R* v. *Walking* (1838) 8 Car. & P. 243, and Justice Coleridge's conception of the prisoner's role in his own defence was again asserted by Justice Patteson in *R* v. *Rider* (1838) 8 Car. & P. 539:

The general rule certainly ought to be, that a prisoner defended by counsel should be entirely in the hands of his counsel, and that rule should not be infringed on, except in very special cases indeed. If the prisoner were allowed to make a statement, and stated as a fact anything which could not be proved by evidence, the jury should dismiss that statement from their minds; but if what the prisoner states is merely a comment on what is already in evidence, his counsel can do that much better than he can. (p. 540)

Thus the role of the accused as 'testimonial resource' is increasingly closed off to the courts, and in its place, counsel is restricted to commentary on the material already in evidence, which cannot include the prisoner's narrative as he is precluded from giving his evidence on oath.

As noted previously, Langbein describes this development as a move from the 'old "accused speaks" theory' of the criminal trial to 'the newer "testing the prosecution" theory', which only became possible with the expansion of a barrister's role and the division of the testimonial and defensive functions of responding to a criminal charge.[61] The testimonial aspect of a prisoner's defence was subordinated to a lawyer's claims of technical expertise which could establish innocence on non-substantive grounds. Although Dickens's concern in both the *Pickwick Papers* and *Bleak House* is for the unjust treatment of the innocent, his angry response to the *Courvoisier* case demonstrates his fear that representation enabled the guilty to evade responsibility. We see this fear of 'sham' defences persisting into the 1860s in Stephen's *General View of the Criminal Law*; here he expresses his regret that the law prevents the interrogation or cross-examination of prisoners (the latter because they do not give evidence on oath):

When an advocate speaks on behalf of his client he can, and often does, say, 'The prisoner's mouth is stopped and he cannot explain; but if he could, he might tell a very different story from the witnesses.' And this way of arguing is favoured by the rule which forbids an advocate to make a statement as the mouthpiece of his client – a rule carried so far, that it has been held that, if a prisoner chooses to make a statement, his counsel cannot address the jury. When the prisoner had to speak for himself, he was practically excluded from the topics which advocates often handle successfully. He could not, without a tacit admission of guilt, insist on the inconclusiveness of the evidence against him, and on its consistency with his innocence. The jury expected from him a clear explanation of the case against him; and if he could not give it, they convicted him. (pp. 194–195, footnote omitted)

Stephen was so concerned at the lack of access to the accused's narrative in the new trial format that he proposed 'the direct and explicit interrogation of the prisoner both at his trial and before the committing magistrates':

It would render sham defences impossible, and would cut down by the roots that bastard ingenuity which counsel acquire in inventing defences for prisoners, which they would never think of setting up for themselves – defences, grounded not on the truth of the case, but on the defects of the prosecutor's evidence.[62] (p. 199)

Dickens clearly shared these anxieties about 'sham defences' and for George in *Bleak House*, integrity was equated with a rejection of legal representation and a preference for straightforward narratives of innocence. The preference for an 'accused speaks' model of the trial is to be found time and time again in Dickens's writings, in Eliot's fiction, in Gaskell's work; just as the reader has access to evidence of Pickwick's and George's innocence in the form of testimonial declarations, so too Eliot confirms Silas's innocence in *Silas Marner*, Hetty's probable guilt in *Adam Bede* and Felix's lack of culpability in *Felix Holt* by providing the reader with confessional confirmation of their various states of criminal responsibility. Similarly, Gaskell ensures that the reader has access to epistolary evidence of Jem's substantive innocence prior to his trial for murder in *Mary Barton*; although the circumstantial evidence weighs against him and his voice is not heard at the trial, Mary's quest to establish his alibi – the tale of genuine innocence – provides the *telos* of the narrative, and his letter to Job Leigh confirms that his acquittal is merited. In Charlotte Yonge's work *The Trial* (1864) Leonard refuses to offer to the court a defence that is plausible but erroneous; despite a 'web of suspicious circumstances', he instructs his counsel 'to contend for his perfect innocence' and his wrongful conviction is followed by a declaration of substantive innocence. Conversely, in *Orley Farm* (1862), Trollope ensures that Lady Mason confesses her guilt to the reader if not to the court. All are reluctant to abandon the view of the accused as a 'testimonial resource'; they insist instead that the discovery of truth is dependent upon the defendants telling their story in their own words, and 'owning' any imputation of criminal responsibility. This is of course, suggestive of the idealistic episte-mology which harks back to Sergeant Hawkins's belief in the ease with which an innocent man may construct a 'plain and honest Defence'. Yet if true innocence can 'speak for itself', then the services of authors are as redundant as the story-telling powers of their legal counterparts. Clearly, the form of the tale must be such that narrative advocacy is not rendered unnecessary. Authors thus adhered to an 'accused speaks' model of the trial whilst simultane-ously moving away from the old epistemology that had initially given rise to it.

Fictional insistence on testimonial declarations of innocence or guilt also stresses the importance of intention in the ideal assessment of criminal culpability. The common law emphasised the role of intention in criminal responsibility, but it was an area where proof was traditionally regarded as difficult.[63] It is part of the author's art to reveal the role of 'true' intentions in just adjudication, and, in acting as a forum for the construction of an accused's story in their 'own words', fictional trials both illuminate the ethical claims of testimony and comment self-reflexively on the reliability of the act of fictional narration itself. Ironically, though, confidence in an 'accused speaks' idea of the trial is undermined by the limited weight to be given to an accused's testimony. In *Bleak House*, George's assurance of the ease with which he can respond to the charge is misplaced, and to satisfy his family that he is whole-heartedly participating in the legal game, he agrees to retain a lawyer and to sacrifice his own narrative of defence (ch. lv, p. 752). But the exposure of the real murderer's identity prompts George's release prior to a trial and his faith in evidentiary procedure is not tested in court.

'WORK . . . UNFIT FOR A GENTLEMAN': DICKENS, TROLLOPE, AND THE 'MANUMISSION OF MURDERERS'

In May 1856, the Bar was subject to further criticism in the press following the trial of William Palmer for the murder of his friend John Parsons Cook, allegedly by the administration of strychnine. Palmer was also suspected of poisoning a number of other people, including his wife and his brother, in order to benefit from the proceeds of their insurance policies and it was feared that he would not receive a fair trial in his home town of Rugeley. A special Act of Parliament was passed to transfer his case to the Old Bailey.[64] Considerable scandal was caused on the seventh day of the trial when Alexander Shee, a prominent Old Bailey lawyer, opened the case for the defence. His lengthy address to the jury reprised the debate of the 1840s about the licence of counsel when he stated 'I commence his defence, I say it in all sincerity, with an entire conviction of his innocence. I believe that there never was a truer word pronounced than the words which he pronounced when he said "Not guilty" to this charge'.[65] In his speech for the prosecution on 24 May 1856, the Attorney-General regretted that Shee had introduced into the trial such an 'unprecedented . . . assurance of his conviction of his client's innocence',[66] and the indignant custodians of ethical representation at *The Examiner* were again mobilised. They reawakened the journalistic memory of the Bar's previous rhetorical excesses and rehearsed again for the edification of the public the great scandals of advocacy – Joseph Chitty weeping for the murderer Jack Thurtell in 1823–1824, which called to mind

Fitzroy Kelly's tears over John Tawell's fate in 1845, and above all
the spectre of Courvoisier's potential acquittal. This was the great
mythology of the Bar's amorality:

Since the trial of Thurtell, there has hardly been a remarkable case in
which the counsel for the prisoner has not wept for his client, or protested
his solemn belief in his innocence. . .

   Is it, then, when the Court becomes dramatic, that belief of innocence
becomes a stage property of the advocate; or is it that in these great cases
the proportionably large fee retains the belief in question, together with the
other services?

The Examiner argued that it is the advocate's duty to 'deal with
evidence' only; he must not become an 'unsworn witness' for the
prisoner. In terms reminiscent of Mrs Gaskell's attack on rhetoric for
hire in the trial of Jem Wilson in *Mary Barton*, the editors concluded
that lawyers should not dispute assertions on the basis of their
honour or their conscience: 'Would it not be more to the purpose to
say, 'I believe on my fee that it is false?' That is a protestation
thoroughly intelligible, and measuring the extent to which it merits
credit'.[67] In his summing-up on the final day of the trial, Lord
Campbell advised the jury 'to try the prisoner on the evidence
before you . . . and by that alone'; 'it is the duty of the advocate to
press his argument upon the jury, and not his opinion'.[68] On the
basis of the (largely circumstantial) evidence, the jury returned a
verdict of guilty.

   Immediately prior to Palmer's execution, the public enthusiasti-
cally awaited his final confession which it was hoped would include
the disclosure of his secret *modus operandi* and perhaps the identity of
further victims. Given a public perception that London was plagued
with poisoning cases at the time, rates of detection and successful
prosecution were subject to anxious analysis.[69] As the law had sealed
Palmer's lips during the trial, this enforced silence attached a
particular resonance to the story of the condemned man which was
shortly to be lost forever. If John Sutherland is right to hypothesise
that Wilkie Collins attended Palmer's trial, then it is likely that this
public desire to uncover Palmer's secrets may have inspired the
famous confession of the poisoner Fosco in *The Woman in White*.[70]
But Palmer preserved his silence on the scaffold and his only
observation was an aside to his solicitor to the effect that Cook was
not poisoned 'by strychnine'. *The Examiner* read his failure to protest
his substantive innocence as proof of his guilt, but also deplored the

public fascination with confessional testimony in so far as it implied that a conviction of guilt could not occur in its absence:

It is to be regretted that endeavours were made to extort confession, for the assumption should always be that the crime has been proved beyond a doubt by the process of law. Nothing more is wanted. If the convict be moved to unburden his mind, well and good, let his confession be received rather for his own satisfaction than that of others. But to solicit it is to imply that the verdict of guilty wants verification; or that some doubt hangs about it. It would be well if the officers of gaols and chaplains were instructed not to solicit the confession of convicts.[71]

In *The Examiner*'s earlier reports of the trial and execution of one Thomas Hocker, who conducted his own articulate defence to a charge of murder and then maintained his innocence to the grave, we see the fears caused by the prisoner's refusal to authenticate the suffering he was about to undergo. *The Examiner* at first criticised the lenient summing-up of the trial judge, Justice Coleridge, which could have allowed a guilty man to escape punishment had not the jury had the sense to convict; *The Examiner* then called for an inconsistency in the evidence to be pursued further before a potentially innocent man was put to death; then finally, when no reprieve was forthcoming, it ridiculed his continued assertion of innocence.[72] To have done otherwise would have been to support Hocker's claim that he died a martyr, and *The Examiner*, for all its criticisms of the Bar, was not prepared to sustain such a claim of illegality and judicial murder. In Palmer's trial, we see how this insistence on the sufficiency of the 'testing the prosecution' theory of the trial to justify the infliction of death displaces the earlier tableau of the spectacle of the scaffold, which privileged the final speech of the condemned as possessing some kind of supernatural sanction. Instead we see an acceptance that crimes committed in secret may be detected by the law without recourse to the felon's story. Where the prosecution succeeds in discharging the burden of proof the accused cannot hide behind his silence.

Both Dickens and Fitzjames Stephen were convinced of Palmer's guilt; writing in his *General View of the Criminal Law*, some seven years after Palmer's execution, Stephen observed that 'it is impossible to doubt the propriety of the verdict' (p. 390). Dickens and his colleagues at *Household Words* used the occasion of Palmer's conviction to assess in some detail the impartiality and fairness of an English trial. Henry Morley, a prolific contributor to the magazine under Dickens's strict editorial control,[73] begins his article 'A Criminal Trial' with the complaint that 'English criminal law displays even more clearly than it enforces, a respect for life'. Although he approves of the amelioration of past injustice – 'the day is still within the memory of many, when men on trial for their lives were not permitted to defend themselves by counsel, and this deprivation was made in the name of fairness, "because", saith Coke, "that the testimony and proof of the crime ought to be so clear and manifest, that there can be no defence of it" ' – he criticises contemporary English justice as 'allowing to the criminal too much chance of escape from punishment'. He extends Lord Campbell's criticisms of Shee's assurances of his client's innocence in a rather startling way; he describes the initial question to the prisoner of 'How say you, guilty or not guilty?' as an extraneous matter of form which should be done away with:

Q. How will you be tried?
A. By God and my country.
Which answer a judicious prisoner once varied by saying, 'Not by God, since He knows all; but by your Lordship and the jury'. The rest of the catechism might also be spared. To expect the prisoner to plead not guilty being guilty, and to say that he does not therein add one more untruth to his offences because it is not falsehood you ask of him but only a legal form, is in truth, the reverse of a solemn and true opening of a most true and solemn trial.

He uses the strategies of prosecution and defence in the trial of 'the Poisoner' to draw some more general conclusions about the integrity and intellectual rigour of each side's performance:

On the part of the Crown there was produced a close chain of the most pertinent testimony. This was urged and there was urged nothing but this. The case for the prosecution was a case of circumstantial evidence, infinitely more convincing than any proof of secret crime from direct testimony . . . On the other hand, counsel for defence – having no other refuge, and being unable to rebut the damning facts – also in accordance with their brief, and in most strict accordance with the spirit of English justice, exhausted their ingenuity in the production of suggestions, suppositions, and surmises.

The prosecution case deals with fact: the defence case only with speculative, imaginative, ingenious fictions of innocence – like the inventions of an author. This perhaps explains why so many novels are cases for the defence, attempts to appropriate for the accused the techniques of the prosecution, and to prove the oppressed hero innocent. This account of circumstantial evidence is again epistemo-logically naive, but what is more interesting in this passage is the way in which the very language of defence is seen as inherently unrelated to any question of proof or to any paradigm of evidentiary analysis. A defence lawyer, Morley argues, may 'use his ingenuity to give a more favourable interpretation to the evidence he is unable to rebut, may suggest any theory he likes, may make any appeal within certain wide limits of common decorum to the feelings and pre-judices of the jurymen'; throughout the trial, 'the business of the prosecution is simply to discover the truth; the business of the defence is personal – to secure, if possible, the prisoner's acquittal'.[74] So the prosecution lawyer adduces evidence in the quest for demon-strable truth; counsel for the defence generates speculation in an attempt to obscure the truth in the exercise of the duty he owes to his client. That Dickens in his fiction undertakes the defence of the unjustly accused is an interesting inversion of this critical anxiety, but George and Pickwick are in good company amongst other protago-nists such as Tom Jones, Caleb Williams, Waverley, Leonard Ward, Jem Wilson, Felix Holt, and even Pompilia in Browning's recreation of a seventeenth-century murder trial in *The Ring and the Book*. The business of the eighteenth- or nineteenth-century author or novelist is also, it seems, to secure the acquittal of the accused.[75]

One clear exception to this generalisation comes to mind. Anthony Trollope's *Orley Farm* (1862) explores the legal profession's move towards the 'testing the prosecution' theory of the criminal trial and it is premised on an inversion of the literary model espoused by Dickens, Eliot, and Gaskell. Like the trial of Courvoisier, the trial of Lady Mason raises the question of how a practitioner should act when he arrives at a conviction of his client's guilt; like the trial of Palmer, *R* v. *Mason* explores the worth and sincerity of a practitioner's protestations of his client's innocence when those statements bear no relation to the merits of the client's case. In *Orley Farm*, many of the main characters are compromised by a transgression of the codes of honour professed by gentle society; Lady Mason has forged a codicil to her husband's will to enable his younger son to inherit the property of the title and she is to be indicted for perjury (although a misdemeanour rather than a felony, dishonesty in speech under-mined the nexus of gentility and veracity discussed in Chapters 1 and 2), the emerging profession of solicitors are struggling to uphold their reputation amongst their fellow commercial travellers on the

railways, criminal defence lawyers are seen to be undertaking 'work
. . . unfit for a gentleman' in their defence of those whom they
'know' to be guilty, and the alternative (writing for the press) does
not generate enough pecuniary reward to support a respectable wife
of good family. The novel contrasts older criminal trial procedures
based on good character and ownership of property with new, more
democratic approaches based only on an impartial assessment of the
evidence. Yet Trollope's sympathy rests with the guilty Lady Mason
and the newer methods of criminal justice fail to convict her; she is
saved from (technically accurate) condemnation by character references from other members of the gentry (in the teeth of the 'plain
facts' of her guilt), by her refusal to confess or plead guilty and tell
her tale in her own words, and by the forensic eloquence of the
barristers Chaffanbrass and Furnival.

Trollope canvasses a variety of ethical positions as he explores the
contrasting attitudes held by various lawyers to the construction of
Lady Mason's defence. On the one hand, Chaffanbrass, the experienced Old Bailey pleader, has no doubt of her guilt; nor does he
experience any discomfort at the prospect of seeking to defend her as
if she had been innocent; 'had she not been guilty, he, Mr Chaffanbrass, would not have been required.'[76] His young colleague Felix
Graham, however, retains an idealistic approach to legal practice,
consistent with his adherence to such tenets as '[t]hou shalt not bear
false witness; thou shalt not steal' (p. 156). Graham is convinced that
lawyers 'give [the defendant] the advantage of every technicality'
and then 'lie for him during the whole ceremony of his trial'. Instead
he insists that work which serves to conceal guilt 'is unfit for a
gentleman and impossible for an honest man' (p. 159). He argues
that '[t]ruth and honour cannot be altered by any professional
arrangements' (p. 169) and, like Pendennis, David Copperfield, and
Clive Newcome before him, he chooses a more artistic calling; in all
these novels the ethical comparison between the two professions
could not be stated more clearly. Yet despite Trollope's sympathy for
Graham's naive idealism, he also presents the plight of the leading
barrister, Thomas Furnival, with non-judgemental insight.

Furnival was to be distinguished from Chaffanbrass – '[h]e had
been no Old Bailey lawyer, devoting himself to the manumission of
murderers, or the security of the swindling world in general' (p. 86) –
yet he is seen to be representative of successful English barristers:
'[n]o living orator would convince a grocer that coffee should be

sold without chicory; and no amount of eloquence will make an English lawyer think that loyalty to truth should come before loyalty to his client' (p. 147). Although he does not hear her confession, Furnival comes to 'believe' that Lady Mason is guilty. But he was prepared to continue acting on her behalf, to 'do many a thing at which . . . an honest man might be scandalized if it came beneath his judgement unprofessionally' (p. 361). However, as the narrator observes, '[t]hat fighting of a battle without belief is . . . the sorriest task which ever falls to the lot of any man' (p. 566).

Lady Mason's son, Lucius, and her chivalric and honourable neighbour, Sir Peregrine Orme, want substantive declarations of her purity announced in court; as Lucius says to his mother, 'Have I your leave to tell [the lawyers] that you want no subterfuge, no legal quibbles – that you stand firmly on your own clear innocence, and that you defy your enemies to sully it?' (pp. 487–488). But, although her voice is not heard in the courtroom, Lady Mason confesses her guilt to Sir Peregrine and the reader just as Dickens and Gaskell have their defendants state their innocence: ' "I – forged the will. I did it all. – I am guilty" ' (p. 407).

At the trial, Furnival presents a closing speech so effective that 'before he had done he had almost brought himself again to believe Lady Mason to be that victim of persecution as which he did not hesitate to represent her to the jury' (p. 655). His narrative involves clear statements of her innocence and he tells the jury that '[y]ou know as well as I do that she has not been guilty of this terrible crime':

And yet as he sat down he knew that she had been guilty! To his ear her guilt had never been confessed; but yet he knew that it was so, and, knowing that, he had been able to speak as though her innocence were a thing of course. That those witnesses had spoken truth he also knew, and yet he had been able to hold them up to the execration of all around them as though they had committed the worst of crimes from the foulest of motives! And more than this, stranger than this, worse than this – when the legal world knew – as the legal world soon did know – that all this had been so, the legal world found no fault with Mr Furnival, conceiving that he had done his duty by his client in a manner becoming an English barrister and an English gentlemen. (pp. 660–661)

Lady Mason is acquitted, and her supporters feel no prolonged discomfort at this disjunction of verdict and actual criminal responsibility. But Lucius resolves to surrender the property and her guilt is

known to the wider court of public opinion. As in the examples from
Dickens's work, to retain legal representation is a tacit admission of
guilt and a consequent need for concealment and duplicity. To be
innocent is to speak freely, unconstrained by the need to test the
solidity of the prosecution case. Yet in George Eliot's work, we see a
recognition that the testimony of personal integrity is not always
sufficient to communicate innocence.

GEORGE ELIOT AND THE PRESENTATION OF UNSWORN
EVIDENCE

In *Felix Holt* (1866), Eliot explores the status and treatment of the
narrative of innocence addressed to the court by the unrepresented
prisoner. The rejection of professional assistance enables Felix to
assert his integrity; as a young man, he had adopted a life of
voluntary poverty because he refused to tell 'professional lies for
profit; or to get tangled in affairs where [he] must wink at dishonesty
and pocket the proceeds, and justify that knavery as part of a system
that [he] can't alter'.[77] But Eliot demonstrates that his confidence in
the construction of a plain narrative of innocence (like the 'artless
tale' of Caleb Williams or the 'straightforward, unvarnished statement'[78] made by Leonard Ward in *The Trial*) is completely unwarranted. Like Dickens, Eliot was familiar with contemporary
debates and developments in the law by virtue of both her association with professional lawyers and her own extensive programme of
reading. Her biographers record that she habitually took great pains
to ensure the accuracy of legal material which was to generate or
resolve issues of narrative emplotment. For example, in 1859, she
consulted a London solicitor, Henry Sheard, in relation to the
bankruptcy procedures which afflict the Tullivers in *The Mill on the
Floss*;[79] in 1866, she sought advice from the renowned positivist
Frederic Harrison of Lincoln's Inn, to ensure the accuracy of the
narrative sequence by which Esther could receive the Bycliffe
inheritance in *Felix Holt*.[80] Her letters record their detailed exchanges on topics such as the statute of limitations, the difference
between settlements and the effects of heirship, the work undertaken
by convicts following transportation and criminal trial procedure
prior to the enactment of the Prisoners' Counsel Act.[81]

In the careful equation of religious and legal sincerity which
characterises the actions of the sympathetic characters in *Felix Holt*

we see something of the consistency which marked the testimony of Jeanie and her father in *The Heart of Midlothian*. After Felix is charged with assaulting a constable, leading a riotous onslaught on a dwelling-house, and manslaughter, Mr Lyon equates his plight with that of the persecuted Church (ch. xxxvii, p. 297) and Felix is seen as a martyr whom neither of the political parties wish to claim as their own (ch. xxxvii, p. 300). The lexicon of Christian suffering ascribes a spiritual significance to his trial as his transparent sincerity brings him into conflict with a legal system which will inevitably undervalue his story. Eliot notes with irony that, for Felix as for George in *Bleak House*, the collation of the eye-witnesses' testimony had seemed a straightforward matter:

Even if the pleading of counsel had been permitted (and at that time it was not) on behalf of a prisoner on trial for felony, Felix would have declined it: he would in any case have spoken in his own defence. He had a perfectly simple account to give, and needed not to avail himself of any legal adroitness. (ch. xxxvii, pp. 300–301)

The desires expressed by the characters for reform – '[i]t is an opprobrium of our law that no counsel is allowed to plead for the prisoner in cases of felony' (ch. xxxviii, p. 311) – are again included in the consciousness that such reforms have indeed occurred in the interim.[82] Yet Felix seriously underestimates the ease with which his behaviour during the riot can be explained to the court. The witnesses' version of events largely corresponds with Felix's own, although the narrator draws attention to the extent to which their evidence has been shaped and moulded by an acute legal mind:

No one else knew – the witnesses themselves did not know fully – how far their strong perception and memory on these points was due to a fourth mind, namely, that of Mr John Johnson, the attorney, who was nearly related to one of the Treby witnesses, and a familiar acquaintance of the Duffield clerk. Man cannot be defined as an evidence-giving animal; and in the difficulty of getting up evidence on any subject, there is room for much unrecognized action of diligent persons who have the extra stimulus of some private motive. (ch. xlvi, p. 369)

This is precisely the argument in favour of the extension of representation to prisoners charged with felony. The mediating mind of a lawyer shapes the narratives of the witnesses without their acknowledgement, allowing for both the prosecutorial arrangement of the allegedly self-evident facts and the more deliberate operation of personal prejudices. Unlike the scheming blackmailers, Christian,

Johnson and Jermyn, Felix refuses to compromise the truthful representation of his narrative by the use of an agent, but the hermeneutics of the courtroom – with its sophisticated manipulation of seemingly unstructured 'fact' by professional men – inevitably operate against him.

At the conclusion of the prosecution case, Felix wishes to adduce in evidence a statement of his own motives. Eliot does not expressly observe that his testimony lacks the validity of an oath, but the presentation of his narrative of innocence is circumscribed by the law of the time; the only way Felix can speak in his own defence is to make an unsworn statement from the dock. Because an unsworn statement enabled the accused to cast aspersions upon the character and testimony of witnesses for the prosecution without himself being subject to the rigours of cross-examination, it has traditionally been regarded as suspect, and certainly not as proof of the facts contained within it.[83] In his integrity, however, Felix chooses not to contest the facts as presented by the prosecution witnesses; he asks only two questions in cross-examination, neither of which seeks to destabilise the prosecution's representation of the narrative sequence of events. His defence is based solely on intent:

'I believe the witnesses for the prosecution have spoken the truth as far as a superficial observation would enable them to do it; and I see nothing that can weigh with the jury in my favour, unless they believe my statement of my own motives, and the testimony that certain witnesses will give to my character and purposes as being inconsistent with my willingly abetting disorder'. (ch. xlvi, pp. 369–370)

This presupposes the importance of 'intention' in the assessment of criminal responsibility[84] and it raises an evidentiary difficulty mentioned earlier, namely whether an accused's statements can be accepted as favourable evidence of intent or whether such declarations can only serve as evidence against him. In the event of the latter, then Felix's intent could only be inferred from his actions during the riot – and these are open to easy misconstruction. His supporters had seen that his defence was a question of 'adjusting fact, so as to raise it to the power of evidence' (ch. xxxviii, p. 311), but Felix rejects any conscious manipulation of factual details. Yet because his exculpatory narrative is vulnerable in two respects – it is unsworn and it is descriptive of intent – it does not carry sufficient probative weight to ensure his acquittal.

Consequently, the character evidence given by Transome and

Esther assumes an even greater significance. The narrator suggests that the adversarial format provides a medium for the 'voice of right and truth' to be heard if it is 'strong enough' (ch. xlvi, p. 375) and it is Esther's recollections of Felix's behaviour prior to the riot which are most persuasive. Eliot's letters to Harrison record her desire to conclude the factual evidence against Felix before the character witnesses could be heard; she wanted to 'produce a certain slackening of interest before Esther comes in' and Harrison assured her that this was consistent with current trial procedure: 'Thus if you need it Esther's speech *might* come in anywhere (last or not) by the special leave of the judge'.[85] The presentation of her evidence in a public forum is a 'confession of faith' in Felix's motives and in the right administration of justice; in Butler's terms, Esther's own integrity is on trial and her testimony also represents the culmination of her journey towards the acquisition of moral nobility: '[h]alf a year before, Esther's dread of being ridiculous spread over the surface of her life; but the depth below was sleeping' (ch. xlvi, p. 376). There is some precedent for the emotional function of Esther's testimony in the trial scene in *Mary Barton* (1848) where the eponymous heroine's evidence reveals her preference for the prisoner over his dead rival.[86] Gaskell's treatment of the evident cynicism and rhetorical excesses of the lawyers is also topical; it too taps into the lengthy debates of the 1840s concerning the licence of advocacy. But Gaskell's representation of the adversarial circus lacks Eliot's sophisticated understanding of the stubbornness of fact and the significance of intent; what for Gaskell is simply unethical behaviour is for Eliot a product of deeper forces of perception. Hence Esther's testimony is insufficient to save Felix from conviction and imprisonment:

The counsel's duty of restoring all unfavourable facts to due prominence in the minds of the jurors, had its effect altogether reinforced by the summing-up of the judge. Even the bare discernment of facts, much more their arrangement with a view to inferences, must carry a bias: human impartiality, whether judicial or not, can hardly escape being more or less loaded. (ch. xlvi, p. 377)

Yonge had observed in *The Trial* that the fate of the accused 'would probably depend on the colouring that the facts adduced would assume in [the judge's] hands';[87] Eliot too shows how the illusory solidity of fact prevails over expressions of intent which are more obviously susceptible to emotive and retrospective manipulation.

The judge is not consciously prejudiced; the biases which accompany the arrangement of facts are not so much deliberate as inherent in the disadvantages which hinder Felix from presenting a truthful defence. In this representation of Felix's trial, Eliot dramatises the very essence of the debate about the extension of legal representation; his unjust conviction rests upon the very prejudices which the proposed reforms of the era were designed to correct. Like Effie in *The Heart of Midlothian* and the eponymous protagonist in *Barnaby Rudge*, Holt owes his release more to 'a very powerfully signed memorial to the Home Secretary' (ch. xlix, p. 388) and his freedom is secured by executive intervention rather than the triumph of natural justice over the hermeneutics of the courtroom.

DICKENS, STEPHEN, AND THE EXCLUSION OF EVIDENCE

If we turn from the plight of the accused for a moment, we see that Dickens also explores the position of other witnesses whose testimony is excluded by the law – notably the plight of the child witness in *Bleak House*.[88] Jo's attempt to give evidence at the inquest into the cause of Hawdon's death is thwarted by his want of religious understanding; in a chilling indictment of the evangelicals' obsession with the plight of the unredeemed in Africa, his testimony cannot be received because he cannot subscribe to the oath to tell the truth:

Can't exactly say what'll be done to him arter he's dead if he tells a lie to the gentlemen here, but believes it'll be something wery bad to punish him, and serve him right – and so he'll tell the truth.

'This won't do, gentlemen!' said the Coroner, with a melancholy shake of the head.

'Don't you think you can receive his evidence, sir?' asks an attentive Juryman.

'Out of the question,' says the Coroner. 'You have heard the boy. "Can't exactly say" won't do, you know. We can't take *that*, in a Court of Justice, gentlemen. It's terrible depravity. Put the boy aside'. (ch. xi, p. 148)

His testimony – that Hawdon was always 'wery good' to him (ch. xi, p. 149) – can only be received by the informal court of public opinion convened at the local public house, Sol's Arms, and by the reader. The evidence is important as an indication of the moral qualities of Esther's father, who dies as the novel opens. As K. J. Fielding and W. Brice point out in their article entitled 'Charles Dickens on "The Exclusion of Evidence"', the rejection of Jo's competence as a witness is central to the novel's epistemological concerns: 'It was a legal question, and it was also a half-philosophical question: men's imaginations were caught by the figure of . . . Jo facing [his] cross-examination (and may still be caught) because they themselves were puzzled by questions like those put by the Coroner'.[89] The common law with respect to the competence of infants was settled in the case of *R* v. *Brasier* (1779) 1 Leach 199, in which the court ruled that 'no testimony whatever can be legally received except upon oath' and that a child may be sworn to give evidence provided he or she 'appears, on strict examination by the Court, to possess a sufficient knowledge of the nature and consequences of an oath':

[T]here is no precise or fixed rule as to the time within which infants are excluded from giving evidence; but their admissibility depends upon the sense and reason they entertain of the danger and impiety of falsehood, which is to be collected from their answers to questions propounded to them by the Court; but if they are found incompetent to take an oath, their testimony cannot be received (p. 200).

Fielding and Brice draw attention to a number of cases, reported in *The Examiner* or in the *Household Narrative*, in which the evidence of child witnesses was excluded because of their inability to answer questions from the Catechism. Dickens was a regular contributor to *The Examiner* throughout 1848 and 1849, after his close friend John Forster assumed the general editorship of the paper in early 1848. Fielding and Brice cannot establish conclusively that Dickens wrote the reports of these cases himself, but given the close association with Forster, they argue persuasively for Dickens's interest in, and knowledge of, each unfortunate child's plight. They argue that Jo is based on one George Ruby, a fourteen-year-old who attempted to give evidence of an assault on a police officer, but who was excluded from the witness-box because he didn't know anything of God or the Devil; all he knew was 'how to sweep the crossing'. The presiding Alderman announced that he 'could not take the evidence of a creature *who knew nothing whatever of the obligation to tell the truth*', but the editorial commentary pointed out that in confessing his ignorance, the boy in fact displayed 'a strict fidelity to truth': 'He was a truthful witness against himself, as society had to its shame suffered him to be; and for the very evidence of his adherence to truth most faithfully, the magistrate puts him aside as not to be trusted as a witness'.[90] Fielding and Brice consider a number of children whose exclusion on the grounds of religious incompetence contributed to Dickens's portrait of Jo, including the unfortunate child of one Sarah French who was tried for the murder of her husband at the Lewes Assizes on 20 March 1852. Her trial was subsequently reported in Dickens's own *Household Narrative* at the time that *Bleak House* was first appearing. The child 'was aware that something would be done to wicked people who told lies, after they were dead, but he did not know what it was', and the court ruled that this was not a sufficient safeguard for the reception of the testimony.[91] As Fielding and Brice point out, this bears a definite similarity to Jo's responses to the questions of the court, and they see Dickens's hand or influence in the editorial criticism of this case in the *Household Narrative*:

A boy of eight years old was thought not to understand sufficiently the moral obligations of an oath, because, though he knew it was a wicked thing to tell a lie, and was aware that something would be done after they were dead to wicked people who told lies, *he did not know what it was*. Now, if this boy had said that he knew what was done to such people (which certainly the learned and conscientious judge would be reluctant himself to say he knew), the law would have been satisfied, and no more questions asked; yet because he did not know how to feign that he did know, he is rejected as untrustworthy. It is a great pity that ordinary common sense has not a larger share in governing such customs of jurisprudence.[92]

Such criticism demonstrates not only the absurd artifice of the tests of a witness's competence, but also a more significant disparity between legal and religious ideas of certainty. The ritual role of the oath tied the law to schematic religious representations which were regarded as overly dogmatic or undemonstrable by the voice of progressive Victorian scepticism.

Jurists like Stephen drew attention to the plight of the child witness to conduct a more general campaign against the retention of the oath as a guarantee of any witness's testimonial veracity. In an article entitled 'Oaths', which appeared in *Cornhill Magazine* in April 1863, Stephen ridicules the scene of the little girl who explains an oath 'with the true Sunday-school beatitude of voice and manner' in the following terms: ' "Please, sir – say my catechism – go to the bad place when I die." "Nothing more required, I think, Mr. — ?" said the chairman to the counsel; and the little lady told her story without further observation'.[93] Hence Dickens's comment in *David Copperfield* that Ham Peggotty was 'a very dragon at his catechism, and [he] may therefore be regarded as a credible witness'.[94] In

Stephen's *General View of the Criminal Law*, he argues that the traditional adherence to the sanction of the oath arises from 'a theory of evidence which in the present day, is deservedly exploded':

> It overlooks the fact that the great security against judicial errors lies in the power of exposing or contradicting false evidence, not in preventing false evidence from being given. It is in fact constantly given and constantly exposed. Hence the guarantee afforded by an oath for the truth of testimony is one to which too much importance may readily be ascribed . . . (p. 289)

Stephen's exposure of such artifice is consistent with the trenchant criticism of the oath expressed in editorial comment in *The Examiner* on 8 December 1849 which Fielding and Brice attribute (in part) to Dickens. One Thomas Hall was accused of an 'atrocious offence' against the person of his twelve-year-old daughter, and when she was excluded from the witness-box on the basis of her religious illiteracy, he was acquitted. *The Examiner* argued that 'the miscreant's first wrong to the wretched child procured his impunity for the second horrible atrocity', but this injustice generated the broader procedural criticism which we have heard in the works of Fielding, and Bentham, and which Stephen was to champion; admit the evidence and then let the jury decide on its creditworthiness:

> [W]hy exclude the evidence? Why not let it go to the jury for as much as it is worth? Why predetermine by the rule of exclusion that it is bad? . . . Though not religiously educated, the child may have been capable of speaking the truth, as pagans and savages are capable of truth. Knowing the child's deficiency, the jury might have heard her testimony with distrust; but such distrust would only have caused them to scrutinise the evidence more narrowly and severely. At the worst they could only, upon the discrediting of it, come to the same conclusion that they did upon the exclusion; but with this difference, that it would have been after having heard and exercised their judgement upon what the witness had to depose.[95] (8 December 1849, p. 771)

The tension here is between the judge's paternalistic protection of the jurors from material which is so prejudicial that they may not know how to deal with it, and a conflicting confidence that a trial jury could reach a just decision based on common-sense. Although Stephen eventually concluded that the oath ought to be retained, he stresses that the 'principal way of finding out liars in courts of justice is by cross-examination'; both circumstantial evidence and testimony may be tested by this comparatively modern tool of advocacy which insists on the scientific hypothesis of falsifiability as the ground of evidentiary truth:

[T]he great leading distinction in the trustworthiness of evidence tested by cross-examination, is whether or not it is capable of being contradicted either by persons or things. If not, cross-examination is no test at all; for, except in novels, people are never, or hardly ever, made to contradict themselves, or to vary materially in a story which they have once told; though, if they are honest though mistaken, the fact that they are or may be mistaken may generally be brought to light.

He rejects the old suggestion that circumstantial evidence may be more reliable than testimony because less susceptible to forgery; the important test is that of the comparison and falsifiability of the evidence which may be effected and demonstrated on cross-examination, and '[h]ence, the difficulty of concocting evidence does not depend on its being direct or circumstantial'.[96]

REALISM IN THE COURTROOM: TRANSPARENT NARRATION AND THE SUPPRESSION OF EVIDENCE

The scope of a witness's testimony, the role of the oath in the generation of truth and the relation of invention to the elucidation of 'real' facts returns us to the heart of issues of narrative construction. In a novel, the testimony of the unjustly accused can be tested against the privileged evidence of innocence (to be found either in circumstances, statements of intention or obvious lack of criminal capacity) presented to the reader. The protagonists' stories are in a sense falsifiable; we are sure of Silas's innocence despite the false testimony, the arrangement of circumstances, and, most problematically, the erroneous judgement of the drawn lots, which combine to condemn him at the beginning of *Silas Marner*; so too Hetty's post-conviction confession in *Adam Bede* suggests both a move towards personal salvation (as in 'Janet's Repentance' where Janet's testimony of guilt generates moral and spiritual renewal) and a tentative confirmation of the court's finding that her intent to harm her child could be inferred from her actions. But whilst characters' stories can be tested and compared to other evidence of their worth presented in the novel, the fictional narrative in itself is not capable of proof – nor habitually does it set itself up as such – and thus the idea of the author as witness, which underpins some of the conventions of realist fiction, raises some difficulty for the reader.

In *Adam Bede*, Eliot's authorial stance is dependent upon the trope of the writer as authentic eye-witness:

[M]y strongest effort is . . . to give a faithful account of men and things as they have mirrored themselves in my mind. The mirror is doubtless defective; the outlines will sometimes be disturbed, the reflection faint or confused; but I feel as much bound to tell you as precisely as I can what that reflection is, as if I were in the witness-box narrating my experience on oath.[97]

Eliot draws on the legal and religious authority of the oath to guarantee the authenticity of her mimetic representations; the pose of the eye-witness is directly implicated in the conventions of her narrative realism.[98] She acknowledges that the oath does not in fact ensure accuracy of recollection, but her description of the ambits of fictional authorship is consistent with the questions which the honest witness must face about the selectiveness of memory, the inadvertent re-arrangement of evidentiary material, and the interposition of a mediating consciousness:

Examine your words well, and you will find that even when you have no motive to be false, it is a very hard thing to say the exact truth, even about your own immediate feelings – much harder than to say something fine about them which is *not* the exact truth. (I, ch. xvii, 268)

Yet the construction of a fictional narrative is essentially an act of artifice and the autonomy of the writer is guaranteed. The reference to the oath – so important to the evidence-based realism of mid-Victorian narrative – simultaneously and paradoxically infringes the 'willing suspension of disbelief' which sustains the reader's involvement in the story. The oath against perjury awakens anxieties about truth-telling in fiction – the suggestion that, in Davis's analysis, fiction itself may be (criminally) deceitful[99] – and the extent to which any imaginative narrative can be compromised by claims of false testimony.

We see this anxiety in Stephen's article on 'The License of Modern Novelists' which assumes a close correspondence between fictional representation and reality. Although naive in his treatment of the essential inventiveness of fiction – for example, he assumes that in writing *Little Dorrit*, Dickens has 'specific accusations . . . to bring against the Government'[100] – Stephen is clearly troubled by an author's immense influence and concomitant lack of public accountability. In the case of Charles Reade's *It is Never too Late to Mend*, he charges the author with libel for exaggerating the criminality of the acts on which the narrative is based. Fielding's idea of fiction as a court of appeal and Shelley's conception of poets as the 'unacknowledged legislators of the world'[101] threaten Stephen with their suggestions of private and inscrutable claims to power; he is disturbed by the possibility that literature may serve as a 'high commission . . . to try offences which elude the repression of the law, and to denounce with hyperbolical violence actions which may not have been committed at all, or which have been committed from very different motives'.[102] Eliot's alliance of the oath and the conventions of narrative realism is designed to generate assent in the reader, but at the same time it compromises fiction by reminding us of its potential association with perjury.

I would like to conclude this chapter by enquiring briefly into some of the anxieties which seem to arise from the mutual pre-occupation of authors and lawyers with issues of representation and the manipulation of evidence. Why was Dickens so enraged by excesses of adversarial licence in the courtroom? He claimed to be exposing injustice to the gaze of what Lord Denman had earlier called 'the tribunal of public opinion'. For Denman, it was crucial to the impartial administration of justice that 'judges . . . should be hourly taught to feel that there is a tribunal to which an appeal constantly lies against their decisions'.[103] Given that Denman had explicitly equated the press with the expression of the public voice,[104] it is not surprising that Dickens's criticisms were happily echoed in *The Examiner*. Yet Dickens was also using a restricted conception of the law as a foil for the definition of his own professional preoccupations. It is tempting to speculate that he was trying to avoid the label of a 'Newgate Novelist' by deflecting criticism onto the one other profession which was required to recite a criminal's story. In fact, his abhorrence of a lawyer's single-minded duty to his client may have helped shape Dickens's sense of social responsibility – that is, that he owed his efforts to a broader audience than that of a single client. Perhaps Pendennis's appreciation of artistic (rather than adversarial) licence is one which Dickens would have countenanced: his work 'necessitates cringing to no patron . . . calls for no keeping up of appearances; and . . . requires no stock in trade save the work-man's industry, his best ability and a dozen sheets of paper'.[105] But there is a defensiveness here, too, about the power of fictional texts to influence action, and Richard Altick records the suspicion that Courvoisier's murderous attack was suggested by his reading of Ainsworth's *Jack Sheppard*.[106] So if the lawyers had almost allowed Courvoisier to get away with it, it may in fact have been the authors who stimulated him to crime. Similarly, in his trial for murder in 1824, Jack Thurtell allegedly drew upon phrases from the speeches of Charles Phillips to construct his own defence;[107] perhaps atrocious crimes revealed a shared discourse of vicarious guilt which troubled both professions.

Perhaps in part perceiving this professional literary defensiveness and self-aggrandisement, Stephen claimed that newspaper reports and the efforts of modern novelists in turn generated the very opprobrium in which the legal profession was held. The title of his article 'The License of Modern Novelists' clearly mirrors Dickens's attacks on 'The License of Counsel' in the 1840s. In a later article entitled 'The Morality of Advocacy', Stephen cites the murder trial in *Mary Barton* as an example of the unrealistic excesses which novelists attribute to contemporary court proceedings; '[t]o judge from the representations given by popular writers, it would appear to be the common opinion that such practices are regarded, both by the bench and by the Bar, as triumphs of ingenuity'.[108] He stresses that, in actuality, improper behaviour by advocates is subject to the internal regulation of the profession and that '[s]uch imputations, as are conveyed in [the trial scene of *Mary Barton*] are not merely unjust, but they are most injurious to the public, because they tend to bring the administration of justice into disrepute'.[109] Dickens and Stephen recognised the power of each other's discourse to either influence public opinion or to sway the fates of unfortunate individuals; each was aware of their ability to generate emotional responses in their respective audiences and each was thus concerned with ethical limitations to imaginative or rhetorical licence.[110] Each was concerned with the locus of authority to speak (should an advocate identify himself completely with his brief, should a realistic novelist confine himself to well-documented facts?) and these are essentially questions about the ethical construction of representations and the manipulation of evidence. Such issues are inherently related to the struggle for influence between the courts and the community with regard to what constitutes true justice in any given case, and what evidence is required to reach the most perfect verdict.

Given this structural similarity between the work of authors and lawyers, the fact that lawyers are often responsible for the crimes perpetrated within a fictional narrative suggests certain anxieties on the part of authors about the extent of power lawyers exercise within both real and fictional communities. In many of the novels I have discussed, lawyers are responsible for a litany of atrocities – in *Amelia* Murphy is hanged at Tyburn for perjury and theft; in both *Felix Holt* and *Bleak House* the lawyers are involved in schemes of blackmail which serve as vehicles for the unfolding and resolution of the plot, and in the following chapter we shall see that *The Ring and the Book* displays a similar fear of the ethical relativity of legal rhetoric. This may be evidence of the author's discomfort at two aspects of legal practice. Firstly, the idea of excluded testimonial evidence (the focus of this chapter) is essentially foreign to the providential and teleological assumptions which underpin many a Victorian narrative. The authors do not want ultimately to withhold evidence from their readers; like the editorial critics of *The Examiner*, they want all the available evidence to go to the jury. As Dickens observed in *Household Narrative*, 'I wonder why I feel a glow of complacency in a court of justice, when I hear the learned judges taking uncommon pains to prevent the prisoner from letting out the truth'; '[i]f the object of the trial is to discover the truth, perhaps it might be as edifying to hear it, even from the prisoner, as to hear what is unquestionably not the truth from the prisoner's advocate'.[111] Nothing could be further from the conclusion of one of his novels where testimonial and authorial or providential confirmation of guilt or innocence is habitually provided. In a later study of the criminal law Stephen noted that 'the fact that the prisoner cannot be questioned stimulates the search for independent evidence',[112] and we see Victorian novelists manipulating the quest for the discovery of oral and material evidence to great effect, delaying the presentation of relevant facts and stories to induce suspense in the reader. But when it comes to narrative closure, the Victorian author's art is that of the carefully crafted recovery and explication of secrets, not the complete exclusion of significant material.

Secondly, the author's interest in the controlled disclosure of secrets is also closely allied to the evidence-gathering activities of the lawyer, and, as Weisberg has noted, there is a sense in which the character of the lawyer in a work of fiction is somehow responsible for the very construction of the narrative. Weisberg suggests that in *Bleak House*, for example, Tulkinghorn 'generates the novel's plot' and perhaps 'even collaborates in its narration'.[113] The power of the lawyers lies partly in the presumed transparency of their subjects;

lawyers are often perceived by other characters as enjoying a privileged access to otherwise hidden intentions and motives. We see this clearly in *Orley Farm* as the prosecutor constructs the story of the protagonist's guilt:

To Lady Mason it appeared as though the man who was now showing to all the crowd there assembled the chief scenes of her past life, had been present and seen everything that she had ever done . . . [I]t seemed to her as though that man who stood before her, telling his tale so calmly, had read the secrets of her very soul. (pp. 616–617)

Furnival, too, is able to read her character; like the narrator, 'he felt sure – almost sure, that he could look into her very heart, and read there the whole of her secret' (p. 374). The author as well as the barrister is vicariously tainted with the guilt of the criminal subject and the very emergence of the novel itself can be related to this simultaneous imitation and critique of the methodologies of the law. In *A Tale of Two Cities* (1859), for example, Dickens adopts the format of cross-examination as both substance and structure of his account of Charles Darnay's trial for treason, and critics such as Bender, Grossman, and Welsh are right to observe the association between the act of defence and the evolution of the third-person 'free indirect' narrative style.[114] What the Prisoners' Counsel Act conferred was the right to narrate a suspected felon's thoughts or intentions. This is the primary trait which the fictional lawyers share with their creator; as Ricoeur notes, the ability of the author to supply the thoughts of his characters creates 'all the magic of the third-person novel.'[115] But it also goes to the heart of the contrast between the ethical agendas of authorial and legal representation. In his article, 'The Demeanour of Murderers' which responded to the conviction of William Palmer, Dickens provided a self-conscious appraisal of the skill of the novelist in terms which explain his anxieties about the ability of the criminal courts to apportion guilt or innocence. Both the criminal law and literature compete to tell tales of transgression, but, in Dickens's analysis, authors do it best. Dickens claimed that he was able to offer an expert reading of Palmer's appearance of guilt as he stood in the dock. He attacked the public assumption that his composure was incompatible with his guilt and instead he argued that 'Nature never writes a bad hand': '[h]er writing, as it may be read in the human countenance, is invariably legible, if we come at all trained to the reading of it'. Dickens clearly felt he had such skills as he assured his readers that the verdict of guilt was in conformity with his reading of the man's appearance; 'the physiognomy and conformation of the Poisoner whose trial occasions these remarks, were exactly in accordance with his deeds; and every guilty consciousness he had gone on storing up in his mind, had set its mark upon him'.[116] The court may have been momentarily fooled into protecting an assumption of his innocence, but Dickens was not. The intervention of the discourse of barristers can only disguise or distort the relationship between appearances and 'reality'; authors, on the other hand, can be entrusted with a right reading of the evidence. That lawyers are often selected to perpetrate the author's darkest deeds – and thus carry the burden of the narrative guilt – is perhaps the product of the author's discomfort at the similarity of their interpretative activities. Perhaps an author does not wish to be reminded that if the rhetoric of the law may be untrustworthy, if a barrister cannot be 'taken at his word', then the rhetoric of fiction may be similarly suspect. To punish the lawyer is to reassure the reader that the author does not share the legal profession's inherent unreliability or unscrupulous pursuit of wealth.

CHAPTER 4

The martyr as witness: inspiration and the appeal to intuition

'If I live yet, it is for good, more love
Through me to men: be nought but ashes here
That keep awhile my semblance, who was John, –
Still, when they scatter, there is left on earth
No one alive who knew (consider this!)
– Saw with his eyes and handled with his hands
That which was from the first, the Word of Life.
How will it be when none more saith "I saw"?'
Robert Browning, 'A Death in the Desert', *Poetical Works 1833–1864*,
ed. by Ian Jack (Oxford University Press, 1970; repr. 1980),
pp. 818–836, at p. 821, lines 126–133.

The previous two chapters have been preoccupied with the ambit and legitimacy of a witness's testimony in a court of law, before a human tribunal and represented by human advocates. To develop more fully the Victorian idea of the transmission of truth in the medium of testimonial speech, we now need to examine the responses of Christian apologists to rationalist agendas of evidentiary analysis.

With the gradual disintegration of the traditional Christocentric paradigm, there arose a need to establish a new impetus for ethical praxis. Whilst theological doctrines were assailed by higher criticism and the implications of the fossil record, the vocabulary of orthodoxy lingered and beatification and martyrdom became fiercely contested motifs of authority. The ideas of duty and selfless resignation epitomised by the sacrifice of the martyr remained important as ethical if not religious virtues, and all sectarian factions sought to claim the heroes of Christian history as their own. For example, Charles Kingsley in *The Saint's Tragedy* (1848) rewrote the story of a popular Catholic saint for the purposes of Protestant propaganda, and George Eliot appropriated Anna Jameson's account of

England's lost heritage of Catholic iconography, using the stylistic features of hagiographical narrative to give a sacred resonance to her representations of Romola and Dorothea. At a time when ethical direction was threatened by the demise of scriptural and sacerdotal authority, the need to find an example by which to live assumed particular significance.

The motif of the martyr as both defendant and witness in literature highlights the aporetics of epistemology and the public attestation of belief; the testimony of the martyrs bears unusual authority because of the importance of their message, the means by which they claim to have received their message (often by such supernatural means as inspiration) and the affirmation which they give to the veracity of their message by their willingness to part with their lives rather than deny it. In this chapter, I explore the attraction of the martyr's testimony for writers in the mid-Victorian age and I trace something of a retreat from the rule-bound methodologies of the courtroom in their enthusiasm for the martyr's claims to an immediate apprehension of the absolute. This inevitably confronts issues of religious and artistic inspiration and emphasises differences between empirical and mystical strategies of interpretation. In the works of John Henry Newman and Robert Browning we see a reservation as to the monopoly which rules of evidence and theories of falsifiability would seek to exercise over the discovery of truth. Bypassing the rules of evidence in favour of an unmediated apprehension of the divine is a polemical and contentious move, however, and we see resistance to it in both the hesitancies of their own narratives and the opposition of the rationalist school.

The example of the Apostles, who endured privation and martyrdom in the quest to promulgate the gospel message, was the foundation of Paley's evidentiary school of theology, and even the higher critics were, on the whole, reluctant to criticise their sincerity. As noted in Chapter 1, most theorists preferred to stress the disciples' errors of perception or pre-scientific judgements; those such as Renan who suggested more deliberate fabrications provoked expressions of distaste, even from otherwise sympathetic agnostics. The violence of their deaths, and the nature of the unique eye-witness testimony they could provide as to the divinity and character of Jesus, ensured that the Apostles remained a source of fascination for those addressing epistemological anxieties. Their proximity to the source of absolute truth as revealed at the resurrection or at

Pentecost is dramatised in a number of nineteenth-century works, such as Bulwer-Lytton's *The Last Days of Pompeii* (1834), which includes the remembrance of an encounter with St Paul, and Robert Browning's 'A Death in the Desert' where we feel a poignant sense of loss at the demise of the man traditionally regarded as the last surviving member of the Apostolic generation: 'How will it be when none more saith "I saw"?'

Yet the privileged claim of the temporal eye-witness ('I saw' the historical Christ), which was to be so directly challenged by the higher critics, is not the only Christian paradigm of revelation. As noted earlier, the allegedly ahistorical operation of the Holy Spirit ensures that any believer, removed in time from the 'facts' of the gospel narrative, is also essentially an eye-witness to the resurrection; perception can be dissociated from an external 'event' and redirected towards the realm of faith and mysticism. In Ricoeur's words:

Primitive Christianity never perceived any fundamental difference between the eyewitness testimonies of the life of Jesus and the encounter with the resurrection Lord. The very editing of the Evangelists proceeds from this direct engagement of the prophetic inspirations attributed to the living Christ and of the memories of the eyewitnesses. There is no intrinsic difference between the facts and gestures of Jesus of Nazareth, or between the appearances of the resurrected Lord and the manifestations of the Spirit in the Pentecostal communities. On the contrary, the continuity of the same manifestation justifies a corresponding extension of testimony given of things seen and heard.[1]

St Paul's conversion on the road to Damascus occupies a position in both paradigms of perception by virtue of his chronological proximity to the historical Jesus and the immediacy of his encounter with the risen Christ. The testimony of many later martyrs and church leaders who could claim to speak directly of their own personal experience of God depends upon the latter approach. Again, this paradigm is well represented in historical fiction; Cardinal Wiseman uses the example of St Agnes to convert his eponymous heroine in *Fabiola* (1854) and both Kingsley and John Henry Newman use the testimony of Church Fathers – St Augustine and St Cyprian respectively – to effect the conversion of their protagonists in *Hypatia* (1853) and *Callista* (1856). For Kingsley and Newman, this reliance on early church example serves an often competing ideological purpose (to be discussed more fully below) but the very appeal to the testimony of the past betrays a common preoccupation with Christian origins and the need to identify an authoritative source of truth. In William James's words:

Dogmatic philosophies have sought for tests for truth which might dispense us from appealing to the future . . . [T]he history of dogmatic opinion shows that origin has always been a favorite test. Origin in immediate intuition; origin in pontifical authority; origin in supernatural revelation, as by vision, hearing, or unaccountable impression; origin in direct possession by a higher spirit, expressing itself in prophecy and warning; origin in automatic utterance generally – these origins have been stock warrants for the truth of one opinion after another which we find represented in religious history.[2]

The testimony of martyrs had a particular claim to authority of utterance as a consequence of Jesus's assurance to the disciples in Luke 12: 11–12: '[a]nd when they bring you unto the synagogues, and unto magistrates, and powers, take ye no anxious thought how or what thing ye shall answer, or what ye shall say: for the Holy Spirit shall teach you in the same hour what ye ought to say'. The Holy Spirit can rupture the proceedings of a trial, revealing the presence of God and the identity of his servants even before an earthly tribunal. The implication of the trial format in the revelation of truth is confirmed in the narrative of Christ's passion. In Stone's analysis of early medieval justice, the tribunal served as merely 'a setting for the revelation',[3] but the Christian model need not obliterate the importance of the legal forum in which such moments of epiphany can occur. As Ricoeur notes, the thematic structure of the trial assumes an archetypal significance; the occasion of Christ's assertion that he came to 'bear witness to the truth'[4] is 'a historic trial before a human court' and the end of Christian eschatology is the judgement of all mankind: '[b]y a strange reversal, the defendant of the earthly trial is also the judge of the eschatological trial'.[5] Hence, the convert, and particularly the martyr, follows the example not only of Christ's passion, but also of his profession of the gospel message in a forum of accusation and denial which serves to reveal God to man. We see this dual motif of suffering and the proclamation of truth in the etymology of the word 'martyr'. It is derived from the Greek root 'martys' meaning 'witness', and, as Robert Cover notes, it may also stem from the Aryan root 'smer' – 'to remember'; hence, '[m]artyrdom functions as a *re*-membering when the martyr, in the act of witnessing, sacrifices herself on behalf of the normative universe which is thereby reconstituted, regenerated, or recreated'.[6]

That the martyrs represented in Victorian fiction were invariably members of the early Christian church draws our attention to the polemical purposes of the historical novel. As George Levine has pointed out, the representation of the historical past in fiction may serve either as utopian model or as point of origin; the former invokes a myth of degeneration and the latter is associated with an evolutionary paradigm of development which gained force with the dissemination of Darwinian ideas.[7] In the debates between Newman and Kingsley regarding the nature of the Victorian church and the need to appeal to the past to legitimise modern praxis, we see something of a tension between the past as model and the past as origin, but in each case history is privileged for its proximity to the source of incarnate truth.

'IT SHALL BE GIVEN YOU IN THAT HOUR WHAT TO SPEAK': NEWMAN AND THE TRIALS OF THE FAITHFUL

Newman acclaimed the primitive church as his 'beau idéal' of Christianity, and the 'imaginative devotion' to the works of the early Church Fathers which arose in his youth had a 'permanent effect on him'.[8] In 1827, E. B. Pusey presented him with a complete set of their works,[9] and in 1828 Newman began to read the Fathers 'chronologically, beginning with St. Ignatius and St. Justin' as research for his first book, *The Arians of the Fourth Century*. In his *Apologia pro Vita Sua* (1864), he notes that primitive Christianity served as an Edenic model for his apprehension of the historical past, but the teleology of preparation for the disclosure of the gospel message also informed his understanding of the classical age; he had long considered 'that antiquity was the true exponent of the doctrines of Christianity' and from the philosophy of Clement and Origen he learnt of the 'various Economies or Dispensations of the Eternal':

I understood these passages to mean that the exterior world, physical and historical, was but the manifestation to our senses of realities greater than itself. Nature was a parable: Scripture was an allegory: pagan literature, philosophy, and mythology, properly understood, were but a preparation for the Gospel.[10]

Newman's early acceptance of the idea of scripture as allegory

implies an awareness of the crucial role of the interpreter. As Ian
Ker has pointed out, Newman believed that 'the present is a text,
and the past its interpretation';[11] '[w]e always judge of what meets
us by what we know already. There is no such thing in nature as a
naked text without note or comment'.[12] Adherence to the past as a
static model, then, is epistemologically naive, and instead Newman
relied upon the organic authority of the Church for the preservation,
transmission and interpretation of religious truth: 'the Creed (i.e. the
Deposit . . .) was delivered to the *Church with the gift of knowing its true
and full meaning*', even though that knowledge may develop 'intermit-
tently, in times & seasons, often delaying and postponing, according
as she is guided by her Divine Instructor'.[13] Unlike its liberal
counterpart, Catholic historicism 'consider[s] that the Church, like
Aaron's rod, devours the serpents of the magicians. They are
hunting for a fabulous primitive simplicity; we repose in Catholic
fulness . . . We consider that a divine promise keeps the Church
Catholic from doctrinal corruption; but on what promise, or on
what encouragement, they are seeking for their visionary purity does
not appear'.[14] Newman's suspicion of literal models of scriptural
interpretation also enabled him to maintain that '[i]t may be almost
laid down as an historical fact, that the mystical interpretation and
orthodoxy will stand or fall together'.[15] Hence, he was to experience
no immediate conflict between the creationist cosmology of Genesis
and the evidence of the fossil record, and in 1858, he was able to
assert, in a letter to Pusey, 'I seem to wish that divine and human
science might each be suffered in peace to take its own line, the one
not interfering with the other. Their circles scarcely intersect each
other'.[16] For Newman, 'reason . . . [was] subservient to faith';[17] the
tendency of the reason 'actually and historically' was 'towards a
simple unbelief in matters of religion' and the action of logic alone
could not prove the existence of the numinous. He also avoided the
Protestant assumptions as to the infallibility of the scriptural text
which had proven so vulnerable to the analysis of rational historicism. For all their differences, Newman did share with Jowett a
suspicion of the scriptural inerrancy proposed by Protestant divines;
Newman argued that the vulnerability of scripture to the destructive
power of rational enquiry (despite its divine origins) arises from an
inappropriate use of the text:

Experience proves surely that the Bible does not answer a purpose for
which it was never intended. It may be accidentally the means of the

conversion of individuals; but a book, after all, cannot make a stand against the wild living intellect of man, and in this day it begins to testify, as regards its own structure and contents, to the power of that universal solvent, which is so successfully acting upon religious establishments.[18]

The ability to look beyond the text – to faith and tradition – preserved Newman from much of the furore generated by higher criticism and geological discoveries.[19] Newman's letter to Pusey also reveals his confidence in the traditional idea of inspiration; scientific methodology posed little threat to Catholic readings of the Bible 'because so little is determined about the inspiration of scripture except in matters of faith and morals'.[20] At this time, Ker notes, the Catholic Church 'had rarely given an authoritative interpretation of any Biblical passage and the inspiration of scripture was not even formally an article of faith': God seemed to be the originator (rather than the author) of the Old and New Testaments.[21] But while Newman's own faith was not shaken by the advances of liberalism and the nascent scientific methodology, he believed that the controversy generated by the publication of *Essays and Reviews* in 1860 had to be addressed if the Church was to survive unscathed. As Ker notes, Newman believed that the doctrine most undermined by the heterodox authors was the status of the Bible as inspired text;[22] he also regarded it as raising difficulties 'which no decision of the Church, no apostolical tradition, no consent of schools or of the faithful, no obvious necessity or reasonableness enables us to solve'.[23] Nevertheless, the provocative position of the Essayists demanded a response. Newman gradually became more familiar with the ideas of the contributors; he refers to Dr Williams's essay in an early draft of an essay on inspiration.[24] In addition to Williams, Wilson and Jowett also dwelt on the difficulties associated with rigid ideas of inspiration in their contributions to the volume, and Jowett in particular asserted that any definition of inspiration 'must conform to all well-ascertained facts of history or science'.[25]

In the early nineteenth century, both the Catholic and the Protestant Churches were prepared to leave the exact definition of 'inspiration' to individual conscience. The sixth of the thirty-nine Articles of the Church of England proclaimed the inspiration of the biblical text, but no further doctrinal direction was provided. In his defence of Dr Williams before the Court of Arches in 1862, Fitzjames Stephen emphasised the Church of England's persistent refusal to narrow the definition of inspiration over the centuries. He traced the

Anglican appreciation of private judgement and liberty of opinion on open questions such as inspiration back to the Reformation itself and he saw Hooker's assessment of the Bible – 'Scripture *is* perfect for the end for which it *was* designed' (and therefore '[i]t is not infallible on other subjects') – as representing the stance of the Church ever since.[26] The work of prominent divines such as Tillotson, Burnet, Butler, Berkeley, and Warburton all contributed to this tradition which Stephen interpreted as limiting the unrestrained operation of inspiration. For example, according to Stephen, Warburton discredited the idea of inspiration in order to emphasise the fidelity of the evangelists as historians:

[H]e puts the authority of the four Gospels upon the genuineness of their contents; upon the broad ground that the ordinary tests of reason and experience show they are substantially true – upon the ground, in fact, on which, if I were addressing a jury, I would ask them to believe a witness in a court of justice.[27]

Stephen noted that as recently as 1816, Bishop Heber had asserted that inspiration in the Church of England remained an open question, an approach affirmed by notable theologians such as Bishops Whately and Thirlwall. In his Introduction to Schleiermacher's *Critical Essay on the Gospel of St. Luke* (1825), Connop Thirlwall gave lengthy consideration to the threat posed to traditional assumptions about inspiration by the advent of 'new critical theories' which describe the gospels as either a summary of oral tradition, the précis of a 'single, large and multifarious original, from which our evangelists made extracts' or a palimpsest of recollections which grew 'in its passage through various hands'.[28] He observed that the belief that 'the sacred writers were merely passive organs or instruments of the Holy Spirit . . . has been so long abandoned . . . by the learned' but it was still popular amongst the laity who tended to venerate more literal interpretations (pp. xi–xii). Stephen, too, conceded that 'the Calvinistic view of the infallibility of the Scriptures prevail[ed] so widely . . . amongst the laity at large, owing to the decline of theological learning, that . . . it has almost come to be received as an article of faith'.[29] But both asserted that leading Anglican divines had moved away from this rigid approach and adopted a 'milder and more flexible theory' which stressed either 'the inspiration of suggestion' or 'the inspiration of superintendency' (pp. xii–xiii). Thirlwall noted that many people conceive of inspiration in hybrid terms, rejecting the idea of dictation, yet 'on the other hand . . .

shrink[ing] from the boldness of the modern theories, by maintaining that whatever was not known to the sacred historians by
[experience or conversation with inspired witnesses] was directly
revealed to them from above' (pp. xiii–xiv). However, Thirlwall
conceded that this comfortable compromise is not immune from
criticism; as a consequence of the new theories which have disclosed
'discrepancies' in the gospel narratives, he is compelled to admit that
'the superintending control of the Spirit was not exerted to exempt
the sacred writers altogether from errors and inadvertencies'. He felt
it was unnecessarily dogmatic to insist that the evangelists must have
been 'first witnesses' of the gospel events and 'unless we make this
totally unfounded supposition, there appears to be no dogmatical
necessity for denying that the evangelists drew from secondary
sources, or for maintaining that the use of these was superseded by
the extraordinary suggestions of the Spirit' (p. xv). As discussed in
Chapter 1, the evidence offered by the evangelists to the truth of the
resurrection was demoted by the advent of higher criticism from the
status of eye-witness testimony, privileged in its representation of
historical 'fact', to that of derivative material whose reliability was
subject to careful scrutiny. And the idea of inspiration underwent a
corresponding change as representations of the evangelist's role
altered progressively from that of passive amanuensis of the Holy
Spirit, to inspired editor of writings supervised by the Holy Spirit,
and finally to fallible secretary or biographer collating equally fallible
traditions and recollections.

The concept of inspiration itself thus changes from being a
moment of epiphany, a divine gift of enlightenment, to becoming
simply an editorial *modus operandi*. For example, Schleiermacher
describes Luke's endeavours in almost mechanical terms; 'we must
content ourselves with considering these narratives as materials
which came separately into Luke's hands, and therefore all that
remains is to make an attempt to discover the law according to
which he arranged them'.[30] Schleiermacher suggests a number of
techniques that the evangelist might have used in order to impose
meaning and structure upon the unwieldy mass of primary documentation. Similarly, Strauss leaves little room for the operation of
the traditional form of divine inspiration; the form of the gospel
narratives 'is governed by the association of ideas, the laws of which
are partly dependent on external relations; and we need not be
surprised to find many passages, especially from the discourses of

Jesus, ranged together for the sole cause that they happen to have in common certain striking consonant words.'[31] We can sense something of Newman's resistance to this theory in his fictional writings as well as his doctrinal pieces.

Newman's treatment of the testimony of a martyr in his second novel, *Callista*, provides an unexpected insight into his understanding of the complexity of the idea of inspiration. Newman's eponymous protagonist was a young Greek girl in Alexandria who was imprisoned on a false charge of Christianity, then converted by the teaching of Caecilius, St Cyprian, and the gospel of St Luke whilst awaiting trial before the Roman tribunal. Callista's trial, like that of the historical Jesus, elicits testimony to his divinity and identity; when interrogated, she is able to assert that 'He is the true son of the True God; and I am His, and He is Mine'.[32] In the construction of Callista's testimony to the existence and attributes of the Christian God, Newman placed particular emphasis upon the historical record of the evidence presented at her trial:

> If, indeed, it could be trusted to the letter, as containing Callista's answers word for word, it would have a distinctly sacred character, in consequence of our Lord's words, 'It shall be given you in that hour what to speak.' However, we attach no such special value to this document, since it comes to us through heathen notaries, who may not have been accurate reporters; not to say that before we did so we ought to look very carefully into its genuineness. As it is, we believe it to be as true as any part of our narrative, and not truer. (p. 360)

This authorial disclaimer raises a number of issues, notably the status of the martyr's testimony to the absolute and the author's understanding of the operation and inerrancy of inspiration itself. Callista's original utterances ('word for word') are understood to exhibit a 'distinctly sacred character' as a consequence of Jesus's promise of direct dictation by the Holy Spirit in Luke 12: 11. Yet the document in which her testimony is recorded is not inspired and free from error as a consequence of the possible intervention of 'heathen notaries, who may not have been very accurate reporters'; inerrancy can only be attributed to the text when its authenticity and provenance are established to the satisfaction of the Church. This is an inversion of the methodology of higher criticism, which suggested the fallibility of the gospels as a consequence of the bias of the Christian reporters and editors. This approach to the question of inspired authorship in turn determines the role of the reader; a reader should approach the text with a moral or religious interest which is distinct from that accorded to other classical works.[33] Jowett's maxim was to '*[i]nterpret the Scripture like any other book*';[34] Newman, on the other hand viewed the scriptures as 'the medium in which the mind of the Church has energized and developed',[35] and Callista's conversion – a product of exposure to the Holy Spirit in both the scriptures and the wider church community – illustrates this.

Yet for all his commitment to the Church as the living embodiment of Christ, Newman was troubled by the idea of direct dictation from God to man. Ker argues that he was disappointed by Vatican moves in the 1870s towards a more rigid view of inspiration which tended to diminish the human component.[36] In his draft article entitled 'The Inspiration of Scripture' (1861), Newman assessed the scriptural and patristic evidence for contrasting attitudes to inspiration; he concluded that an external approach to the definition is essentially the issue of canonicity – the 'attestation of the Holy Ghost . . . to the book' – whilst an internal definition must address the question of dictation or suggestion and supervision of the evangelists' work. At this point in time, Newman decided the internal definition could be formulated in inclusive terms:

[T]he Bible is the Word of God *such*, by virtue of its being throughout written, or dictated, or impregnated, or directed by the Spirit of Truth, or at least in parts written, in parts dictated, in parts impregnated, in parts directed, and throughout preserved from formal error, at least substantial, by the Spirit of Truth.[37]

This version of the article remained unpublished. However, in February 1884, Newman published an article entitled 'On the Inspiration of Scripture' in *The Nineteenth Century* which revealed his later thoughts on the subject; he asserted that whilst the Bible clearly contained a human element, 'by reason of the difficulty of always drawing the line between what is human and what is divine, [it] cannot be put on the level of other books, as it is now the fashion to do, but [it] has the nature of a Sacrament, which is outward and inward, and a channel of supernatural grace.'[38] Newman noted that the Council of Trent insists that the evangelists are inspired whilst the more recent Council of the Vatican (1870) claimed inspiration for the books themselves, and he insists that both are internally consistent 'dogmatic truths'; the books are inspired, because the writers were inspired to write them. Thus there are 'two agencies, divine grace and human intelligence, co-operating in the production of the Scriptures' which are essentially 'man's writing, informed and quickened by the presence of the Holy Ghost':

Hence we have no reason to be surprised, nor is it against the faith to hold, that a canonical book may be composed, not only from, but even of, pre-existing documents, it being always born in mind, as a necessary condition, that an inspired mind has exercised a supreme and an ultimate judgement on the work, determining what was to be selected and embodied in it.

For Newman, then, the doctrine of inspiration is dependent upon the idea of an 'inspired Editor' – 'that is, an inspired mind, authoritative in faith and morals, from whose fingers the sacred text passed'.[39] Thus, the scriptures were not a product of direct dictation. Similarly, Callista's testimony is weakened by its transmission through 'heathen notaries' and it has not been generated and preserved by inspired Christian editorial practice.

Newman's description of the status of the testimony Callista provides at her trial raises one further issue. In disclaiming inerrancy, Newman asserts that the record of her privileged witnessing is 'as true as any part of our narrative and not truer'. In one sense, this is an obvious acknowledgement of the story's fictionality; despite the artifice of documentary material which claims to ground the narra-tive in historical 'fact' (a popular convention of the nineteenth-century historical genre), Newman admits that the tale of Callista's conversion is not indebted to any primary source material. But as Stephen Prickett has observed, there is also a sense in which Newman's disclaimer of 'fact' serves the contrary purpose; it seeks to claim inspiration as a quality of fictional art, to invest imaginative endeavour with a kind of truth value, to elevate poetics to the service of religion. Newman would have rejected the romantic appropria-tion of religious inspiration as a travesty of the sacred, and it is most unlikely that he conceived of his own sense of vocation (as a Christian writer persecuted for the truths of Catholicism and theoretically open to the same source of inspiration as the disciples) as directly given by God. He states dogmatically in his early writings on inspiration that it ceased with the close of the apostolic age – 'the Apostles were inspired, and the Fathers were not'.[40] But he notes that he did not 'writ[e] or publish . . . without a *call*' or 'invitation, or necessity, or emergency':

The Essay on Assent is nearly the only exception. And I *cannot* write without such a stimulus. I feel to myself going out of the way, or impertinent

– and I write neither with spirit nor with point. As to the 'Assent', I had felt
it on my conscience for years, that it would not do to quit the world without
doing it. Rightly or wrongly, I had ever thought it a duty, as if it was
committed to me to do it.[41]

In his article 'On the Inspiration of Scripture', Newman observed
that it is not '*de fide* . . . that inspired men, at the time when they
speak from inspiration, should always know that the Divine Spirit is
visiting them'. In other words, it is not a prerequisite of inspiration
that a saint should feel 'that every word he uttered was not simply
his, but another's'[42] and this seems to leave open the possibility of
his own inspiration. But, he upholds the judgement of the Vatican
Council that in order to be categorised as sacred and canonical, it is
not enough 'for a book to be a work of mere human industry, [even
if] it be afterwards approved by the authority of the Church', nor is
it enough 'if it contains revealed teaching without error': 'Neither of
these views supposes the presence of inspiration, whether in the
writer or the writing; what is contemplated above is an inspired
writer in the exercise of his inspiration, and a work inspired from
first to last under the action of that inspiration.'[43] Yet whilst
Newman may not have described his own literary career, with its
periods of doubt and uncertainty, as 'inspired', more liberal theologians were reluctant to maintain the distinction between polemical
writing in the service of religious truth and the generation of purely
fictional narratives. Some twenty-five years earlier, Hennell had
conceived of the evangelist not as earth-bound editor but as inspired
artist; '[m]any of the finer thoughts and feelings of mankind find a
vent in fiction, expressed either by painting, poetry, or the poetic
tale; and the perception of historical inaccuracy does not prevent
our sharing the thoughts and feelings which have embodied themselves in this manner.'[44] Williams, too, regarded inspiration as
available to the artist. Unlike his prosecutors in the Court of Arches,
who sought to 'draw a line between the influence which produced
the Holy Scriptures and the other influences of the Holy Ghost',
Williams maintained that the activities of the Spirit continued to be
felt in a variety of callings in the present day.[45] In Stephen's words,

The truth is, that what [the prosecutors] object to is not that Dr. Williams
maintains that the Bible is not inspired; but that he maintains the
possibility that other persons may in their own degree, and for their own
purposes, be inspired: that he contends that it is possible that it was not
without the influence of God prompting them to it, that Luther undertook

what he did, or that Milton wrote the works which still instruct and delight mankind.[46]

The continuing operation of the Holy Spirit thus ensures that poetics may serve the promotion of Christian truth in vehicles other than the scriptural canon.

The distinction between ideas of religious and artistic/secular inspiration arises in part from competing views of the relationship between the disintegration of the tenets of Christian orthodoxy and the emergence of the realist novel in England. The demise of traditional Christian typology is seen as a necessary cause of, or at least corollary of, the teleological evolution of the novel as a genre designed to explore the psychological dramas of introspection and persuasion. Hence, Levine's claim that the novel 'is so firmly grounded in the realities of this world that it can only achieve the slightest hints and intimations about the other'.[47] Such an approach assumes both the unknowability of God and the unutterability of religious experience – that the apprehension of the absolute is the point at which narration breaks down. It also embodies Strauss's anxieties, cited earlier, about the means by which to prove the existence of the numinous; 'it is inadequa[te to] appeal, in a scientific enquiry, to a popular notion, such as that of the aid of the Holy Spirit'.[48] The reconciliation of such differing *a priori* assumptions is virtually impossible, but Newman's belief in the occurrence of miracles justifies their inclusion in a fictional representation of Catholic religious experience. And in *Origins of Narrative: The Romantic Appropriation of the Bible*, Stephen Prickett challenges some of the long-standing assumptions about the progress of secularisation and the origins of fictional realism in the eighteenth and nineteenth centuries. After a reappraisal of the romantic indebtedness to the Bible as metatype, he claims that 'there is a very real sense in which the Roman and early Christian novels of Lockhart, Ware, Kingsley and Newman may better reflect the acknowledged biblical origins of the genre than the more realistic novels of contemporary life'. Prickett concedes that the 'innate religiosity in the nineteenth-century novel may equally well be interpreted as both a covert secularisation and a fictionalisation of what was once immutable Holy Writ',[49] but the ambiguity and the possibility of competing interpretative strategies is precisely the point. To see the historical development of narrative in evolutionary or progressive terms, with Newman sidelined because of his adherence to the representation of the absolute in fiction, is to ignore the extent to which he shared with other writers of his age (in John Coulson's terms) a common 'grammar' of belief.

The interpretation of martyrdom – and especially, in Ricoeur's phrase, the hermeneutics of testimony – goes to the heart of nine-teenth-century debates about the existence of the miraculous and the limits of man's knowledge of the divine. Both Kingsley's *Hypatia* and Newman's *Callista* use the motif of martyrdom to explore Christian history; whilst Kingsley's heroine is murdered by the church as she moves towards an appeal to Christ unmediated by sacerdotal authority, the relics of Newman's heroine are translated to the altar of the church and incorporated into Catholic history. Powell had confidently asserted that 'no testimony can reach to the supernatural', but for Newman this proposition is refuted by the very process of conversion – the point at which the individual encounters God – and the acquisition of religious certainty. That the motif of martyrdom becomes a special source of interpretative conflict is not surprising; the quest for truth becomes particularly compelling when the price to be paid by a witness for her testimony may be death, and an analysis of these cases discloses the power implicit in all acts of adjudication:

Martyrdom, for all its strangeness to the secular world of contemporary American Law, is a proper starting place for understanding the nature of legal interpretation. Precisely because it is so extreme a phenomenon, martyrdom helps us see what is present in lesser degree whenever interpretation is joined with the practice of violent domination. Martyrs insist in the face of overwhelming force that if there is to be continuing life, it will not be on the terms of the tyrant's law . . . Their triumph – which may well be partly imaginary – is the imagined triumph of the normative universe – of Torah, Nomos, – over the material world of death and pain.[50]

The violent sanctions which can attend a finding of guilt in a court of law thus stand revealed, and the literary representation of martyrdom in Victorian fiction draws on a rich fund of both religious and secular associations. The criminal defendant is often said, in texts such as *Orley Farm*, *The Trial*, or *Felix Holt*, to be martyred by the very process of accusation and proof, and one who is unjustly executed is said to fall as a martyr to the law itself. The representa-tion of criminal trials in Victorian narratives often gestures towards both human and divine tribunals of justice; in *The Trial*, for example, Yonge reminds us that the accused is simultaneously innocent of the temporal charge, yet not 'guiltess in God's sight', and therefore liable to conviction at the Great Assize.[51] The representation of the religious defendant is similarly paradoxical; Callista is guilty of the temporal charge (failing to worship the emperor, for example) yet eternally innocent through her appropriation by faith of Christ's sacrificial atonement for her sins. The paradox is sustained by the nexus of belief between subject and narrator, and hence the stories of Callista, Hypatia or Savonarola are told by the communities which seek to find in their otherwise shameful deaths a transcendent justification of the beliefs to which they themselves subscribe.[52]

If the extreme sanction of martyrdom enables issues of legal adjudication to be analysed with greater clarity, there is also the reciprocal sense in which a trial is the essential arena for the generation and assessment of the martyr's claims to truth and inspiration. *Callista, Romola* and *The Ring and the Book* all rely upon the mechanism of trial or interrogation to reveal the nature of a witness's understanding of truth and religious experience. As noted earlier, the archetypal association of trial and truth is confirmed in the proceedings of Christ's passion which are re-enacted in each subsequent martyrdom of a disciple or believer. For Ricoeur, the revelatory possibilities of testimony require a paradoxical form of self-surrender and self-transcendence which is essentially personal in its operation, and he observes that neither the exemplary lives of heroes or saints nor the function of symbol can supply an experience of the absolute:

The example is historic but is obliterated as the case before the rule. The symbol is not obliterated so easily; its double meaning, its opacity, renders it inexhaustible and causes it never to cease giving rise to thought. But it lacks – or can lack – historic density; its meaning matters more than its historicity. As such it constitutes instead a category of the productive imagination. Absolute testimony, on the contrary, in concrete singularity gives a caution to the truth without which its authority remains in suspense. Testimony, each time singular, confers the sanction of reality on ideas, ideals, and modes of being that the symbol depicts and discovers for us only as our most personal possibilities.

The personal confrontation with the absolute must combine the universality of symbol with a moment of specific 'historical density'. Following Jean Nabert, Ricoeur argues that the central ontological dilemma is thus the difficulty of 'invest[ing] with an absolute character a moment of history'[53] and this is exacerbated where the relevant 'moment' of time is to be represented in fictional or historiographical narrative. Yet it is this very act of investiture –

where the eternal impacts upon the individual in the act of conversion or martyrdom – which Newman attempts to narrate in *Callista*, which Eliot explores in Romola's examination of Savonarola's confessions, and which Browning investigates in the testimony of Pompilia and the Pope.

In Prickett's analysis, the repeated use of the word 'I' in Callista's narrative is 'the authentic voice of romanticism'; '[t]he kind of "romantic" self-consciousness attributed . . . to Christianity and to the influence of the Bible is probably a necessary prerequisite for what we would understand as genuine martyrdom . . . *Callista* is supremely a novel of interior consciousness'.[54] Callista is no Christian cipher or *tabula rasa* on which dogmatic truths may be impressed. Her representation as martyr and witness in fact involves a heightened awareness of self which both facilitates and results from the pursuit of divine truth; the knowledge in which her testimony is grounded is both rational (based on an assessment of 'Evidences' such as Caecilius's preaching and the gospel of St Luke) and mystical (the suggestion that, in the forum of the trial, her very defence may be provided by the Holy Spirit). For Newman, the testimony of the martyr can reach to the divine and Powell's conception of testimony as a second-hand assurance lacking in phenomenological value is rejected.

Newman, Eliot and Browning share another central preoccupation which is effectively addressed by Ricoeur's analysis; 'what is a true witness, a faithful witness?'.[55] Callista's main objection to Agellius's pursuit of her hand in marriage is that he has 'had much to tell of [him]self, but nothing of Him!' (p. 131):

'You profess to believe in One True God, and to reject every other; and now you are implying that the Hand, the Shadow of that God is on my mind and heart. Who is this God? where? how? in what? O Agellius, you have stood in the way of Him, ready to speak of yourself, using Him as a means to an end.' (p. 129)

In contrast, the faithful witness must become a transparent medium through which God may be seen. In Ricoeur's analysis, the Christian becomes, for the benefit of others, a sign of the absolute – emptied of self but filled with an intimation of the divine presence. Thus testimony 'proceeds from an absolute initiative as to its origin and its content'.[56] Newman's belief in a personal revelation for which it is possible to suffer martyrdom willingly ensures that Callista embraces death as a true witness, giving testimony to her own encounter with the absolute. In fact, Newman – like Paley – seems to believe that no-one could be a martyr for anything less than a vision of the reality of absolute truth:

The heart is commonly reached, not through the reason, but through the imagination, by means of direct impressions, by the testimony of facts and events, by history, by description. Persons influence us, voices melt us, looks subdue us, deeds inflame us. Many a man will live and die upon a dogma: no man will be a martyr for a conclusion . . . No one, I say, will die for his own calculations: he dies for realities.[57]

Newman's belief that an individual can assent to a religious mystery (which is comprehensible to man because we can assent to the language of dogma and spiritual experience)[58] enables Callista to choose death rather than repeat the narrative formulation which would undo her linguistic and religious world. According to Prickett, this romantic self-expression is a distinctive legacy of the Christian consciousness to which literature is permanently indebted.

'THE LIGHT I SAW WAS THE TRUE LIGHT': THE CONFESSIONS OF SAVONAROLA

George Eliot, in contrast, was interested in the disconsolate suffering of those who face death without doctrinal assurance or affirmation. Although *Romola* is deeply indebted to Catholic hagiographical narratives, she emphasises the contingent character of the interpretative act which seeks to read the significance of an act of martyrdom. In *Loss and Gain*, Newman ridicules the possibility that the name of 'martyr' can rightly be given to one 'who dies professing that [Truth] is a shadow' or that '[a] life-long martyrdom is this, to be ever changing'.[59] Eliot, on the other hand, is aware that one generation's heretic may become a future generation's martyr, and the hermeneutics of a martyr's testimony is at the heart of the quest for religious certainty in *Romola*.

In Eliot's novel, the charismatic priest, Savonarola, shares the communal journey of the persecuted as he moves from the empty rhetoric of martyrdom to a reenactment of Christ's passion. The mechanism of the trial, in which the prophet is both witness and defendant, also places the hermeneutic act at the culmination of Romola's journey towards wisdom and the reader's journey towards narrative closure. Her interpretation of Savonarola's passion enables her to define ethical action for the benefit of Lillo and the future generation of Florentines. But a reading of Savonarola's death is difficult, because his martyrdom is problematic. As his execution approaches, he feels only that '"I am not worthy to be a martyr: the Truth shall prosper, but not by me"'.[60] In David Carroll's analysis, Eliot (like Newman) is exploring the question of 'What is a hero? Who is the true martyr?'[61] Yet, unlike Callista, in death Savonarola experiences only a profound self-abasement:

There is no jot of worthy evidence that from the time of his imprisonment to the supreme moment, Savonarola thought or spoke of himself as a martyr . . . And through that greatness of his he endured a double agony: not only the reviling, and the torture, and the death-throe, but the agony of sinking from the vision of glorious achievement into that deep shadow where he could only say, 'I count as nothing: darkness encompasses me: yet the light I saw was the true light.' (ch. lxxi, p. 581)

Like the implied audience of the early Christian community in *Callista*, Romola waits anxiously for news of his confessions and proclamations as he is tortured in prison – he both asserts and denies the divine basis of his utterings, a 'twofold retraction' which 'fill[s her] with dismayed uncertainty'. Firstly, he denies his initial fear that 'God has withdrawn from [him] the spirit of prophecy'; '[t]he things that I have spoken, I had them from God'. Then, under renewed torture, he states that he confessed only that he 'might *seem* good' (my italics); 'the truth' is an alternative narrative (ch. lxxii, p. 582). Seeking an authoritative reading of these oral texts transmitted by unsympathetic auditors, Romola hopes to witness his final moments, to hear his ultimate assessment of his own inspiration:

'[T]here will come a moment when he may speak. When there is no dread hanging over him but the dread of falsehood, when they have brought him into the presence of death, when he is lifted above the people, and looks on them for the last time, they cannot hinder him from speaking a last decisive word. I will be there'. (ch. lxxii, pp. 582–583)

She seeks the privileged position of the ocular eye-witness, whose own evidence of the senses can generate a reliable act of judgement. Savonarola's supporters retain hope 'even at this eleventh hour, that God would interpose, by some sign, to manifest their beloved prophet as His servant'. Romola, in contrast, hopes for a clear declaration that he was 'innocent of deceit' (ch. lxxii, p. 583). Romola yearns for his public acquittal, but her act of witnessing, burdened with hope and expectation, is ultimately frustrated. At his brutal death, she sees no final sign of divine acclamation; she experiences instead a sympathetic transference of sensory perception which imparts to her his silent suffering: 'in the same moment expectation died, and she only saw what he was seeing – torches waving to kindle the fuel beneath his dead body, faces glaring with a yet worse light; she only heard what *he* was hearing – gross jests, taunts, and curses' (lxii, p. 584). There is no long-awaited epiphany; there is no transcendent insight to be transmitted to the watching witness.

As Carroll has observed, Romola's interpretation of Savonarola's confessions is a seminal episode of the novel. He argues that Savonarola's doubts as to his identity, his role and his mission are reminiscent of the representation of Jesus in Hennell's *Inquiry*, and that in interpreting whether or not Savonarola is a genuine martyr, Romola 'practises a form of higher criticism' on evidence that is of 'doubtful authority': '[the text] was obtained under torture, it is an unofficial second edition printed after the first was withdrawn, and the digest of the confession was made by a corrupt notary'. Carroll argues that Romola's quest for the correct interpretation of Savonarola's death is 'an imitation of the priest's struggles which were in turn an imitation of Christ', and hence some kind of salvation is possible; '[a]fter the crucifixion [of Savonarola] comes the resurrection of her faith in this man "who had been for her the incarnation of the highest motives". The final reading depends on what has been transferred to the reader'.[62] Carroll claims that in this act of interpretation, Romola 'represent[s] the author, the narrator and the reader'.[63] She decides for herself which interpretation of Savonarola's calling will help her to live a life of exemplary self-sacrifice, and she chooses to keep the day of his death sacred for private reasons which are not widely shared: '[p]erhaps I should never have learned to love him if he had not helped me when I was in great need' (Epilogue, p. 588). Clearly the typological antecedent of Savonarola's martyrdom is a reading of the gospel message which is radically distinct from the exemplary life held up by theologically orthodox writers such as Newman, Wiseman and Kingsley for the edification of their Christian audience. Yet Eliot avoids the slide into total relativism; as John Coulson has observed, '[t]he traditional metaphors of religious description are retained as essential mediating structures: they are not *mere* similes'.[64]

BROWNING AND EYE-WITNESS TESTIMONY TO THE ABSOLUTE

Whilst acknowledging important formal and structural differences between the poetic and the fictional genres, I want to conclude this chapter with reference to two works by Robert Browning which illustrate most effectively some of the mid-Victorian anxieties about the status of testimony in religious and legal hermeneutics. He too uses the demythologising typology of the higher critics to explore the status of St John's eye-witness testimony in 'A Death in the Desert'. Like the records of the confessions of Callista and Savonarola, the parchment of Pamphylax the Antiochene, which supposedly conserves the final declarations of the evangelist, is of uncertain provenance. The personal identity of the narrator is not disclosed. The poem opens with a number of fellow believers attending to the comfort of the dying John, ministering to his needs and, like Romola, awaiting a final ocular authentification of the divine message he had preached; they 'laid him in the light where [they] might see . . .[t]he last of what might happen on his face' (lines 32, 28).[65] John is aroused from unconsciousness for the last time by the repetition of Jesus's words at the raising of Lazarus, as recorded in his own gospel (11: 25).[66] That these words are also spoken in the Anglican burial service contributes to the confusion as to John's ontological state at the time of the address; he seems to hover on the brink of life and death – traditionally a time of privileged access to the realities of the absolute – but the final insights which he offers into the truth of the events that he 'saw' are destructive rather than supportive of orthodox Christian historicism.

As he looks back over his long life and assesses the truth value of the revelation he has been granted, John repeats his claim that he had '[seen] and heard, and could remember all' (line 117). Initially, his dissemination of Christ's teachings, his composition of the Book of Revelation under the guidance of the Holy Spirit ('[w]ith nothing left to my arbitrament / To choose or change', lines 143–144), and his own 'reasoning from . . . knowledge' enabled men to believe (line 147), but now, as his life draws to a close, men ask ' "[w]as John at all, and did he say he saw? / Assure us, ere we ask what he might see!" ' (lines 196–197). In his attempt to articulate the broader truths of love and power which 'o'erfloods [his] soul' (line 217), John wrestles with the uncertainty of the traditional Christian 'Evidences', and, in doing so, transcends any reliance on the accuracy of the historical

record. To encourage those who doubt and yearn for the miraculous
certainties of the vanishing apostolic age, John argues that his
eventual assurance of God's love did not arise from what he had
seen:

> 'Ye know what things I saw; then came a test,
> My first, befitting me who so had seen:
>> "Forsake the Christ thou sawest transfigured, Him
>> Who trod the sea and brought the dead to life?
>> What should wring this from thee!" – ye laugh and ask.
> What wrung it? Even a torchlight and a noise,
> The sudden Roman faces, violent hands,
> And fear of what the Jews might do! Just that,
> And it is written, "I forsook and fled:"
> There was my trial and it ended thus.'   (lines 302–311)

That fear of the Roman garrison could outweigh the conviction
arising from John's eye-witness knowledge of the transfiguration and
the performance of miracles in the course of Christ's public ministry
inevitably raises questions as to precisely what John has in fact seen,
and whether or not the gospel account is report or invention. More
significantly, as Shaffer points out, he acknowledges that in his
cowardice, he fled from the scene of the crucifixion,[67] thus confirming the synoptic accounts (Mt. 26: 56, Mk 14: 50), in preference to
the assertion in his own gospel that Jesus, from the cross, bound him
to the service of his mother and that 'he who saw it bore this
testimony, and his testimony is true' (John 19: 35).

In Browning's poem, John is aware of this appearance of inconsistency and he seeks to justify his interpretation of Christ's mission to
those whom he perceives to be the sceptics of the current generation.
An imagined auditor pleads with John for an admission of the
'factual' truth of the gospel narratives: 'Has [Christ] been? Did not
we ourselves make Him?' (line 377). John's answer is to embrace a
progressive revelation which harnesses the miraculous to the service
of higher symbolic truths which men are as yet unable to grasp.
When pressed by his implied audience to reveal the historical kernel
of the healing of the blind man (John 9), he questions the accuracy
of any eye-witness claim to the representation and recollection of
factual 'events':

> 'I say, that miracle was duly wrought
> When, save for it, no faith was possible.
> Whether a change were wrought i' the shows o' the world,

> Whether the change came from our minds which see
> Of shows o' the world so much as and no more
> Than God wills for his purpose, – (what do I
> See now, suppose you, there where you see rock
> Round us?) – I know not; such was the effect,
> So faith grew . . .'   (lines 464–472)

However, he does not quite succeed in evading the allegations of fraudulent misrepresentation and there is substance to the imagined auditor's complaint that inaccuracy in the literal account of gospel events hinders those in pursuit of divine truth from grasping the greater symbolic significance of Christ as love incarnate. Orthodox Christianity is then equated with the mythology of pagan antiquity, and the prophet or evangelist is only an artist: ' "Is John's procedure just the heathen bard's?" ' (line 530). Eye-witness testimony, with its claims to immediate apprehension of personal experience, is subsumed within the realm of poetic vision or imaginative devotion. Even John's last defence of the creed of progress – 'man's distinctive mark alone' (line 586) – and his hope of continuing in the work of the growing church are closed ironically by his sudden death, and the representation of his passing evokes the finality of the end of the apostolic age. With John's death, the conclusion of his gospel and its apparent promise of the evangelist's survival until the return of Christ ('what was darkly spoke/ At ending of his book', lines 657–658) are problematised.

At the poem's conclusion, John's narrative is distanced from the reader by the mediation of several successive generations of the Christian community at Ephesus or perhaps Antioch. Time has passed since John's death – 'By this, the cave's mouth must be filled with sand' (line 647) – and the anonymous narrator is in turn relating his own 'dying declaration' of faith to an amanuensis of his own; '[s]o, lest the memory of this go quite, / Seeing that I to-morrow fight the beasts, / I tell the same to Phoebas, whom believe!' (lines 651–653). The record of his memories is then subject to later glosses and interpretative notes which further emphasise the manuscript's provenance and gently question the reliability and authenticity of John's words. 'A Death in the Desert' is both a resurrection and a burial – a resurrection of the past in art which imitates the higher critics's conception of the resurrection of Christ as a visionary, literary 'event', and a burial of a kernel of 'truth' (either historically grounded or poetic) within a complicated matrix of documentary material of uncertain transmission (both oral and written) stretching back over a number of years (but never quite attaining to the 'historical' point of origin). And yet 'A Death in the Desert' questions the very legitimacy or wisdom of the search for historical origins; for although the figure of Jesus is tantalisingly near in John's claims – ' "It was so; so I heard and saw" ' (line 137) – he remains elusive, and the evangelist refuses to answer the repeated requests for a literal presentation of ' "plain truth from man to man" ' (line 529) concerning the 'events' of Jesus's life. The search for historical certainty is seen as misguided; John's imagined auditors are asking the wrong questions. Browning gives us an alternative account of Christian origins; the genesis of orthodoxy lies in John's imaginative, visionary grasp of Christ's love and God's power, and the historical Jesus becomes almost a peripheral figure in this mythology of the beginning. John himself is the origin of the Church's orthodox tenets of belief, and these tenets are slippery and loose in their relation to 'fact' rather than firmly grounded in external 'events'. As the eyewitness gives testimony to what he has seen, his narrative is so highly dependent upon his own preconceptions and beliefs that it does not reach to the realm of the 'real' or the historical past. It is, then, arguable whether John's conception of truth transcends the historical or retains something of the stigma of fraud.

Shaffer has revealed the extent of Browning's indebtedness to the work of Strauss and Renan in her incisive analysis of 'A Death in the Desert' in *'Kubla Khan' and the Fall of Jerusalem*. Shaffer notes that Browning uses Renan's idea of John as a man who 'outlived his first vision of Christ'[68] and she argues that the major achievement of the poem is the successful evocation of the concept of 'community' in which the tenets of Christian orthodoxy grew and developed in the years after Christ's death. Shaffer suggests that the transition from a dependence on the historical record to a visionary mysticism necessarily entails the 'attenuation of direct witness' and a recognition of the essential inventiveness of memory and perception:[69]

'A Death in the Desert' shows the process by which the claim to ocular witness was transformed into the claim to valid Christian spiritual experience. It is Browning's peculiar merit to have exhibited this change, which took place over centuries, which indeed was complete only in his own day, as the experience of 'John'. This 'John', then, is neither the aged apostle nor his gnostic disciples and interpolators, but 'John' as inherited and interpreted by Christians. That he can be taken thus is shown by Browning as the triumph of Christianity over historical fact.[70]

The privileged claim of the eye-witness is thus replaced by a communal exercise in collective construction and interpretation, with only a tenuous appeal to the 'Evidences' of traditional Paleyian apologetics.

Browning's magnum opus, *The Ring and the Book* (1864–1869) purports to function as an extension of this sceptical paradigm. As in 'A Death in the Desert' Browning observes that the 'event' which he hopes to re-enact has 'fallen stonewise' into a past from which it cannot be recovered except by a sensitive reading of the ripples which its descent has generated.[71] To augment this historical relativism, Browning concludes this work with his famous maxim; 'our human speech is naught, / our human testimony false' (xii, lines 834–835), with truth to be found only in the interstices of conflicting statements (x, lines 228–230). But Browning's relativism is rhetorical rather than substantive and it does not conform to the relentless defence of injured innocence which drives the poem. In the collection of pamphlets known as the *Old Yellow Book* which inspired the poem, Browning found statements of evidence and law regarding the trial of Count Guido Franceschini for the murder of his young wife Pompilia and her parents in Rome in 1698. Guido claimed her flight from their house with the priest Caponsacchi justified both his inference of her adultery and his consequent defence of his wounded honour. An editor of the *Old Yellow Book* has argued that the weight to be given to Pompilia's testimony of innocence (recorded after the infliction of the fatal wounds) is questionable:

The authorities on the subject in such a case as Pompilia's are not clear, but it would seem from an examination of them, that even if her declarations were entitled to some consideration, they did not by any means give rise to a very strong presumption, much less to positive proof.[72]

What is most interesting here is why Browning feels that he must undertake her defence, and more than that, her beatification. Did he fear that without his powerful interpretation, the evidence would not in fact disclose Pompilia's innocence?

Like Wilkie Collins in *The Woman in White*, Browning in *The Ring and the Book* displays a disparagingly ambivalent attitude to the law. On the one hand, his poem claims to be an imitation of the legal form. Seventeenth-century Italian trials differed from their English counterparts in that the former were based solely on the submission of written documentation by the legal representatives of each party (although in this case, the lawyers are shown to be rehearsing their speeches rather than presenting written argument to the court). This enabled Browning to claim a special status for the *Old Yellow Book* as 'absolutely truth, / Fanciless fact', 'real summed-up circumstance' just as it would have been presented to 'the eye o' the Court' (I, lines 143–150). There is thus less risk that these reports would have been altered in the course of oral transmission, or repeated transcription, like the gospel in 'A Death in the Desert'. It reduces the trial to the sum of its evidences:

> . . . – the trial
> Itself, to all intents, being then as now
> Here in the book and nowise out of it;
> Seeing, there properly was no judgement-bar,
> No bringing of accuser and accused,
> And whoso judged both parties, face to face,
> Before some court, as we conceive of courts.   (I, lines 152–158)

Since each lawyer 'only spoke in print / The printed voice of him lives now as then' (I, lines 166–167), and each reader of the *Old Yellow Book* enjoys the same access to the representation of the 'real' as the Roman Court itself (without an imperative power to sanction the parties). The reader of the source material, as well as of the poem, must attend to the 'voices we call evidence' (I, line 833). This enables Browning's appropriation of the contents of the *Old Yellow Book* to compete with the legal evidence, but also to address, in Goodrich's terms,[73] that which is excluded by legal analysis. As his imagination resurrects and 'resuscitates' the figures of the past (I, lines 707–719) – '[t]he life in me abolished the death of things' (I, line 520) – he is able to offer an instinctive assessment of Pompilia's testimony of innocence which invokes literary representations of martyrdom and revelation for its authority.

Browning uses the model of the documentary-based civilian trial to marshall his evidence and also to claim for his own work something of the status of the factually-based court reports. To this extent he is trying to validate his poetic method by reference to more empirical methodologies as he asks – is the 'fiction which makes fact alive fact too?' (I, line 705). He thus accepts the evidentiary paradigm as valid; imagination is just one more 'circumstance' to be considered in a reading of the evidence, and fiction can be conceived of as a form of proof. But if he seeks momentarily to claim for his poem a share in the authority of 'fact', he evinces simultaneously a loathing for all that the law represents – not only in terms of the ethical relativity of its practitioners, but also for its very adherence to evidentiary analysis and its insistence that facts require interpretation. Browning seeks an unmediated appreciation of purity, an innocence that 'speaks for itself' in the words of the old epistemology. The presence of the lawyers reminds him of its impossibility; it is easier to satirise them than acknowledge his discomfort. Paradoxically, though, it is the very need for such a defence which elicits his own creative interpretation; he simply claims for poetic advocacy a higher truth than that available to its forensic counterparts.

In Welsh's analysis, '[p]recisely in the respect that trials are an institution for finding the truth, Browning despises them' (p. 206).[74] Browning eschews the rule-bound methodologies of the courtroom in favour of Pompilia's transcendent testimony of innocence and divine approbation. In contrast to the rhetorical ambiguity of the courts, Pompilia, Caponsacchi and the Pope instinctively recognise each other's inherent goodness – a quality, like so many other aspects of their dialogue, 'not explained but known' (VII, line 1767). Pompilia and Caponsacchi receive confirmation of their intuitively righteous judgement in the Pope's monologue; he praises the instinct which enables her to 'plant firm foot / On neck of man . . . / . . . and obey God all the more!' (X, lines 1060–1062), and he imaginatively reconstructs her self-abnegating explanation of her own purity; ' "I know the right place by foot's feel, / I took it and tread firm there; wherefore change?" ' (X, lines 1885–1886). There is a gesture here towards the artless statements of innocence preferred by the eighteenth-century jurists, but the assertion of her purity is carefully crafted, and, as he 'tries' Pompilia's actions, he predetermines the verdict and renders an acquittal inevitable. Ultimately, Browning pays only lip-service to the rules of evidence (such as the status of 'dying declarations' as discussed in *The Old Yellow Book*)[75] and the tests of witness credibility which impact upon the presentation of Pompilia's testimony. Pronounced '[p]erfect in whiteness' by the Pope, Pompilia narrates her own passing in terms which both enact and confirm her salvation – 'And I rise' (VII, line 1845).

It is arguable that in implementing this strategy of defence, Browning exceeds his brief – that he makes assertions which cannot be supported by the evidence. To this extent, his fictions are those of a bad advocate and his conventional criticisms of the lawyers' rhetorical excesses are ultimately self-referential. His own retort – that the fiction which reanimates the past is also authentic 'fact' – mirrors that of the dying John in 'A Death in the Desert'. The poet-lawyer is also poet-theologian; both point to the 'resurrection' of the past in the service of truth. Hence, Browning's success in evoking both the divine vision and possible fraud in 'A Death in the Desert' serves almost to deconstruct his efforts to proclaim Pompilia's purity in *The Ring and the Book*. He tries to move beyond the fact-finding model which ties truth to the assessment of evidence and which proportions assent to proof, but he is unable to evade the suspicion of fraud which this engenders. His efforts to reach to the absolute – to illuminate the eternal goodness which generated Pompilia's testimony – are ultimately undermined by a failure to address the very evidence which he makes a decision to discard. The authoritative testimony of the religious martyr is invoked in a number of nineteenth-century works, but with the advent of higher criticism, the scepticism generated by an obsession with evidence is constantly present as an alternative hermeneutic paradigm, namely the model which Welsh so aptly calls 'the hermeneutics of suspicion' (p. 150 and p. 211).

It is a tribute to the power of the aesthetic imagination that, aside from 'A Death in the Desert', none of the texts referred to in this chapter suggest that truth cannot be discovered by a careful, cautious reading. Despite contrasting attitudes to Christian dogma, both Newman and Browning emphasise the inter-relationship of secular and spiritual hermeneutics. Newman pondered the movement from the act of reading to the act of worship and he argued that meditation on the sacred text can 'make the facts which they relate stand out before our minds as objects, such as may be appropriated by a faith as living as the imagination which apprehends them'.[76] This type of claim has led Coulson to suggest that 'the real assent we make to the primary forms of religious faith (expressed in metaphor, symbol, and story) is of the same kind as the imaginative assent we make to the primary forms of literature'; '[i]n the articulation of this assent, the theologian and the literary critic share . . . a common grammar, if by grammar is understood that underlying form or structure which is revealed as we learn and use a language'.[77] Even for Browning and Eliot – who engaged more closely with higher criticism and who felt unable to retain an orthodox faith – the hermeneutic act was central to the development of personal powers of judgement: hence Browning's claim in *The Ring and the Book* that reading can 'save the soul beside' (xII, line 863). Like Kingsley and Newman, they too are wrestling with a fundamental epistemological difficulty – is assent instinctual (an innate faculty, a gift of God, an act of grace) or is it tied to an assessment of evidence? The trope of the martyr-as-witness serves both models; her speech may be divinely inspired but the records of her testimony become evidence for her community to test, to 'try'. It is for this reason that the religious fictions of Eliot, Browning, Kingsley, and Newman illuminate so clearly many of the anxieties of greatest significance to the Victorian age.

Conclusion

When Mrs Humphry Ward's *Robert Elsmere* appeared in 1888, it seemed to many that the efforts of the eponymous clergyman to reconcile his Christian faith with his rigorous intellectual honesty were representative of the struggles of the mid-Victorian age. It can be read as a fictionalised response to the progressive theorising of the contributors to *Essays and Reviews*. In the novel, it is Squire Wendover's work, *The Idols of the Market Place*, which serves instead of the controversial volume to import continental thought 'into a startled and protesting England'.[1] But in his conversations with the Squire which begin his disaffection with orthodoxy, Elsmere learns that *The Idols of the Market Place* was merely a digression from Wendover's life-work. The Squire had ultimately hoped to meet 'the great want of modern scholarship' by compiling 'a History of Evidence, or rather, more strictly, "A History of Testimony"' (vol. II, p. 240).

Wendover instructs Elsmere that the Darwinian account of origins also informs theological paradigms. This emphasis on the limitations of the observer's ability to record the truth of an experience reveals the historicity of all acts of interpretation. In the words of the Squire:

'Testimony like every other human product has *developed*. Man's power of apprehending and recording what he sees and hears has grown from less to more, from weaker to stronger, like any other of his faculties, just as the reasoning powers of the cave-dweller have developed into the reasoning powers of a Kant'. (vol. II, p. 245)

The gospel narratives are not immune from forensic analysis by virtue of their sacred subject matter and the cultural presumptions of their authors must be recognised:

'The witness of the time is not true, nor, in the strict sense, false. It is merely incompetent, half-trained, pre-scientific, but all through perfectly natural. The wonder would have been to have had a life of Christ without miracles . . . The Resurrection is partly invented, partly imagined, partly ideally

174

true – in any case wholly intelligible and natural, as a product of the age, when once you have the key of that age'. (vol. II, pp. 246–247)

Elsmere eventually eschews the claims of Anglican orthodoxy, which are vulnerable to criticism as a consequence of their reliance on the documentary record, and he undertakes the journey of the age towards a theistic position dependent less on external evidence than on internal convictions of belief. Faith 'is its own witness' (vol. II, p. 249).

But as William Gladstone pointed out in his famous review of *Robert Elsmere*, published in *The Nineteenth Century* in May 1888, Elsmere's defence of Christian orthodoxy is flawed; '[a] great creed, with the testimony of eighteen centuries at its back, cannot find an articulate word to say in its own defence . . .'[2] Gladstone claimed that Ward had 'skipped lightly . . . over vast mental spaces of literature and learning relevant to the case, and ha[d] given sentence in the cause without hearing the evidence'.[3] There is certainly substance to this allegation, although Gladstone invokes the same legalistic model of evidence-based analysis as Ward. Gladstone is not so much unhappy that Christianity has been put on trial as that it has not been adequately defended. But it is arguable that the evidence-based paradigms of the courtroom invariably place Christian apologetics on the defensive; as Powell had observed in *The Order of Nature*, the obsession with 'proofs in support of faith' is 'a peculiarly *protestant* prejudice' which 'might easily be construed into a confession of its weakness'.[4] Can Christian truth be proven in any other way? Need it be 'proven' at all?

The problem is to find an alternative model which is also intellectually satisfying. Newman questioned whether it is appropriate to conceive of the spiritual in terms of its evidentiary and probative value. Speaking of the reliability of the evangelists, he notes:

It has been said . . . that no testimony can fairly be trusted which has not passed the ordeal of a legal examination. Yet, calculated as that mode of examination undoubtedly is to elicit truth, surely truth may be elicited by other ways also. Independent and circumstantial writers may confirm a fact as satisfactorily as witnesses in Court.[5]

Newman here seeks to ascribe reliability and the generation of assent to the acts of reading and writing rather than the technique of cross-examination; the power to judge resides with the informed reader rather than the Court. Yet he still invokes the criteria of independence and circumstantiality as tests of evidentiary weight, which returns us to the 'Old Bailey' theologians who purported to try the testimony of the evangelists. The evidentiary paradigm proves hard to escape, and indeed, as noted throughout this study, the trial format is also part of Christian heritage as the passion of Christ and of subsequent martyrs illustrates. The fundamental ambiguity of the trial – in its roles as both a fact-finding forum and the venue for revelation – ensures that testimony (as a rational mode of proof or as the product of inspiration) retains a special place in the Victorian quest for truth.

IS TESTIMONY A SPECIES OF EVIDENCE?

Inevitably, a reconciliation of contrasting ideas about the scope and reliability of testimony founders on such contrasting *a priori* assumptions about the existence and accessibility of God. A comparison of the thought of two of the major figures whose work has featured prominently in this study reveals the extent of the gulf between the various schools of thought. Throughout his mature Christian life, Newman cherished the assumption that

certitude was a habit of mind, that certainty was a quality of propositions; that probabilities which did not reach to logical certainty, might suffice for a mental certitude; that the certitude thus brought about might equal in measure and strength the certitude which was created by the strictest scientific demonstration; and that to possess such certitude might in given cases and to given individuals be a plain duty. . .[6]

He propounded this assertion more fully in his *Essay in Aid of a Grammar of Assent* (1870), where he argued that an individual could assent to a religious mystery which shares its linguistic structure with the vocabulary of everyday affairs; '[t]he same act, then, which enables us to discern that the words of the proposition express a mystery, capacitates us for assenting to it'.[7] The similarities between Newman's paradigm of capable judgement and Browning's Pope in *The Ring and the Book* are well documented. Newman praised an intuitive grasp of the facts as the basis of the 'illative sense', his term for man's inherent ability to assent to moral or religious truths, and he too appeals to the exemplary value of 'some great lawyer, judge or advocate, who is able in perplexed cases, when common minds see nothing but a hopeless heap of facts, foreign or contrary to each other, to detect the principle which rightly interprets the riddle, and, to the admiration of all hearers, converts a chaos into an orderly and luminous whole'.[8] This appeal to immediate apprehension rather than the careful assessment of the evidence is ultimately dependent upon a subscription to dogmatic truths which he acknowledges that his peers cannot always share. In the *Grammar of Assent*, he asserts that he is 'suspicious of scientific demonstrations in a question of concrete fact, in a discussion between fallible men'; '[f]or me, it is more congenial to my own judgement to attempt to prove Christianity in the same informal way in which I can prove for certain that I have been born into this world, and that I shall die out of it'. He holds that from 'an *accumulation* of various probabilities . . . we may construct legitimate proof, sufficient for certitude',[9] a contentious position which generated much debate.

This is the heart of the Victorian apologist's difficulty. In an article comparing Newman's conception of judgement with the work of juries, Colin Moran is prepared to accept that 'a conclusion can be stronger than its weakest link'.[10] But he poses a second and more problematic question, namely 'whether one's assurance can exceed the *sum* of the evidence, viewed as a corroborative whole'.[11] Newman does concede that the attainment of certitude 'about things in the concrete' is essentially a personal quest, as 'men differ from each other, not so much in the soundness of their reasoning as in the principles which govern its exercise'. And he concludes that 'where there is no common measure of minds, there is no common measure of arguments, and that the validity of any proof is determined, not by any scientific test, but by the illative sense'.[12] As Moran notes, Newman is not admitting a lack of evidence for Christian belief, simply that those grounds of assent are not always 'articulable' in such a way as to satisfy all men.[13] But to Stephen, immersed in the philosophy of J. S. Mill, this leap, from the probable (which tied judgement to the realm of evidence) to the certain (which closed off the prospect of revision to one's conclusions should further evidence arise) was untenable. In Stephen's critique of Newman's work we see revealed the contrasting epistemologies of witnessing on which the two schools of thought base their claims for the scope of testimony.

In his *General View of the Criminal Laws of England* (1863), Stephen addresses the relationship between belief and the evidence which generates that belief, and his biographer K. J. M. Smith traces in this work a profound indebtedness to Mill's *System of Logic* (1843).[14] Stephen compares two possible views of the human faculty which 'believes' in a piece of evidence; firstly, that the tendency to believe is 'part of the constitution of the human mind, and is the ultimate ground of all the credit which we give to testimony', and secondly, the contrasting theory derived from Hume and Mill which states that 'our experience of the agreement between the testimony and the facts testified, is the sole ultimate reason for our belief' (p. 239). Stephen argues that the psychology of belief may begin with our acquisition of language skills as a child rather than with a strict adherence to the rules of evidence, and, like Newman, his 'grammar of belief' is in part dependent on 'the qualities of the mind in which the belief is to be produced' (p. 241).

Stephen concludes that the jury's test of guilt or innocence, the beyond reasonable doubt standard of proof, is not a magical formula invoking ideas of certainty:

> In every intelligence which is not omniscient there is room for doubt on every subject, for such an intelligence can never assert, that if its knowledge were increased its present belief would not be changed . . . Notwithstanding this, every one does, in fact, believe entirely . . . that a probable story sworn to by credible witnesses is true. The reason is, that the business of life could not otherwise be carried on, and it is better to run some risk of being mistaken than to sit in helpless inaction for fear of a possible error.

For Stephen, the 'state of mind described as absolute certainty, is one which either does not exist at all, or is not conceivable by man' (pp. 260–261), and in two subsequent essays Stephen undermined Newman's idea of assent based on 'probabilities which [do] not reach to logical certainty'. In Stephen's terms, 'the "principle of dogma" is nothing else than an obscure way of describing the process of begging the question'.[15]

Just as Stephen accuses Dickens of exceeding the licence of a novelist, he sees Newman as exceeding the brief of a theologian; Newman fails to 'bear in mind the fact that it is a probability on which he is acting, and to keep himself open to conviction in case further evidence should be discovered'.[16] This, in Stephen's analysis, is the 'modern Protestant view'. The Catholic exaltation of 'authority at the expense of reason' invariably depends on 'inferring from difficulties in the evidence, a radical defect in the instrument which weighs the evidence and recognizes the existence of the difficulties':[17]

> He views the adverse evidence, not as a possible guide to an unwelcome truth, but as an objection which, by some means or other, is to be answered;

and he certainly does show inexhaustible ingenuity in finding answers. He is like a thorough-going advocate, who never will abandon his cause . . . His client's innocence is the one fixed point in a world of doubt and supplies the key to every part of the evidence. The 'pull devil pull baker' system on which English justice is administered, may justify this at the Bar; but Dr. Newman's voluntary advocacy goes beyond that of a professional advocate – he justifies it on principle.[18]

In terms redolent of Dickens's criticisms of the licence of counsel in the 1840s, Stephen accuses Newman of placing his duty to his client (the Pope) above that of his commitment to the higher ideals of 'truth'. His *a priori* convictions have determined the treatment of the evidence, and Stephen regards this as a kind of perjury, like a juror reaching a verdict before the case is closed or because he takes an irrational partiality to one piece of evidence above another.[19] Following Bentham and Hume, Stephen sees intuitive apprehensions of God as probative only to the 'degree in which they are verified by experience'.[20] The willingness of martyrs to die for their own beliefs is no attestation of their veracity; 'no inference at all can be drawn from the warmth with which any belief is held, to the truth of the matter believed'.[21] Instead he asserts that 'there is no assignable connection between belief and truth, except through the medium of evidence, because evidence is what connects belief with truth'.[22]

The constant point of comparison for Stephen is the role of the jury in the criminal trial; the theologian, like the juror, must act only on the evidence before the court. Both men adopt the language of legal procedure to illustrate their preferred processes of judgement; for Newman, it is the autocratic mind of the great judge who can immediately apprehend the 'truth' of a web of facts; Stephen's model is the assessment of evidence undertaken by the trial jury. In Butler's paradigm of life as a state of probation, Newman sees life as a trial of his faith, and Stephen sees him working to secure his ultimate acquittal by adhering to a religious belief which must cast aside alleged evidence to the contrary. For Stephen, faith (or at least the authority of the Catholic church) is in the dock and the trial must be conducted according to the same rules of investigation which govern other aspects of human affairs.

In an attempt to reconcile these contrasting stances, it is not surprising that some theologians and religious theorists came to adopt a purely spiritual approach to faith, like Powell, or a psychological approach to the question of belief, like William James. We see a glimpse of this in Mansel's Bampton Lectures of 1858 as he asserts that '*[t]he primary and proper object of criticism is not Religion, natural or revealed, but the human mind in its relation to Religion*'. He hoped that conflicting traditions might find common ground in his philosophical enquiry as to 'the limits of our faculties, and the conditions of their legitimate exercise'.[23] James took this approach further in the Gifford Lectures on Natural Religion, delivered in Edinburgh in 1901 and 1902. Without discussing the proofs of religion, which he saw, post-Kant, as incapable of generating conclusive assent or persuasion, he took his stand on 'feeling [as] the deeper source of religion', and he asserted that 'philosophic and theological formulas are secondary products, like translations of a text into another tongue'.[24] Yet he concluded that religious experience is a valid species of evidence:

Is [the religious man] like the traveller, whose testimony about foreign countries we should be foolish not to believe? May he instruct us as to the actual existence of a higher world with which our world is in relation, even though personally he be in other respects no better than ourselves? To say yes to this question is to side with supernaturalism taken in a wide sense, in its world-old quarrel with naturalism.

He avowed that he did in fact 'side' with supernaturalism,[25] but his determination 'to use human standards to help us decide how far the religious life commends itself as an ideal kind of human activity'[26] would have satisfied Stephen rather than Newman.

WHY IS THE EVIDENTIARY STATUS OF TESTIMONY IMPORTANT? LAW, LITERATURE, AND THE COMPETITION TO CONTROL REPRESENTATIONS OF THE REAL

In this study we have seen something of how the definition of a witness and the limitations of testimonial credibility altered with a movement away from the medieval reliance on the oath as a guarantee of veracity to the mid-Victorian jurist's interest in the falsifiability of evidence as the test of its authority. Yet the actual classification of testimony as valuable evidence in courts of law remained secure.

That testimony ultimately retained the status of reliable proof is important because of the ways in which Victorians attempted to clarify the responsibilities of the fictional author and the value of the realist novel. Victorian debate about how the real should be represented invariably suggested that fiction should imitate the strategies of the courtroom. As George Craik, editor of an English edition of *Causes Célèbres*, noted in 1840, legal records were themselves a type of literature and he upheld their distinctive qualities as a model for the endeavours of modern authors:

There are few things that enchain the attention of all sorts of people like the chains of evidence in an interesting trial at law. Some of the most successful fictions have been in the main merely imaginary trials at law – ingeniously contrived imitations of the same long, apparently conflicting, but ultimately concurring, trains of incident, the gradual development of which keeps curiosity on the stretch in a real trial.[27]

Stephen's insistence that novels should bear a close representational relationship to the 'real' was influential. Writing in the *Cambridge Essays* of 1855, he conceded the popularity of modern fiction but he assessed its value in the following terms; are novels so like real life that their content 'can be accepted as additions to [the reader's] experience'?[28] For Stephen, the question was one of genre – a novel must be a fictitious biography which generates assent by its adherence to the honest and direct representation of the probable. Too strict an adherence to fact produces history; too loose an adherence to fact produces legend which can no longer command a modern reader's assent. Stephen couches his criticisms of modern authors in terms of their treatment of the evidence which makes up the flux of real life; as an author interprets such evidence selectively (what Ricoeur called the pre-understanding of the world of action)[29] in order to emphasise that which appeals to the heart and to minimise that which is tedious, he edits out much that should not, in the interests of veracity, be excluded:

One of the most obvious causes which makes novels unlike real life is the necessity under which they lie of being interesting, an object which can only be obtained by a great deal of *suppressio veri*, whence arises that *suggestio falsi* of which it is our object to point out the principal varieties.

Foreshadowing his claims in 'The License of Modern Novelists' which was to appear two years later, Stephen argues that the representation of trials at law in fiction is invariably a distortion of actual practice:

The *State Trials* would give a juster notion of the interminable length of the indictments, the apparently irrelevant and unmeaning examinations and cross-examinations of witnesses, the skirmishing of the counsel on points of law, and the petition of the prisoners, often painfully reasonable, for some relaxation of the rules of evidence, or procedure; but to any one who seeks mere amusement, such reading is intolerably tedious, and even when accomplished, it gives a very faint representation of the actual scene as it appeared to those who sat or stood, day after day, in all the heat, and dust, and foul air of the court-house at Carlisle or Southwark, half-understanding, and – as the main points at issue got gradually drowned in their own details – half-attending to the proceedings on which the lives and deaths of their friends depended.[30]

In this passage we hear Stephen's protective proclamation of the greater seriousness and worthiness of the law; no one's life is at stake in the act of reading a novel, and legal proceedings can only really be grasped and fairly represented by the practitioners initiated into their mysterious significance. He judges fiction accordingly; his most favoured novel at the time was one 'which adds to the information and excites the feelings of its readers in a manner almost as natural and complete as if it were a real history of real facts' – *Robinson Crusoe.* Defoe undertakes the most accurate representation of the evidence; Stephen finds no significant 'variations from real life introduced into it for artistic purposes'[31] and Crusoe is an ordinary man who puts his business on the island first, followed by his reflections on 'the principles upon which he lived, his reflections upon Providence, and the Divine plans of which he conceived himself to be the subject'.[32] Purely personal meditation on love and marriage is kept to himself. That Stephen acclaims this as the most perfect realist novel tells us much about his own mind and his emphasis on the prudent execution of his own duties. That he seeks to justify his choice in evidentiary terms – Defoe suppresses the least evidence and distorts the least facts – speaks of the preoccupations of the age. To a certain extent, Stephen's assumption that novels must deal with evidence in turn engendered much criticism of the legal profession; as we saw in Chapter 3, authors and journalists in mid-Victorian times were scathing in their criticisms of the exclusory rules of evidence which often prevented relevant evidence from going to the jury in cases where certain formal conditions could not be satisfied. Lawyers prided themselves on the rules which kept 'tainted' evidence from the untrained minds of the jury; journalists and authors called for all relevant material to go before the jurors who had sufficient common sense to know how such material should be assessed. Stephen was astute enough to see that fictional mimesis was a selective activity; but authors, who could sway public opinion against the law, could retort that the legal profession itself adopted an institutionalised selectivity which was not above criticism when it allowed for the 'manumission of murderers'.

Victorian authors also saw themselves as witnesses – as witnesses, perhaps, of a higher truth than that which the lawyers could prove in court, in the tradition of cultural appreciation which acclaimed poets as the 'unacknowledged legislators' of the world. Their self-conscious assertions of factual fidelity – for example, Eliot's statement in *Adam Bede* that her narrative is that of a witness on oath – created an evidentiary rivalry which required of both professions a combative delimitation of their discourses. Each profession then sought to justify its model of reality by accusing the other of 'misrepresentation', or a failure to present evidence responsibly. This assumption, shared in the mid-Victorian age by Dickens, Eliot, Gaskell, and Stephen (with the exception perhaps of Thackeray), that fiction must be tied to a paradigm of evidentiary realism, created the conditions for the conflict of literature and the law after the enactment of the Prisoners' Counsel Act. Theodore Ziolkowski has identified similar convergences of literary and legal preoccupations at various points in the history of western thought, and he has concluded that '[j]ustice gazes most often into her literary mirror at times when she has been disheveled by the winds of social and political upheaval', when 'the existing law has just undergone, or is threatened by, a major transformation: when, for one reason or another, the law finds itself out of phase with the prevailing community passions, and justice is wracked'.[33] In this context, it is interesting to note that the controversial Victorian legal cases (such as *Courvoisier* and *Palmer*) which generated the most debate at the Bar are the same cases which stimulated intense fictional and journalistic commentary by the likes of Collins, Dickens, and Fonblanque. This was at least in part due to their subject matter; murder trials and the extinction of the guilty offender's life were subjects of great interest to writers and readers alike, and perhaps as Welsh suggests, the Victorian enthusiasm for the conviction of murderers arose from their enhanced desire to punish those responsible for temporal death at a time when the assurance of eternal life was fast receding from the cultural imagination (pp. 165–178). The trial provided for the recreation of the past, the narration of subjects' thoughts, the provision of a verdict – an imitation of divine judgement and eventually an alternative in its completeness and its closure to the

Christian idea of history. And the law made claims for itself which invited authors to use it as a model for their own activities. But this is not to suggest that fiction invariably mimics the law as Craik had asserted. Authors came to define their own story-telling powers by critical analysis of the law's treatment of the evidence to be drawn from 'real life'.

Newman and Browning tried bravely to move beyond the restrictions imposed by this paradigm, to question whether legal standards were the only test of truth or whether the trial was the only effective fact-finding model, but critical discomfort at their methods suggests that they may not have entirely succeeded in escaping the weighty traditions of the Anglican indebtedness to an assessment of Christian 'Evidences'. With the gradual demise of widespread *a priori* beliefs in the existence of God, Stephen's refraction of the philosophy of Mill prevailed over Newman's philosophy of certitude. Assent, to fictional narratives, to legal judgements and to religious belief, was increasingly seen as proportional to proof.

Counterbalancing the sceptical trend engendered by higher criticism was the Victorian authors' adherence to the 'providential aesthetic' which enabled the Christian conception of justice to retain its power in fictional narratives long after the demise of an unquestioned communal commitment to religious orthodoxy. Stories which depend on the invocation of oaths and which invest the verdicts of a court with the imagery of the final Assize often rely on a secularised conception of providence to secure narrative closure. As Frank Kermode notes in *The Sense of an Ending*, 'there is an irreducible minimum of geometry – of humanly needed shape or structure – which finally limits our ability to accept the mimesis of pure contingency'.[34] Hence, we see a persistence in fiction not only of the providential assumptions of design, judgement, and reward, but of quasi-doctrinal symbols and religious 'Evidences' which retain an aura of sanctity despite the erosion of their strict dogmatic content. In Mrs Humphry Ward's *Robert Elsmere* and *Helbeck of Bannisdale* (1898), we see the survival of traditional beliefs in the evidentiary value of a 'good death' both as an art-form which concludes a life, and as an opportunity for a moment of supernatural revelation as the veil is drawn from the eyes of the soul. In *The Heart of Midlothian*, the oath can still invoke the deity; in *The Ring and the Book*, Pompilia narrates her own ascension. Both Best's *Treatise on the Principles of Evidence* and Jameson's work on the rediscovery of Catholic iconography contributed to the metaphors and methods of Eliot's later fiction.

It is of course possible to observe the beginning of a transition 'from a literature which assumed that it was imitating an order to a literature which assumes that it has to create an order, unique and self-dependent',[35] and to construe the post-Enlightenment development of narrative as a linear process of secularisation, with the novel as well as the format of the criminal trial dependent upon the weakening of dogmatic truths which impact on representations of guilt, certainty, and judgement. Despite the rich (and mutually referential) legal and religious implications of the concept of martyrdom, we could argue, for example, that representations of criminal trials in Victorian fiction increasingly *lost* their metaphorical connections to the Great Assize. But this is to overlook the range of responses to the challenge to traditional Christian ideas of narrative and judgement; *Callista*, *The Trial*, *Orley Farm* and *Felix Holt*, with their overlapping but distinct approaches to Christian and/or legal judgement, all appeared within roughly a decade of one another. With the exception perhaps of Thackeray, (although he too moved from the novel without a hero, *Vanity Fair*, to the more idealised world of *The Newcomes* within less than a decade), we can see in the enthusiasm of the mid-Victorian age for heroes, heroines, and hagiography something of a reaction against the agendas of rational enquiry. Inevitably, such a transition is not linear, and the old vocabulary of piety and voluntary self-sacrifice persisted, invested on occasion with altered meanings but still tied to older providential assumptions. The transmission of 'truth' or 'fact' remained the primary purpose of testimony in the works of these writers, and their narratives reveal a resistance to the idea of a multivalent plurality of subjective 'truths'.

Welsh posits a decline in the popularity of circumstantial evidence in the mid- to late Victorian period and he sees in fiction a concomitant return to the provision of first-person testimony in narrative (that is, testimony valued as stories of personal experience rather than as a form of proof). As I argued earlier, I place the decline of the old epistemology of 'facts speaking for themselves' in the early part of the nineteenth century and I do not automatically equate this anti-hermeneutic paradigm with the doctrine of circumstantial evidence familiar to Bentham or Stephen. But Welsh is right to note that the evidentiary basis of fictional realism declined in importance towards the end of the nineteenth century. Literature did finally move beyond the interpretative strategy which insisted that assent be strictly proportional to evidentiary proof.[36] In Joseph Conrad's work, for example, we see a refusal to clarify the ambiguity of 'events' within the text at the point of narrative closure; in *Lord Jim* or *The Heart of Darkness*, evidence of 'facts' remains beyond recovery. There are more stories to be told about the relationship between law and literature as the nineteenth century drew to an end and fiction both looked back to Romantic, promethean ideas of the artistic imagination and experimented with the radical instability of fact which became the heritage of modernism. Law, too, moved away from the exclusion of testimonial material; as noted earlier, prisoners with counsel were increasingly allowed to make their own unsworn statements to the jury in the 1880s and the accused were given the right to testify on oath just as the century closed. To trace the treatment of testimony in fiction is thus to identify what was most unique about mid-Victorian narratives of guilt and innocence.

GUILT, INNOCENCE, AND THE 'GOLDEN THREAD' OF THE ENGLISH COMMON LAW

In his *Commentaries* (1764), Blackstone provided one of the earliest statements of what has since come to be cherished as the 'golden thread' of the English common law, that a man is presumed to be innocent of a charge brought against him until proven otherwise by the prosecution. In Blackstone's famous phrase, 'it is better that ten guilty persons escape, than the one innocent suffer'.[37] Paley criticised this maxim as tending to produce injudicious acquittals. He argued that when the public interest required the effective eradication of crime, courts ought to consider 'that he, who falls by a mistaken sentence, may be considered as falling for his country; whilst he suffers under the operation of these rules, by the general effect and tendency of which, the welfare of the community is maintained and upheld'.[38] Yet Lord Denman, writing in the *Edinburgh Review* in 1824, felt the need to criticise Bentham's tendency to follow Paley in 'cast[ing] some ridicule on the homely adage of English law, which pronounced it better that ten, or perhaps a hundred guilty should escape, than that one innocent man should suffer death by legal process'.[39] Despite the perceived antiquity of such a maxim, and despite the fact that it appeared in settled form in Starkie's *Treatise* in the same year, Denman reminded his audience of the need to cherish such a heritage: 'to punish is no matter of indispensable necessity, even where guilt is manifest, while, to refrain from punishing without a perfect legal warrant, is a simple but a most sacred duty'.[40] His analysis reminds us of the formative state of the maxim in the early nineteenth century and it is perhaps no surprise that fiction also responded to the law's attempts to address such fundamental issues. The perceived humanity of the common law was of definitive significance to the identity of the English nation. Denman noted that '[h]uman beings are never to be run down, like beasts of prey, without respect to the laws of the chase':

If society must make a sacrifice of any one of its members, let it proceed according to general rules, upon known principles, and with clear proof of necessity: 'let us carve him as a feast fit for the gods, not hew him as a carcase for the hounds' . . . [We] maintain that it is desirable that guilty men should sometimes escape, by the operation of those general rules, which form the only security for innocence.[41]

This is the rhetoric of both procedural fairness and of gentlemanly pursuit, and this insistence on detection was to become the teleological engine of many a Victorian narrative; as the policeman states of Jem Wilson's appearance of guilt in *Mary Barton*, '[t]here would be no fun in fox-hunting, if Reynard yielded himself up without any effort to escape'.[42] Yet if the detective figure lacks skill and traces of guilt remain unrecovered, the rhetoric of the common law will nevertheless prefer the protection of the potentially innocent.

But against this enlightened narrative of the safeguards of innocence must be placed Langbein's articulation of the 'accused speaks' model of the trial, in which a defendant could not hope for acquittal unless he was able to adduce some positive evidence to support his assertion of innocence. The nascent presumption of innocence thus remained divorced from the labouring class's daily experience of the criminal law in action. The absence of defence lawyers in felony trials in the early eighteenth century may indeed have been an incentive for authors to imagine the ambit and duties of just such a role. Because the history of criminal legal procedure can be read as a progressive amelioration of prisoners' rights (for example, from the extension of legal representation to those accused of treason in 1696, to the extension of the oath to the defendant's witnesses in 1702, to the abolition of the felony counsel restriction in 1836, to the ultimate extension of the oath to the accused himself in 1898), the authors of early modern novels may have sought to remedy in imaginative works the injustices caused by such procedural inequities. It is perhaps this desire to experiment which lies behind the contrasting attitudes seen in the fictional and non-fictional pieces of both Fielding and Dickens. Outspoken critics of the lenience of the system in their non-fictional commentaries, in their fictional narratives they became equally outspoken defenders of the innocent and the unjustly accused. Their social criticism bemoans the legal system's failure to protect the property of the middle classes from predation at the hand of hardened criminals; their fiction imagines what crimes they would most fear being accused of wrongfully (murder, perjury, meanness of spirit) should they be perceived to transgress the law. With the development of professional criminal advocacy, defence work came to be associated with speculation, with fiction and with lying, in contrast to the prosecution's rigorous insistence of the proof of fact alone, yet neither authors nor lawyers seem to have realised that their vehement criticisms of each other were self-referential.

That the burden of proof evolved to require the demonstration of guilt rather than innocence sat somewhat uncomfortably with the initial need for the defendant to construct a 'plain and honest Defence'. This ultimate divergence of emphasis between eighteenth-century literature and law is of interest; fiction, like law, began with the assumption that innocence, like a prisoner's story, must be proven, yet fiction did not follow the law in moving towards the 'golden thread' of a *presumption* of innocence and the possibility that the defendant may mount a defence which consists solely of 'testing the prosecution's' construction of the evidence. With the exception of Trollope in *Orley Farm*, the Victorian authors discussed here continued to adhere to the requirement that innocence must be substantive to secure a verdict of not guilty and, as Welsh observes of Fielding, they appropriated the strategies of prosecution counsel to bring about proof of innocence.[43] Authors acknowledged more promptly than the legal profession that facts do not always speak for themselves. If they did, then fictional representation would have been as unnecessary as legal representation. By Stephen's time, it had become a ploy of defence counsel to suggest that a piece of evidence was 'only circumstantial'; Fielding had been emphasising the misleading transience of 'fact' many years before.

Why did authors share this commitment to strategies of ac-quittal? In this work I have been arguing that reliance on testimony is often insisted on by Victorian authors as an index of substantive innocence even where the law has sealed the lips of the prisoner and offered him legal representation in lieu of his own hesitant narrative of events. The provision of testimony as to genuine innocence is a prerequisite for many a protagonist of literary narratives from *Clarissa* through to Pompilia's tale in *The Ring and the Book*. Victorian fiction has little room for innocence established on a technicality or a sham defence, and unlike *The Examiner*'s wise rejection of a prisoner's confession as verification of the verdict in a court of law, fiction insists on the 'accused speaks' model of the trial. In Bentham's terms, silence is the realm of guilt and speech the province of the innocent. This motif implies an arguably naive expectation that accusatory circumstances can be explained by honest testimony; in contrast, in a society of increasing surveillance, guilt seeks to evade detection, to cover its traces. This may be due to the persistence in fiction of the Christian paradigm of judgement which (prior to say, Thomas Hardy's *Tess of the D'Urbervilles*) is reluctant to apportion punishment without blame or offer reward without corresponding merit. It may also be due to anxieties about legal process and a system of adjudication which increasingly came to reach a verdict based on material other than the testimony of the accused. In fiction, where the author is responsible for the creation of all the evidentiary material to come before the reader (an autonomy which surely weakens their criticisms of criminal procedure), a crime must be 'owned' before the infliction of punishment is justified; the narration of a protagonist's intention in his 'own words' is crucial to just adjudication. A wrong verdict may be rendered temporarily to serve as a foil to the greater justice of fictional narrative, but in mid-Victorian fiction it is rare for an unjust judgement to stand at the novel's conclusion. In the narratives I have analysed, there is nothing to equal the ferocity of Justine's wrongful execution for murder in *Frankenstein* after her 'plain and simple explanation of the facts' was rejected in favour of the circumstantial evidence against her, a travesty which is described by Frankenstein as the inversion of the cherished presumption of innocence; 'all judges had rather that ten innocent should suffer, than that one guilty should escape'.[44] In contrast, in the one mid-Victorian example I have discussed where an inaccurate verdict does remain at the point of closure – *Orley Farm* – it is interesting to note that fiction follows the law in sanctioning the escape of the occasional guilty party in preference to the potential conviction of the innocent.[45]

But *Orley Farm* is an exception. If Victorian readers seem to have expected an innocent character to announce his or her innocence, on the whole obvious guilt is rarely broadcast aloud – think of the tortured testimonies of intent which Hetty, Lydgate or Gwendolen Harleth offer in explanation of the deeds which 'determine' their moral characters. There are surprisingly few works in the realist genre which include specific testimony of guilt without some gesture towards exculpation; Moll Flanders tells her story after she has 'pretended' to penitence, and Miss Wade's 'History of a Self-Tormentor' in *Little Dorrit* is scarcely confessional in intent. Aside from the Faustian heroes of Romantic tradition who saw themselves above the law, literary convention seems to have required that the heroes and (more often) heroines of the new realist narratives be tried and found honourable before they could enjoy the temporal and spiritual rewards to be conferred by narrative closure. Butler's conception of life as a trial remained a fertile narrative paradigm; in appropriating this model for the analysis of sexual worth, the novelists were clearly expressing their own anxieties about female constancy as well as their imaginative exploration of transgression and criminality in general. Testimonial veracity in women (in their capacity as either witness, defendant or Christian martyr) is thus consistent with authorial investigation of broader cultural notions of honour and worth.[46]

Perhaps expressions of culpability are displaced into the gothic genre, for it is here that we find testimonies of guilt celebrated with the most relish. The testimony of the villain to the effect that 'I did it' is a sensational device employed most effectively in the thrillers of the gothic and the detective narratives. In the gothic genre and the detective novel, the *telos* of the plot and the drive towards narrative closure reassure the reader that evil can be identified and expelled from the fictional community. James Hogg's *The Private Memoirs and Confessions of a Justified Sinner* (1824) is a skilful combination of prosecutorial narratives which reveal the guilt, and finally culminate in the miserable death, of the deluded murderer Robert Wringham. *The Woman in White* shares this drive towards the conviction and execution of the guilty, despite its realist and probabilist aspirations; the goal and end of all Walter Hartright's detective work is the recording of Fosco's narrative of guilt which in turn supplies gaps in the painstakingly compiled evidences of Laura's identity and returns her to her rightful place in society. If circumstantial evidence could be criticised as incomplete, then authors preferred confessional confirmation of guilt even where the court was unlikely to obtain it. That realist narratives may prefer to repress the representation of articulate evil is revealed in critical commentary of the era; works seen as morally reprehensible or as overly salacious in detail were effectively excluded from the canon of acceptable texts.[47] Perhaps legal history again played a part in the 'rise' of detective fiction in Victorian times. Given that narrative advocacy is closely allied to forensic advocacy, it is tempting to speculate that the Victorian enthusiasm for detective fiction, with its emphasis on the confession and disclosure of guilt, arose in part because of the effective protection now afforded to those wrongfully accused of felony by the enactment of the Prisoners' Counsel Act. In other words, in the context of this study, fiction could more effectively experiment with the prosecution of guilt once the wrongful conviction and execution of the innocent had receded as a possible outcome of a criminal trial.

The question 'who is a witness of the truth?' receives a variety of answers during the period I discuss, as the restrictive rules of competence of the late eighteenth century gave way to a more liberal definition of who could speak. Benthamite reforms ensured that objections to a witness's character or reliability increasingly went to issues of creditworthiness rather than competence. With the advent of full representation for felons in 1836, the court lost access to the represented prisoner's own narrative of innocence or culpability; if unrepresented, the prisoner's story was devalued because it could not be given on oath. Whilst Welsh considers the emergence of the paradigm of circumstantial evidence as the great threat to the dominance of testimony in legal hermeneutics, a reading of Langbein's work suggests that it was the 'lawyerization' of the trial in the late eighteenth century and the early nineteenth century that really altered the court's access to the testimony of the accused and influenced its representation in the cultural imagination. That novelists continued to prefer access to the testimony of their protagonists, even where legal representation would act to deny it, is a function of the importance attributed to intention in English conceptions of criminal responsibility. Eighteenth-century fictional authors showed the injustices of the belief that 'it requires no manner of Skill to make a plain and honest Defence', but their mid-Victorian successors, whilst continuing on the whole to work for their characters' acquittals, refused to follow the law and silence their own protagonists. The authors resisted the stubborness of allegedly self-evident facts which would have rendered interpretations nugatory; in their representations of ideal justice, they sought to retain the 'accused speaks' model of the trial whilst severing it from the naive epistemology of self-evident fact which was incompatible with the urge to undertake fictional advocacy. Facts may not 'speak for themselves' but if the first-person testimonial declarations of the protagonist at his trial are similarly untrustworthy, then the act of fictional narration is itself undermined. Hence 'telling one's own story' is crucial to the recovery of truth, and to this extent the speech of the accused acts as a locus of resistance in the gradual move towards the instability of all fact.

The treatment of testimony, as evidence of intention, thus marks the point at which legal and literary strategies of interpretation diverge. The 'free indirect' syle of narration described by Bender and Welsh may have arisen, at least in part, from the imitation of the rhetorical strategies of defence counsel, but authors were not prepared to deny readers access to the story of the accused. An honest defence in the mid-Victorian era usually incorporated the defendant's own words and his or her assessment of his or her own accountability. The secularised quest for personal redemption required no less. Justice should not be dependent on rhetorical flourishes or the exploitation of evidentiary technicalities; to that extent Victorian fiction adhered to the hope that justice should reach towards an accurate representation of the 'real'. The struggle of literature and law to monopolise the representation of the real in the cultural imagination occurs in the realm of evidence, in the space between the apprehension of the actual and the speculative. Evidence and testimony are thus at the heart of the Victorian quest for certainty, truth, and reliability in fictional narration.

Notes

INTRODUCTION

1 James Bradley Thayer, *A Preliminary Treatise on Evidence at the Common Law* (London: Sweet & Maxwell, 1898), pp. 518–519.

2 [John Hawles], *The English-man's Right. A Dialogue between a Barrister at Law and a Jury-man: Plainly setting forth* I. The Antiquity II. The excellent designed use III. The Office and just Priviledges, of Juries, by the law of England (London: Fineway, 1680), p. 8.

3 Geoffrey Gilbert, *The Law of Evidence*, 2nd edn (London: Owen, 1760), p. 4.

4 Michael McKeon, *The Origins of the English Novel 1600–1740* (Baltimore: Johns Hopkins University Press, 1987), p. 27.

5 Ibid., p. 20.

6 John Sutherland, 'Wilkie Collins and the Origins of the Sensation Novel', *Dickens Studies Annual: Essays on Victorian Fiction* 20 (1991), 243–258.

7 Nuel Pharr Davis, *The Life of Wilkie Collins* (Urbana: University of Illinois Press, 1956), p. 211. Davis is here citing from Louis Dépret's *Chez les Anglais* (1869).

8 2 & 3 Phil & Mar. c. 10 (1555).

9 See Chapter 1, below, for a general discussion of early modern trial procedure.

10 Shoshana Felman and Dori Laub, *Testimony: Crises of Witnessing in Literature, Psychoanalysis, and History* (New York: Routledge, 1992), p. 5.

11 Elie Weisel, 'The Holocaust as a Literary Inspiration', in Weisel, ed., *Dimensions of the Holocaust* (Evanston: Northwestern University Press, 1977), p. 9.

12 Richard Weisberg, 'Editor's Preface', *Cardozo Studies in Law and Literature* 3 (1991), no. 2, i–iii.

13 Felman and Laub, *Testimony*, p. xvii.

14 Anne Frank, *The Diary of a Young Girl: The Definitive Edition*, trans. by Susan Massotty (London: Viking, 1997), p. 334.

15 Paul Ricoeur, *Time and Narrative*, trans. by Kathleen Blamey, Kathleen McLaughlin and David Pellauer, 3 vols. (University of Chicago Press, 1984–1988), vol. I, p. 75.

193

16 Again, much of the discussion which explores the status of auto-biography as testimony has arisen in response to the literary treatment of the Holocaust. Theorists have emphasized both the fictional qualities which inevitably impact upon any attempt to 'capture a prior experience in language' (Weisberg, 'Editor's Preface', i – iii, at i) and also the ways in which extreme experience such as suffering and torture can destabilise and disrupt subsequent efforts to represent them within the conventions of narrative: see for example, Lea Fridman Hamaoui, 'Art and Testimony: The Representation of Historical Horror in Literary Works by Piotr Rawicz and Charlotte Delbo', *Cardozo Studies in Law and Literature* 3 (1991), 243–259. A comprehensive assessment of the value of testimony in the historiography of the Holocaust is provided in Felman and Laub, *Testimony.*

17 Michiel Heyns, *Expulsion and the Nineteenth-Century Novel: The Scapegoat in English Realist Fiction* (Oxford: Clarendon Press, 1994).

18 Douglas Lane Patey, *Probability and Literary Form: Philosophic Theory and Literary Practice in the Augustan Age* (Cambridge University Press, 1984). See also Ian Hacking, *The Emergence of Probability* (Cambridge University Press, 1975).

19 Barbara Shapiro, *Probability and Certainty in Seventeenth-Century England: A Study of the Relationships between Natural Science, Religion, History, Law, and Literature* (Princeton University Press, 1983), especially chs. 1 and 5, and 'The Concept "Fact": Legal Origins and Cultural Diffusion', *Albion* 26 (1994), no. 2, 227–252. For a general appraisal of the value of testimony, see C. A. J. Coady, *Testimony: A Philosophical Study* (Oxford: Clarendon Press, 1992), and Steven Shapin, *A Social History of Truth: Civility and Science in Seventeenth-Century England* (University of Chicago Press, 1994, especially chs. 1–3 and 5), both of which seek to uncover the extent of historical reliance upon ancient authorities (the testimony of tradition) and the post-enlightenment insistence on the primacy of personal experience and perception (the testimony of the senses). For a general introduction to testimony and proof in law, see Glanville Williams, *The Proof of Guilt: A Study of the English Criminal Trial* (London: Stevens, 1955) and Richard Eggleston, *Evidence, Proof and Probability*, 2nd edn (London: Weidenfeld & Nicolson, 1983).

20 Jeremy Bentham, *Treatise on Judicial Evidence* (London: Baldwin, Cradock & Joy, 1825), p. 241.

21 John P. Zomchick, *Family and the Law in Eighteenth-Century Fiction: The Public Conscience in the Private Sphere* (Cambridge University Press, 1993). See also, John Bender, *Imagining the Penitentiary: Fiction and the Architecture of Mind in Eighteenth-Century England* (University of Chicago Press, 1987).

22 *The Morning Chronicle*, Thursday, 23 June 1836, p. 4.

23 Wilkie Collins, *The Moonstone*, 3 vols. (London: Tinsley, 1868), vol. II, pp. 64–65.

24 Alexander Welsh, *Strong Representations: Narrative and Circumstantial Evidence in England* (Baltimore: Johns Hopkins University Press, 1992), p. 30. Frequent reference will be made throughout this study to Welsh's seminal work and page numbers will be included in the text.

25 Richard A. Posner, *Law and Literature: A Misunderstood Relation* (Cambridge, MA: Harvard University Press, 1988), p. 15.

26 Ibid., p. 71.

27 Richard H. Weisberg, *The Failure of the Word: The Protagonist as Lawyer in Modern Fiction* (New Haven: Yale University Press, 1984), p. xii.

28 Weisberg, *Poethics: And Other Strategies of Law and Literature* (New York: Columbia University Press, 1992), p. x.

29 Ricoeur, *Time and Narrative*, vol. I, p. 59.

30 Ricoeur, *From Text to Action: Essays in Hermeneutics II*, trans. by Kathleen Blamey and John B. Thompson (London: Athlone Press, 1991), p. 175.

31 C. R. B. Dunlop, 'Literature Studies in Law Schools', *Cardozo Studies in Law and Literature* 3 (1991), 63–110, at 79.

32 Ibid., 70.

33 Robin West, *Caring for Justice* (New York University Press, 1997), pp. 184–185.

34 Ricoeur, *Time and Narrative*, vol. III, p. 249.

35 Robin West, *Narrative, Authority, and Law* (Ann Arbor: University of Michigan Press, 1993), pp. 93–94. Likewise, Robert Cover has argued that the legal vocabulary must not be divorced from the force which is available to ensure individual compliance with its commands:

Legal interpretation takes place in a field of pain and death . . . Legal interpretive acts signal and occasion the imposition of violence upon others: A judge articulates her understanding of a text, and as a result, somebody loses his freedom, his property, his children, even his life.

See Cover, 'Violence and the Word', in *Narrative, Violence, and the Law: The Essays of Robert Cover*, ed. by Martha Minow, Michael Ryan and Austin Sarat (Ann Arbor: University of Michigan Press, 1993), p. 203.

36 Stanley Fish has argued that meaning is generated by such communities rather than by any objective constraints located within the text itself: see *Is there a Text in this Class?: The Authority of Interpretive Communities* (Cambridge, MA: Harvard University Press, 1980). For a critique of the application of Fish's theories to legal interpretation, see West, *Narrative, Authority and Law*, ch. 3, 'Adjudication is not Interpretation', which is also to be found in *Tennessee Law Review* 54 (1987), 203–278.

37 See for example, M. Lindsay Kaplan, *The Culture of Slander in Early Modern England* (Cambridge University Press, 1997), pp. 1–33, and David Lawton, *Blasphemy* (Hemel Hempstead: Harvester Wheatsheaf, 1993). On the traditional belief in the ameliorative role of satirical literature as a response to the inefficacy of the law, see McKeon, *Origins of the Novel*, p. 269.

38 Jonathan H. Grossman, 'Representing Pickwick: The Novel and the Law

Courts', *Nineteenth-Century Literature* (1997), 171–197. See also, Dickens, *The Old Curiosity Shop*, ed. by Elizabeth M. Brennan (Oxford: Clarendon Press, 1997). Note in particular the irony in the speech of Samuel Brass:

'I am of the law. I am styled "gentleman" by Act of Parliament . . . I am not one of your players of music, stage actors, writers of books or painters of pictures, who assume a station that the laws of their country don't recognise.' (p. 465)

39 Coral Lansbury, *The Reasonable Man: Trollope's Legal Fiction* (Princeton University Press, 1981), especially ch. 5.

40 R. D. McMaster, *Trollope and the Law* (Basingstoke: Macmillan, 1986), chs. 1 and 3.

41 Wilkie Collins, *The Woman in White* (Oxford University Press, 1996), p. 5. Other references to this edition are included in the text.

42 Victor Sage, *Horror Fiction in the Protestant Tradition* (Basingstoke: Macmillan, 1988), p. 221.

43 See Patey, *Probability and Literary Form*, pp. 197–212.

44 William Makepeace Thackeray, *The History of Pendennis* (Harmondsworth: Penguin, 1986), p. 318.

45 Thackeray, *Pendennis*, p. 317.

46 See Chapter 3, p. 117.

47 On the relationship of the novel to the earlier genre of criminal biography, see Lennard J. Davis, *Factual Fictions: The Origins of the English Novel* (New York: Columbia University Press, 1983), especially chs. 5 and 7; Lincoln B. Faller, *Turned to Account: The Forms and Functions of Criminal Biography in Late Seventeenth- and Early Eighteenth-Century England* (Cambridge University Press, 1987); and Jonathan Grossman, 'The Art of Alibi: A History of the Novel and the Law Courts' (Unpublished PhD thesis, University of Pennsylvania, 1996), pp. 16–71.

48 As Peter Goodrich points out, premodern discourses of the law were more pluralist and more able to accommodate or incorporate languages of the body, of conscience, of spirituality, or of ethics. He sees the science of the law, with its repression of the sensate and the spiritual, as arising in the second half of the seventeenth century, thus quashing other minor jurisprudences which had previously enjoyed a voice in legal history: *Law in the Courts of Love: Literature and other Minor Jurisprudences* (London and New York: Routledge, 1996). A number of authors identify women as embodying the discourse of passion most alien to the law; see for example, Weisberg, *Poethics*, p. 71, Lynne Marie Decicco, *Women and Lawyers in the Mid-Nineteenth Century Novel: Uneasy Alliances and Narrative Misrepresentation* (Lewiston: Edwin Mellen, 1996), p. 31. On Trollope's conception of the language of the law, see Lansbury, *The Reasonable Man*, ch. 5, and Glynn-Ellen Fisichelli, 'The Language of Law and Love: Anthony Trollope's *Orley Farm*', *ELH* (1994), 635–653. On the comparative scope of the language of law and of literature, see

James Boyd White, *The Legal Imagination: Studies in the Nature of Legal Thought and Expression* (Boston: Little, Brown & Co., 1973).

49 See John Barrell, *The Birth of Pandora and the Division of Knowledge* (Basingstoke: Macmillan, 1992), p. 119, and Goodrich, *Law in the Courts of Love*, pp. 1–8.

50 Goodrich, *Law in the Courts of Love*, p. 113.

51 On physical experience as an example of that which is excluded by the language of the law, see White, *Legal Imagination*, pp. 83–127.

52 Samuel Richardson, *Clarissa* (Harmondsworth: Penguin, 1985), Letter 218, p. 701.

53 Dickens, *The Posthumous Papers of the Pickwick Club* (London: Oxford University Press, 1948; repr. 1959), ch. 45, p. 643.

54 Henry Longueville Mansel, *The Limits of Religious Thought Examined in Eight Lectures, Preached before the University of Oxford, in the Year 1858* (Oxford: John Murray, 1858), p. v.

55 Ibid., p. 257, pp. 30–31, p. 234.

56 Benjamin Jowett, *The Epistles of St. Paul to the Thessalonians, Galatians, Romans*, 2 vols. (London: John Murray, 1855), vol. II, p. 88.

57 Ibid., vol. II, p. 97.

58 John Henry Newman, *Loss and Gain* (London: Burns, 1848), p. 385. The emphasis is mine.

59 Ricoeur, *Time and Narrative*, vol. I, p. 45.

60 See for example, Hanna Fenichel Pitkin, *The Concept of Representation* (Berkeley: University of California Press, 1967), pp. 69–71.

61 Barbara J. Shapiro, *'Beyond Reasonable Doubt' and 'Probable Cause'* (Berkeley: University of California Press, 1991), p. 135.

62 See Patey, *Probability and Literary Form*, p. 37.

63 See Chapter 1, p. 27.

64 See Chapters 1 and 3 below.

65 In Patey's terms, these are the 'conditions of knowing in Augustan fiction': see *Probability and Literary Form*, ch. 6.

66 See Shapiro, 'The Concept "Fact"', 233, 244 and 252.

67 For a discussion of how to describe the unspeakable in the context of the Holocaust, see for example Robert McAfee Brown, 'The Holocaust as a Problem in Moral Choice', in Weisel, (ed.) *Dimensions of the Holocaust*, pp. 47–63. I am grateful to Anne Henry for discussions on this topic.

1 EYE-WITNESS TESTIMONY AND THE CONSTRUCTION OF NARRATIVE

1 Ian Watt, *The Rise of the Novel* (London: Chatto & Windus, 1957), p. 31.

2 Thomas Hill Green, 'An Estimate of the Value and Influence of Works of Fiction in Modern Times', in *Works of Thomas Hill Green*, ed. by R. L.

Nettleship, 3 vols. (London: Longmans, Green, 1885–1888), vol. III, p. 32.

3 See for example Zomchick, *Family and the Law in Eighteenth-Century Fiction* and Bender, *Imagining the Penitentiary.*

4 See Patey, *Probability and Literary Form*, Part One: Barbara Shapiro, *Probability and Certainty in Seventeenth-Century England* and *'Beyond Reasonable Doubt'*; and Shapin, *A Social History of Truth.*

5 Watt, *Rise of the Novel*, p. 32.

6 See Introduction, p. 5.

7 Shapin, *Social History of Truth*, pp. 201–202.

8 Ibid., p. 236.

9 Shapiro, 'The Concept "Fact"', 233.

10 The Authorized Version of the *Holy Bible* (London: Longmans, Brown, 1841), Hebrews 11: 1. Other references to this edition are included in the text.

11 Shapiro, *Probability and Certainty*, p. 104.

12 McKeon, *History of the Novel*, pp. 75–76.

13 Ricoeur, 'The Hermeneutics of Testimony', p. 135. On received opinion as testimony, see Patey, *Probability and Literary Form*, pp. 3–13.

14 Julius Stone, *Evidence: Its History and Policies*, rev. by W. A. N. Wells (Sydney: Butterworths, 1991), pp. 345–346.

15 Thomas Starkie, *A Practical Treatise on the Law of Evidence*, 3 vols. (London: Clarke, 1824) vol. II, pp. 48 and 53.

16 *R* v. *Warickshall* (1778) 1 Leach 263.

17 Henry Joy, *On the Admissibility of Confessions and Challenge of Jurors in Criminal Cases in England and Ireland* (Dublin: Milliken, 1842), p. 22.

18 Ibid., p. 51.

19 Peter Brooks, 'Storytelling without Fear? Confession in Law and Literature', in Brooks and Paul Gewirtz (eds.), *Law's Stories: Narrative and Rhetoric in the Law* (New Haven: Yale University Press, 1996), pp. 114–134, at p. 121.

20 See Gregory Dart, *Rousseau, Robespierre and English Romanticism* (Cambridge University Press, 1999) ch. 2.

21 Samuel Richardson, 'Hints of Prefaces' in *Clarissa: Preface, Hints of Prefaces, and Postscript* (Los Angeles: William Andrews Clark Memorial Library, 1964, Augustan Reprints Society, no. 103), p. 5.

22 William Hazlitt, 'On the English Novelists' in *Lectures on the English Comic Writers, and Fugitive Writings* (London: Dent, 1963), pp. 117–118.

23 Walter Wilson, *Memoirs of the Life and Times of Daniel De Foe*, 3 vols. (London: Hurst, Chance, 1830), vol. III, p. 428.

24 Ricoeur, *Time and Narrative*, vol. I, p. 45.

25 McKeon, *Origins of the Novel*, p. 120.

26 Ricoeur, *Time and Narrative*, vol. I, p. 54.

27 Sidney Lee, (ed.), *Dictionary of National Biography*, 69 vols. (London: Smith Elder, 1885–1912), vol. 55, p. 93, p. 98.

28 William Thackeray, *The Newcomes* (Harmondsworth: Penguin, 1996), pp. 237–238 and pp. 817–818.

29 In his first *Discourse*, Woolston had criticised the Anglican clergy for their adherence to literal schemes of scriptural interpretation which problematised the accounts of Christ's ministry: *A Discourse on the Miracles of Our Saviour, in View of the Present Controversy between Infidels and Apostates*, 6th edn (London, 1729), p. 63. Woolston was tried on the 4th of March, 1729, for 'wrest[ing] the literal Scope and Meaning' of the text and representing it 'as idle Romance and Fiction' (p. 2). In defence, Woolston's Counsel argued that the tracts were written and published without blasphemous intent; indeed, Woolston wished only to place Christianity on a more solid footing and to promote the metaphorical interpretation of the miracles (p. 2). His conviction rested on the basis that the laws of God formed 'the chief Part of the Laws of the Kingdom' (p. 8); the report of the trial is appended to Thomas Ray, *A Vindication of the Miracles of our Saviour, or a Compleat Answer to all Mr. Woolston's Discourses, with an Appendix for Scripture Revelation, to which is Annexed an Expostulatory Letter to Mr. Woolston; With His Tryal, and Sentence passed upon him for Publishing the said Books*, 2nd edn (London: John Marshall, 1731). Woolston was unable to pay the fine imposed by the court and he subsequently died in prison: see Anon., *The Life of Mr. Woolston, with an Impartial Account of his Writings* (London: Roberts, 1733). For further material on the history of the offence of blasphemy, see Leonard W. Levy, *Treason Against God: A History of the Offense of Blasphemy* (New York: Schocken, 1981), and Lawton, *Blasphemy*.

30 Thomas Sherlock, *The Tryal of the Witnesses of the Resurrection of Jesus* (London: Roberts, 1729), p. 8. Other references to this edition are included in the text.

31 Mark Pattison, 'Tendencies of Religious Thought in England 1688–1750', in *Essays and Reviews* (London: Parker, 1860), pp. 254–329, at p. 303. Other references to this edition are included in the text.

32 Paul Ricoeur, 'The Hermeneutics of Testimony', in Lewis S. Mudge (ed.), *Essays on Biblical Interpretation* (London: SPCK, 1981), p. 125.

33 For further discussion of this motif, see Welsh, *Strong Representations*, p. 169.

34 Henry Venn, *Man a Condemned Prisoner, and Christ the Strong Hold to Save Him: Being the Substance of a Sermon preached at the Assizes held at Kingston, in Surry (sic) before The Hon. Sir Sidney Stafford Smythe, one of the Barons of His Majesty's Court of Exchequer, on Thursday March 16, 1769* (London: Dilly, 1769), pp. 8–9. The historian John Beattie observes that at the beginning of the Assizes, the sheriff's chaplain preached a sermon which was usually 'some variant on the theme of the Great Assizes before which in time every man would be called, or a homily on the wisdom of the laws and the rightfulness of the punishments that would be imposed in the

coming session': *Crime and the Courts in England 1660–1800* (Oxford: Clarendon Press, 1986), p. 31.

35 George Levine, *Darwin and the Novelists: Patterns of Science in Victorian Fiction* (Cambridge, MA: Harvard University Press, 1988), p. 24.

36 Benjamin Jowett, 'Essay on Natural Religion', in *Theological Essays of the Late Benjamin Jowett*, ed. by Lewis Campbell (London: Henry Frowde, 1906), p. 155.

37 Joseph Butler, *The Analogy of Religion, Natural and Revealed, to the Constitution and Course of Nature* (London: Knapton, 1736), p. 248.

38 Ibid., p. 228, p. 221.

39 William Paley, *A View of the Evidences of Christianity*, 2 vols. (London: Faulder, 1794), vol. I, pp. 109–110. Other references to this edition are included in the text.

40 David Hume, *Enquiries Concerning Human Understanding and Concerning the Principles of Morals*, ed. by L. A. Selby-Bigge, 3rd edn (Oxford: Clarendon Press, 1975), p. 113.

41 Thomas Vargish, *The Providential Aesthetic in Victorian Fiction* (Charlottesville: University Press of Virginia, 1985), p. 31.

42 Levine, *Darwin and the Novelists*, p. 25.

43 Elinor S. Shaffer, *'Kubla Khan' and the Fall of Jerusalem: The Mythological School in Biblical Criticism and Secular Literature 1770–1880* (Cambridge University Press, 1975), p. 6.

44 Samuel Taylor Coleridge, *Lectures 1795 on Politics and Religion*, ed. by Lewis Patton and Peter Mann (London: Routledge & Kegan Paul, 1971), p. 152.

45 Shaffer, *'Kubla Khan'*, p. 50, p. 52.

46 Samuel Taylor Coleridge, *Aids to Reflection*, ed. by John Beer (London: Routledge, 1993), p. 188.

47 Bonnier, *Traité des Preuves*, s. 205, cited in W. M. Best, *A Treatise on the Principles of Evidence* (London: Sweet, 1849), pp. 122–123.

48 See, for example, the treatment of St John's gospel in Arthur Penrhyn Stanley, *Sermons and Essays on the Apostolical Age* (Oxford: John Henry Parker, 1847). Stanley explores the character and influence of Peter, Paul and John and concludes that the latter, occupying as he does 'the point of transition between the miraculous and the natural, between the age of the Apostles and the age of the Church, between the times of the earthly and the times of the spiritual Jerusalem' (p. 146), speaks with particular significance to his own generation. In his Bampton Lectures of 1866, Henry Liddon described St John's gospel as the 'battle-field' of the New Testament as it contained the 'most conspicuous written attestation' of Christ's divinity: Henry Parry Liddon, *The Divinity of our Lord and Saviour Jesus Christ: Eight Lectures Preached before the University of Oxford in the Year 1866* (London: Rivingtons, 1867), pp. 311–312.

49 Shaffer, *'Kubla Khan'*, p. 47.

50 Ibid., p. 210.
51 Friedrich Schleiermacher, *A Critical Essay on the Gospel of St. Luke*, trans. by Bishop Thirlwall (London: John Taylor, 1825), p. iv. Other references to this edition are included in the text.
52 See Jack C. Verheyden's Introduction to Schleiermacher's *The Life of Jesus*, trans. by S. MacLean Gilmour (Philadelphia: Fortress Press, 1975), pp. xi–lx, at p. xx.
53 Charles C. Hennell, *An Inquiry Concerning the Origins of Christianity* (London: Smallfield, 1838), p. 30. Other references to this edition are included in the text.
54 Shaffer, *'Kubla Khan'*, p. 4.
55 David Friedrich Strauss, *The Life of Jesus Critically Examined*, trans. by George Eliot, 3 vols. (London: Chapman, 1846), vol. I, pp. 63–64.
56 Ibid., vol. II, pp. 182–183. Footnotes omitted.
57 Ibid., vol. II, p. 345. Footnotes omitted.
58 Ibid., vol. III, p. 21. Footnotes omitted.
59 Ludwig Feuerbach, *The Essence of Christianity*, trans. by George Eliot (London: John Chapman, 1854), p. 129.
60 Liddon, *Divinity of our Lord*, pp. 398–400.
61 Ernest Renan, *The Life of Jesus*, trans. by anon. (London: Trübner, 1864), p. 130.
62 Liddon, *Divinity of our Lord*, p. 405.
63 Charles Kingsley, *Hypatia*, 2 vols. (London: Parker, 1853), vol. I, pp. 180–181.
64 Ibid., vol. I, p. 197.
65 As Gillian Beer has noted, the impact of Darwinian science was not always felt immediately, nor was the response to his work monolithic. For a discussion of how various authors engaged with Darwinian theory, see for example, Gillian Beer, *Darwin's Plots* (London: Routledge & Kegan Paul, 1983) and Levine, *Darwin and the Novelists*. On the vitriolic response to the publication of *Essays and Reviews*, see Joseph Altholz, *Anatomy of a Controversy: The Debate over 'Essays and Reviews' 1860–1864* (Aldershot: Scolar Press, 1994), and Ieuan Ellis, *Seven Against Christ: A Study of 'Essays and Reviews'* (Leiden: E. J. Brill, 1980). *Essays and Reviews* was condemned by the Convocation of Canterbury in 1864 and the two contributors who held ecclesiastical benefices, Williams and Wilson, were prosecuted and convicted of heresy by the Court of Arches in 1862. On appeal to the Privy Council in 1864, the convictions were quashed. See for example, James Fitzjames Stephen, *Defence of the Rev. Rowland Williams, D. D, in the Arches' Court of Canterbury* (London: Smith, Elder, 1862).
66 Shaffer, *'Kubla Khan'*, p. 191.
67 Henry Wilson, 'Séances Historiques de Génève – The National Church', in *Essays and Reviews*, pp. 145–206, at p. 151.

68 Jowett, 'Essay on Natural Religion', pp. 128–129. For a discussion of interpretative approaches to the idea of the 'still small voice' see Stephen Prickett, *Words and the Word* (Cambridge University Press, 1986), ch. 1.

69 William James, *The Varieties of Religious Experience: A Study in Human Nature, Being the Gifford Lectures on Natural Religion Delivered at Edinburgh in 1901–1902* (Cambridge, MA: Harvard University Press, 1985), p. 67.

70 Baden Powell, 'The Burnett Prizes: The Study of the Evidences of Natural Theology', in *Oxford Essays* (London: John W. Parker, 1857), pp. 175–176.

71 Baden Powell, *The Order of Nature Considered in Reference to the Claims of Revelation* (London: Longman, Brown, Green, Longmans, & Roberts, 1859), p. 230.

72 Ibid., p. 296.

73 Ibid., p. 439.

74 Ibid., p. 279.

75 Baden Powell, 'On the Study of the Evidences of Christianity', in *Essays and Reviews*, pp. 94–144 at p. 106. Other references to this edition are included in the text.

76 Victor Sage, *Horror Fiction in the Protestant Tradition* (Basingstoke: Macmillan, 1988).

77 Ibid., p. xx.

78 Ibid., pp. 127–186.

79 Beer, *Darwin's Plots*, p. 45.

80 See for example, George Levine, *The Boundaries of Fiction: Carlyle, Macaulay, and Newman* (Princeton University Press, 1968), p. 259.

81 See Douglas Hay, 'Property, Authority, and the Criminal Law', in Hay et al., *Albion's Fatal Tree: Crime and Society in Eighteenth-Century England* (London: Allen Lane, 1975), pp. 17–63.

82 William Blackstone, *Commentaries on the Laws of England*, 4 vols. (Oxford: Clarendon Press, 1765–1769), vol. I, p. 38.

83 John Austin, *The Province of Jurisprudence Determined*, 2nd edn (London: John Murray, 1861), pp. 2–4.

84 Jowett, *Epistles*, vol. II, pp. 193–195.

85 Ibid., vol. II, pp. 196–197. The phrase 'parcel of the law of the land' echoes the famous judgement of Matthew Hale in the case of *R* v. *Taylor* (1676) 1 Vent. 293; for discussion of this case, see Alan Cromartie, *Sir Matthew Hale 1609–1676: Law, Religion and Natural Philosophy* (Cambridge University Press, 1995), pp. 174–175.

86 Jowett, *Epistles*, vol. II, p. 197.

87 See for example, Stephen, *Defence*, p. 15.

88 See Stone, *Evidence*, pp. 1–11, and Thomas Andrew Green, *Verdict According to Conscience: Perspectives on the English Criminal Trial Jury 1200–1800* (University of Chicago Press, 1985), pp. 3–27.

89 Green, *Verdict According to Conscience*, p. 3 and pp. 11–14.

90 See Green, *Verdict According to Conscience*, pp. 16–20; Stone, *Evidence*, pp. 16–20; and Thomas A. Green and J. S. Cockburn (eds.), *Twelve Good Men and True: The Criminal Trial Jury in England, 1200–1800* (Princeton University Press, 1988), pp. 358–399.

91 Stone, *Evidence*, p. 18.

92 Stone, *Evidence*, pp. 20–23. Blackstone speaks of the practice as recently discarded in the interest of fairness to the accused and in response to procedural changes in the treatment of juries; see *Commentaries*, vol. III, pp. 359–360 and pp. 374–375.

93 Stephan Landsman, 'The Rise of the Contentious Spirit: Adversary Procedure in Eighteenth Century England', *Cornell Law Review* 75 (1990), 497–609, at 498–499. Footnotes omitted.

94 1 Ann stat. 2, c. 9.

95 Beattie, *Crime and the Courts in England*, p. 378. See also Beattie, 'Scales of Justice: Defense Counsel and the English Criminal Trial in the Eighteenth and Nineteenth Centuries', *Law and History Review* 9 (1991), 221–26, at 222.

96 Langbein, I, 275.

97 [Lord Thomas Denman], 'Law of Evidence – Criminal Procedure – Publicity', *Edinburgh Review* 79 (1824), 169–207, at 200. This article is unsigned but it is attributed to Denman by *The Wellesley Index to Victorian Periodicals*, ed. by Walter T. Houghton et al., 5 vols. (Toronto: University Press; London: Routledge & Kegan Paul, 1966–1989), vol. I, p. 465.

98 Hay, 'Property, Authority and the Criminal Law', p. 28. For further information on the operation of the criminal justice system in the nineteenth century, see Allen, *Victorian Evidence*; David J. A. Cairns, *Advocacy and the Making of the Adversarial Criminal Trial 1800–1865* (Oxford: Clarendon Press, 1998), ch. 1; David Bentley, *English Criminal Justice in the Nineteenth Century* (London: Hambledon, 1998), in which chs. 11 and 12 relate to the appearance of criminal lawyers; and V. A. C. Gatrell, *The Hanging Tree: Execution and the English People 1770–1868* (Oxford University Press, 1994), pp. 529–542.

99 Hay, 'Property, Authority and the Criminal Law', p. 52.

100 John H. Langbein, '*Albion's* Fatal Flaws', *Past and Present* 98 (1983), 96–120.

101 Langbein, III, 1047–1048.

102 Ibid., 1053 and footnote 30.

103 Ibid., 1055.

104 *The Times* 19 March 1858, p. 6. See also Blackstone, *Commentaries*, vol. IV, p. 353, and Allen, *Victorian Evidence*, pp. 162–163.

105 Langbein, I, 307–308.

106 Beattie, *Crime and the Courts in England*, pp. 271–272.

107 William Hawkins, *A Treatise of the Pleas of the Crown*, 2nd edn (London: Walthoe, 1724), Book II, p. 400.

108 Langbein, III, 1053.
109 Langbein, II, 124.
110 Langbein, I, 283.
111 Bender, *Imagining the Penitentiary*, pp. 174–175; and also Grossman, 'The Art of Alibi', pp. 11–13.
112 McKeon, *Origins of the Novel*, pp. 104–105, and p. 109.
113 7 & 8 Gul. III, ch. 3.
114 Rupert Cross, *Evidence*, 4th edn (London: Butterworths, 1974), pp. 164–165.
115 On the 'felony counsel restriction', see Cairns, *Advocacy*, p. 3. On the constitutional discourses used to ground radical defences in the Romantic period, see James Epstein, *Radical Expression: Political Language, Ritual, and Symbol in England, 1790–1850* (New York and Oxford University Press, 1994), ch. 2. On the treason trials of 1794, see Barrell, *Birth of Pandora*, ch. 4.
116 Grossman, 'The Art of Alibi', p. 48.
117 [Denman], 'Law of Evidence', 192.
118 Langbein, I, 311.
119 Ibid., 311–313.
120 Landsman, 'Rise of the Contentious Spirit', 548–564.
121 Langbein, I, 313. Bentham states that at the time he composed his work on evidence, 'nine-tenths' of defendants were too poor to enjoy legal assistance, but even in those rare cases where the accused could afford representation, 'the tongue of the defendant's advocate . . . is but half let loose. Questions, – interrogations and counter-interrogations, for the extraction of testimony, – he is allowed to put. Statements, or observations on the evidence, it is not allowed to him to make': *A Rationale of Judicial Evidence, Specially Applied to English Practice*, 5 vols. (London: Hunt & Clarke, 1827), vol. v, p. 384.
122 Langbein, II, 130–131.
123 Bender, *Imagining the Penitentiary*, p. 176.
124 Langbein, II, 130.
125 See Langbein, III, 1066–1071, and Shapiro, *'Beyond Reasonable Doubt'*, p. 199.
126 Langbein, III, 1047–1048.
127 Ibid., 1068.
128 Thayer, *Treatise on Evidence*, pp. 180–181, p. 509.
129 Langbein, I, 306.
130 Bender, *Imagining the Penitentiary*, p. 176.
131 Michel Foucault, *Discipline and Punish: The Birth of the Prison*, trans. by Alan Sheridan (London: Allen Lane, 1977), and Gatrell, *The Hanging Tree*, pp. 14–17.
132 See Gatrell, *The Hanging Tree*, pp. 589–611.
133 Grossman, 'The Art of Alibi', p. v.
134 On the history of the English Bar, see Raymond Cocks, *Foundations of*

the Modern Bar (London: Sweet & Maxwell, 1983), pp. 118–120. On consolidation in the status of precedent, see Jim Evans, 'Change in the Doctrine of Precedent during the Nineteenth Century', in Laurence Goldstein, (ed.), *Precedent in Law* (Oxford: Clarendon Press, 1987), pp. 36–72.

135 Matthew Hale, *The History of the Common Law of England* (London: Walthoe, 1713), p. 257. For analysis of this work, see Cromartie, *Matthew Hale*, pp. 104–109.

136 Hale, *History*, pp. 256–257.

137 Ibid., pp. 257–259.

138 Shapiro, *'Beyond Reasonable Doubt'*, p. 22 and p. 225.

139 Geoffrey Gilbert, *The Law of Evidence*, 2nd edn (London: Owen, 1760), pp. 4–6.

140 Landsman, 'Rise of the Contentious Spirit', 594–597.

141 Patey, *Probability and Literary Form*, pp. 50–62.

142 Shapiro, *'Beyond Reasonable Doubt'*, pp. 217–218.

143 (1753) 18 *State Trials*, p. 1230. The earlier case of *R* v. *Blandy* is described on p. 1299.

144 Summarised in Stephen, *General View*, pp. 338–356.

145 *R* v. *Blandy* (1752) 18 *State Trials* 1118, p. 1187. See also Patey, *Probability and Literary Form*, pp. 50–62, and Welsh, *Strong Representations*, p. 29.

146 *R* v. *Blandy*, p. 1130. See also, Susan Sage Heinzelman, 'Guilty in Law, Implausible in Fiction: Jurisprudential and Literary Narratives in the Case of Mary Blandy, Parricide', in Susan Sage Heizelman and Zipporah Batshaw Wiseman, (eds.), *Representing Women: Law, Literature, and Feminism* (Durham: Duke University Press, 1994), pp. 309–336.

147 William Paley, *The Principles of Moral and Political Philosophy* (London: Faulder, 1785), p. 551.

148 Bentham, *Rationale*, vol. I, p. 197. Austin, on the other hand, regarded testimony as reliable 'in many departments of [empirical] science' but as untrustworthy in the science of ethics where '[t]here is not *that concurrence or agreement of numerous and impartial inquirers*, to which the most cautious and erect understanding readily and wisely defers': *Province of Jurisprudence*, pp. 56–57.

149 Bentham, *Rationale*, vol. III, pp. 7–8.

150 *R* v. *Blandy*, p. 1187.

151 Welsh, *Strong Representations*, ch. 1, and Shapiro, *'Beyond Reasonable Doubt'*, pp. 216–220. See also Barbara Shapiro, 'Circumstantial Evidence: Of Law, Literature, and Culture', *Yale Journal of Law and the Humanities* 5 (1993), 219–241.

152 For the Victorian definition of circumstantial evidence, see Stephen, *General View*, pp. 265–266. Stephen's report of *R* v. *Donellan*, which appears as an appendix to his *General View*, also includes a very interesting anecdote which in fact suggests his suspicion of circumstantial evidence: he recites an admission passed on to his father by

Donellan's attorney which seemed to confirm his client's guilt. It is as if he felt that Donellan's conviction required testimonial endorsement (albeit in the form of hearsay): Stephen, *General View*, pp. 348–349.

153 Cairns suggests that the complexity of circumstantial evidence was a significant factor in the abolition of the felony counsel restriction: Cairns, *Advocacy*, pp. 79–81.

154 Anon., 'Preface' in *Illustrated Life and Career of William Palmer of Rugeley: Containing Details of his Conduct as School-boy, Medical Student, Racing-man, and Poisoner . . .* (London: Ward & Lock, 1856), p. 6.

155 James Fitzjames Stephen, *The Indian Evidence Act with an Introduction on the Principles of Judicial Evidence* (Calcutta: Thacker, Spink, 1872), pp. 6–7.

156 See also Bentham, *Rationale*, vol. III, pp. 7–8.

157 See for example, Starkie, *Treatise on Evidence*, vol. I, p. 19.

158 Shapiro also suggests an earlier date for the erosion of the paradigm: 'Circumstantial Evidence', 228; and judicial reluctance 'to condemn a criminal upon circumstantial evidence, be it ever so decisive' is referred to in *Frankenstein* in 1818; Mary Shelley, *Frankenstein: or, the Modern Prometheus* (Harmondsworth: Penguin, 1985; repr. 1992), p. 83.

159 The Attorney-General, John Copley (later Lord Lyndhurst), speaking on the proposal to extend full legal representation to those accused of felony before the House of Commons, 25 April 1826, in *Parliamentary Debates, 20 March 1826–31 May 1826*, 15 (London: Hansard, 1827), cols. 602–603.

160 Shapiro, *'Beyond Reasonable Doubt'*, p. 13.

161 Ricoeur, *Oneself as Another*, trans. by Kathleen Blamey (University of Chicago Press, 1992), pp. 42–43.

162 Ibid., pp. 21–22.

163 See Shapiro, *'Beyond Reasonable Doubt'*, p. 6; Cross, *Evidence*, p. 170.

164 Allen, *Victorian Evidence*, p. 1.

165 Allen also raises the possibility that the rule which excluded the parties on the grounds of interest may be due as much to the desire to protect members of the gentle classes from being placed in a position where they may be tempted to commit perjury (thus breaching their code of honour and damaging their social standing) than to any automatic assumption that those with an interest in the outcome of a case would be unreliable: *Victorian Evidence*, p. 97.

166 Bentham, *Rationale*, vol. IV, pp. 490–492.

167 Bentham, *Rationale*, vol. V, p. 743.

168 Stone, *Evidence*, p. 38. Opinion is divided on the extent of Bentham's influence on the subsequent legislative developments; see Allen, *Victorian Evidence*, pp. 4–13.

169 9 Geo. IV, c. 32, 3 & 4 Will. IV, c. 49 and 1 & 2 Vict., c. 77.

170 See Allen, *Victorian Evidence*, ch. 3 for his analysis of 'Incompetence due to Religious Principle'.

171 6 & 7 Vict., c. 85.
172 14 & 15 Vict., c. 99.
173 *The Times*, 19 March 1858.
174 Allen, *Victorian Evidence*, pp. 132–144.
175 61 & 62 Vict., c. 36.
176 Stone, *Evidence*, p. 65. For discussion of whether this reform was designed to assist the defence case or the prosecution, see Allen, *Victorian Evidence*, pp. 144–180, and W. R. Cornish et al., *Crime and Law in Nineteenth Century Britain* (Dublin: Irish University Press, 1978), p. 58.

2 THE ORIGINS OF THE NOVEL AND THE GENESIS OF THE LAW
OF EVIDENCE

1 McKeon, *Origins of the Novel*, p. 131.
2 Shapin, *Social History of Truth*, p. 69. Other references to this edition are included in the text. See also J. Douglas Canfield, *Word as Bond in English Literature from the Middle Ages to the Restoration* (Philadelphia: University of Pennsylvania Press, 1989), p. xii.
3 But cf. J. S. Mill's attitude towards the unreliability of the labouring class: 'Thoughts on Parliamentary Reform', in J. M. Robson (ed.), *Essays on Politics and Society* in *Collected Works*, 33 vols. (University of Toronto Press, 1977–1991), vol. xix, p. 338.
4 Patey, *Probability and Literary Form*, pp. 89–109.
5 Christopher Hill, *Society and Puritanism in Pre-Revolutionary England* (London: Secker & Warburg, 1964), p. 418.
6 McKeon, *Origins of the Novel*, p. 207.
7 Simon Schaffer, 'Defoe's Natural Philosophy and the Worlds of Credit', in John Christie and Sally Shuttleworth (eds.), *Nature Transfigured: Science and Literature, 1700–1900* (Manchester University Press, 1989), pp. 13–14.
8 Schaffer, 'Worlds of Credit', p. 24.
9 Shapiro, *'Beyond Reasonable Doubt'*, p. 13: Shapiro, *Probability and Certainty*, pp. 186–187.
10 Gilbert, *Evidence*, pp. 157–158.
11 *Walton v. Shelley* (1786) 1 T. R. 296 at 300.
12 *R v. Atwood & Robbins* (1788) 1 Leach 464 at 464–465.
13 Langbein, I, 303–305.
14 Fielding, 'An Enquiry into the Causes of the Late Increase of Robbers', in *An Enquiry into the Causes of the Late Increase of Robbers and Related Writings*, ed. by Malvin R. Zirker (Oxford: Clarendon Press, 1988), pp. 63–172, at p. 159.
15 'An Enquiry', p. 163.
16 Martin C. Battestin, *Henry Fielding: A Life* (London: Routledge, 1989; repr. 1993), pp. 225–237, 271–272, 448–449.
17 Langbein, II, 56.

18 Bender, *Imagining the Penitentiary*, chs. 5 and 6 (quote on p. 173); Langbein, II, 63.

19 Patrick Reilly, 'Fielding's Magisterial Art', in *Henry Fielding: Justice Observed*, ed. by K. G. Simpson (London: Vision Press, 1985), pp. 76–83: Welsh, *Strong Representations*, pp. 48–49: Patey, *Probability and Literary Form*, ch. IV.

20 It appeared several decades later in Blackstone's *Commentaries*; Beattie, 'Scales of Justice', 248. Anthony Morano emphasizes that the presumption of innocence may be found in an inchoate form in the writings of much earlier jurists such as Hale and Fortescue; Morano, 'A Re-examination of the Development of the Beyond Reasonable Doubt Rule', *Boston University Law Review* 55 (1975), 507–528, at 509. The presumption of innocence was clearly articulated by 1824; it appears in settled form in Starkie's *Treatise of the Law of Evidence*, vol. III, p. 1248.

21 Fielding, *The Journal of a Voyage to Lisbon*, ed. by Austin Dobson (London: Henry Frowde & Oxford University Press, 1907), pp. 16–17.

22 Morano, 'Beyond Reasonable Doubt', 515–519.

23 Shapiro, *'Beyond Reasonable Doubt'*, p. 22 and p. 225.

24 'A Charge Delivered to the Grand Jury', in *An Enquiry*, pp. 1–30, pp. 11–14.

25 Bender, *Imagining the Penitentiary*, p. 104; Langbein, II, 97.

26 'An Enquiry', p. 158.

27 Langbein, II, 100–101.

28 'An Enquiry', pp. 159–160.

29 Langbein argues that '[b]oth the law of evidence and the adversary system, those epochal creations of the second half of the eighteenth century, were responses to the perception that the safeguards in the criminal trial had been inadequate to deal with the dangers posed by the prosecutions that were coming before the courts': II, 106.

30 'An Enquiry', pp. 162–163.

31 Henry Fielding, *The History of Tom Jones: A Foundling*, intro. by Martin C. Battestin and ed. by Fredson Bowers (Oxford: Clarendon Press, 1974), vol. I, Book VIII, ch. v, p. 420. Other references to this edition are included in the text.

32 This rule was hardening in Fielding's time; see Landsman, 'Rise of the Contentious Spirit', 564–572.

33 Fielding, *Joseph Andrews*, ed. by Martin C. Battestin (Oxford: Clarendon Press, 1967), Book III, ch. i, p. 189. Other references to this edition are included in the text.

34 See Patey, *Probability and Literary Form*, pp. 136–154.

35 Langbein, II, 19.

36 See for example, Landsman, 'Rise of the Contentious Spirit', 514–517.

37 Zomchick, *Family and the Law*, pp. 147–149.

38 Fielding, *Amelia*, ed. by Martin C. Battestin (Oxford: Clarendon Press,

1983) Book 1, ch. ii, pp. 24–25. Other references to this edition are included in the text.

39 In his edition of *Amelia*, Battestin notes that this maxim is to be found in Coke's *Reports* of 1658, and that Fielding made a significant alteration to the original; he changed 'existentibus' to 'insistentibus', thus suggesting the power of rhetoric – that which is not insisted on is to be treated as unapparent: *Amelia*, Book 1, ch. x, p. 61. Welsh argues that Fielding's amendment emphasizes the ease with which evidence may be employed to mislead or deceive the court: *Strong Representations*, p. 61.

40 Ian Bell, *Literature and Crime in Augustan England* (London: Routledge, 1991), p. 204.

41 Ibid., p. 209, p. 216.

42 Richardson, 'Hints of Prefaces', in *Clarissa: Preface*, p. 13.

43 Watt, *Rise of the Novel*, p. 30.

44 Samuel Richardson, *Clarissa, or the History of a Young Lady* (Harmondsworth: Penguin, 1985), Letter 183, p. 882. Other references to this edition by letter as well as page numbers are included in the text.

45 Zomchick, *Family and the Law*, p. 84.

46 Terry Castle, *Clarissa's Ciphers: Meaning and Disruption in Richardson's 'Clarissa'* (Ithaca: Cornell University Press, 1982), p. 54.

47 Ibid., p. 67.

48 Ibid., p. 115.

49 Judy M. Cornett, 'The Treachery of Perception: Evidence and Experience in *Clarissa*', *University of Cincinnati Law Review* 63 (1994), 1, 165–193, at 168–169.

50 Castle, *Clarissa's Ciphers*, p. 57.

51 Cornett, 'Perception', 172, 176.

52 Ibid., 187, 190.

53 Ibid., 191–192.

54 Castle, *Clarissa's Ciphers*, p. 93.

55 Pamela Clemit, *The Godwinian Novel: The Rational Fictions of Godwin, Brockden Brown, Mary Shelley* (Oxford: Clarendon Press, 1993), p. 36.

56 William Godwin, Preface to Second Edition of *Caleb Williams*, reprinted in *Caleb Williams* (Harmondsworth: Penguin, 1988), p. 4. Other references to this edition are included in the text.

57 William Godwin, *Cursory Strictures on the Charge Delivered by Lord Chief Justice Eyre to the Grand Jury* (London: Eaton, 1794), p. 25.

58 Barrell, *Birth of Pandora*, p. 141.

59 Ibid., p. 130.

60 William Godwin, *An Enquiry Concerning Political Justice, and its Influence on General Virtue and Happiness*, 2 vols. (London: Robinson, 1793), vol. II, p. 767. Other references to this edition are included in the text. On the other hand, despite his belief in the ideal transparency of all speech (discussed below), in the *Enquiry* Godwin concedes that because people can be misunderstood or misheard, and sincere speech is not always

translated into accurate evidence in courts of law, 'words ought seldom or never to be made a topic of political animadversion' (vol. II, p. 763).

61 Randa Helfield, 'Constructive Treason and Godwin's Treasonous Constructions', *Mosaic* 28 (1995), 2, 43–62, at 49.

62 For a summary of the political context of the novel and the ways in which Caleb's plain speech was designed to counter the rhetoric of Burke, see Clemit, *Godwinian Novel*, ch. 2. See also Gary Handwerk, 'Of Caleb's Guilt and Godwin's Truth: Ideology and Ethics in *Caleb Williams*', *ELH* 60 (1993), 4, 939–960, which explores the ethical implications of Caleb's assumption of guilt at the conclusion of the narrative.

63 Zomchick, *Family and the Law*, chs. 6 and 8.

64 John Sutherland, *The Life of Walter Scott: A Critical Biography* (Oxford: Blackwell, 1995), pp. 48–49, p. 71, pp. 109–110.

65 David Brown, *Walter Scott and the Historical Imagination* (London: Routledge & Kegan Paul, 1979), p. 124.

66 Walter Scott, *The Heart of Midlothian*, ed. by Claire Lamont (Oxford University Press, 1982), ch. v, p. 55; also ch. xxii, pp. 217–218. Other references to this edition are included in the text.

67 On the trials of heroines in fiction, see Welsh, *Strong Representations*, pp. 227–228.

68 For an analysis of the rhetorical traditions which inform Scott's representation of Jeanie's plea to the Queen, see Marie Secor, 'Jeanie Deans and the Nature of True Eloquence', in Don H. Bialostosky and Lawrence D. Needham, *Rhetorical Traditions and British Romantic Literature* (Bloomington & Indiana: Indiana University Press, 1995), pp. 250–263.

69 See Chapter 2, pp. 67–68.

3 CRIMINAL ADVOCACY AND VICTORIAN REALISM

1 Langbein, III, 1048.

2 Wilfrid Prest, *The Rise of the Barristers: A Social History of the English Bar 1590–1640* (Oxford: Clarendon Press, 1986), p. 5. He argues that '[t]he main force which opened up the central courts to barristers was a massive expansion in the volume of litigation during the second half of the [seventeenth] century, when the amount of business handled by the two major central courts of Common Pleas and King's Bench appears to have more than trebled': Prest, pp. 5–6.

3 On the education, social status, and social mobility of those trained in the Inns of Court in early modern England, see J. H. Baker, 'Counsellors and Barristers', *Cambridge Law Journal* (1969), 205–229, and *An Introduction to English Legal History* (London: Butterworths, 1990), ch. 10; Cairns, *Advocacy*; Cocks, *Foundations of the Modern Bar*; David Duman, 'Pathway to Professionalism: The Legal Profession in the Nineteenth Century', *Journal of Social History* 13 (1980), 615–628; David Lemmings, *Gentlemen and Barristers: The Inns of Court and the English Bar 1680–1730*

(Oxford: Clarendon Press, 1990); J. R. Lewis, *The Victorian Bar* (London: Hale, 1982); Prest, *Rise of the Barristers*. On the representation of lawyers in literature, see E. F. J. Tucker, *Intruder into Eden: Representations of the Common Lawyer in English Literature 1350–1750* (Columbia: Camden House, 1984), and *Coram Paribus: Images of the Common Lawyer in Romantic and Victorian Literature* (Charleston: Citadel, 1986); Kathleen Loncar, *Legal Fiction: Law in the Novels of Nineteenth-Century Women Novelists* (London: Minerva, 1995); and Beth Swan, *Fictions of Law: An Investigation of the Law in Eighteenth-Century English Fiction* (Frankfurt: Peter Lang, 1997).

4 The popular trope of the barrister offering rhetoric for hire is itself illustrative of the literary perversion of legal history; Baker observes that the insistence on payment for speech was initially designed to avoid the tort or misdemeanour of 'maintenance' which could arise when a practitioner interfered with a third party's litigation: Baker, 'Counsellors and Barristers', 212. Central to the status of the barrister as a gentleman was the claim that his payment for services rendered was an honorarium rather than a wage: Baker, *Introduction to English Legal History*, p. 187.

5 *Clarissa*, L516, p. 1441.

6 James Fitzjames Stephen, *A General View of the Criminal Law of England* (London: Macmillan, 1863), pp. 284–285. Other references to this edition are included in the text.

7 Cairns, *Advocacy*, p. 3.

8 William Holdsworth, *Charles Dickens as a Legal Historian* (New Haven: Yale University Press, 1929), p. 81.

9 Stephen, 'The License of Modern Novelists', *Edinburgh Review* 106 (1857), 124–156, at 127. The article is unsigned, but attributed to Stephen by *The Wellesley Index to Victorian Periodicals*, vol. 1, p. 506.

10 See for example, Norman Vance, 'Law, Religion and the Unity of *Felix Holt*', in *George Eliot: Centenary Essays*, ed. by Anne Smith (London: Vision Press, 1980), pp. 103–123, at p. 106.

11 Cairns, *Advocacy*, p. 68.

12 [Denman], 'Law of Evidence', 187–188.

13 From his speech on 25 April 1826, recorded in *Parliamentary Debates, 20 March 1826–31 May 1826*, 15 (London: Hansard, 1827), col. 628.

14 Ibid., cols. 598–599.

15 *Second Report from His Majesty's Commissioners*, in *Parliamentary Papers: Reports from Commissioners: Church, Education, Law etc*, 36 (London, 1836), p. 193.

16 Ibid., p. 189.

17 Ibid., p. 196.

18 Ibid., p. 200.

19 Cairns, *Advocacy*, pp. 77–82.

20 Stephen, 'The License of Modern Novelists', 128.

21 Fred Kaplan, *Dickens: A Biography* (London: Hodder & Stoughton, 1988), pp. 47–60.
22 Holdsworth, *Charles Dickens*, p. 7.
23 Phillip Collins, *Dickens and Crime*, 3rd edn (Basingstoke: Macmillan, 1962; repr. 1994), pp. 174–176.
24 On the role of the criminal in fiction , see Davis, *Factual Fictions*, ch. 7, and Faller, *Turned to Account*, Preface and pp. 194–211.
25 Thomas Hatton and Arthur H. Cleaver, *A Bibliography of the Periodical Works of Charles Dickens* (London: Chapman & Hall, 1933), p. 94. Previously called 'The Old Bailey', its title was altered for the second series of *Sketches by Boz* (1837).
26 Charles Dickens, *Sketches by Boz* (London: Oxford University Press, 1957), pp. 198–199.
27 For the history of the Newgate genre, see Keith Hollingsworth, *The Newgate Novel 1830–1847: Bulwer, Ainsworth, Dickens, and Thackeray* (Detroit: Wayne State University Press, 1963), especially ch. 5.
28 *Punch* 2 (1842), 62.
29 William Makepeace Thackeray, *Vanity Fair* (1848) (Harmondsworth: Penguin, 1985), p. 796.
30 Hatton and Cleaver, *Bibliography*, p. 101.
31 Dickens, *Sketches by Boz*, p. 209.
32 On the *Murder Act* of 1752 and the subsequent *Anatomy Act* of 1832 which substituted the bodies of the unclaimed poor for the condemned criminal as the subject of experimental dissection, see Ruth Richardson, *Death, Dissection and the Destitute* (London: Routledge & Kegan Paul, 1987).
33 Dickens, *Oliver Twist*, ed. by K. Tillotson (Oxford: Clarendon Press, 1966), p. 52.
34 Collins, *Dickens and Crime*, p. 224.
35 See for example, *The Letters of Charles Dickens*, ed. by Madeline House, Graham Storey et al., 8 vols. (Oxford: Clarendon Press, 1965–1989), vol. i, p. 153; also Holdsworth, p. 68.
36 Dickens, *Letters*, vol. i, p. 153.
37 Dickens, *The Posthumous Papers of the Pickwick Club* (Harmondsworth: Penguin, 1986), ch. xx, pp. 266–267. Other references to this edition are included in the text.
38 Dickens, *Letters*, vol. ii, pp. 86–87. Holdsworth also cites this possibility, but notes that the physical appearance of Buzfuz was based on that of one Serjeant Bompas: Holdsworth, *Charles Dickens*, p. 68.
39 On the rhetorical training of lawyers in the nineteenth century, see Bege Bowers Neel, 'Lawyers on Trial: Attitudes Towards the Lawyers' Use and Abuse of Rhetoric in Nineteenth-Century England' (Unpublished PhD thesis, University of Tennessee, 1984), ch. 2.
40 It is interesting to note that in *Norton* v. *Melbourne*, the Attorney-General was specifically instructed by the defendant Prime Minister to assert his substantive innocence to the charge of adultery, but this was not

evidence and hence the jury was 'not to be swayed by this solemn declaration [. . .]'. It probably served a valuable rhetorical purpose, however, and may have been important to the deliberations of the jury: *The Morning Chronicle*, 23 June 1836, p. 4.

41 Dickens, *Letters*, vol. II, p. 86.

42 Ibid., vol. II, pp. 88–89.

43 Ibid., vol. II, p. 491, and see also Cairns, *Advocacy*, p. 133.

44 Dickens, *Letters*, vol. II, pp. 491–492.

45 Ibid., vol. II, p. 91.

46 28 February 1846. Reproduced in *Selected Letters of Charles Dickens*, ed. by David Paroissien (Basingstoke: Macmillan, 1985), pp. 217–223, at p. 220.

47 'License of Counsel', *The Examiner*, 12 July 1840. Neel attributes this article to Fonblanque himself; Neel, 'Lawyers on Trial' p. 46.

48 For a concise summary of the positions, see the debate in *The Examiner* following the executions of Frederick and Maria Manning, 24 November 1849. For a discussion of changing ideas of adversarial licence in the profession throughout the decade, see Cairns, *Advocacy*, ch. 6.

49 *The Examiner*, 16 August 1845, and also 15 November 1845. See also 'War between the Press and the Bar', *Punch* 9 (1845), 64–65, and 128, and Neel, 'Lawyers on Trial', pp. 58–65. Lewis notes that peace was restored in November 1845 when the Attorney-General advised that barristers were allowed to report for newspapers: *Victorian Bar*, p. 45. See also *The Law Times* 6 December 1845. For the legal profession's response to the press's criticisms, see 'The Newspapers Against the Bar', *Law Magazine* NS 3 (1845), 165–187.

50 In a leading article entitled 'Effects of Examples of Impunity', *The Examiner* said of Kelly, '[t]he fate of the victim does not touch the heart of Mr Fitzroy Kelly. He has no retainer for emotion, no fee for sensibility in that cause'; 29 March 1845. See also *The Examiner* 16 August and 15 November 1845. Tawell's trial was reported in *The Examiner* on the 15 March and his execution on the 29 March 1845.

51 [Thomas Noon Talfourd], 'On the Principle of Advocacy as Developed in the Practice of the Bar', *Law Magazine* 4 (1846), 1–34, at 21. The article is unsigned, but Cairns explains how it represents the culmination of ideas which Talfourd developed throughout his career; Cairns, *Advocacy*, pp. 146–149.

52 [Talfourd], 'Principle of Advocacy', 12.

53 Thackeray, *The Newcomes*, p. 817.

54 William Forsyth, *Hortensius: An Historical Essay on the Office and Duties of an Advocate* (London: John Murray, 1849), p. 436.

55 See for example, *The Examiner*, 27 October, 24 November and 8 December 1849.

56 Collins, *Dickens and Crime*, p. 235, p. 280 and p. 344.

57 Dickens was contributing to *The Examiner* at the time (see p. 135) and

I would argue that Dickens was familiar with the article on Phillips for the following reasons: he had followed the trial and execution of the Mannings with interest, and their defence had helped to re-open the controversy about adversarial licence, the second article in the paper on the same day discusses a response to some of Dickens's views on capital punishment, and in the light of his letters to *The Morning Chronicle* in 1840, he no doubt took a keen interest in Phillips's explanation of his behaviour in the *Courvoisier* case.

58 Charles Dickens, *Bleak House* (Oxford University Press, 1948; repr. 1978), ch. lii, p. 704. Other references to this edition are included in the text.

59 Zelman Cowen discusses judicial confusion on this point and notes that Baron Aldeson allowed both counsel and the accused to make representations to the court in *R* v. *Dyer* (1844) 1 Cox C. C. 113. However, this practice seems to have been unusual until the 1880s when both Justice Cave and Justice Stephen suggested that a prisoner should be allowed to make an unsworn statement to the jury even though he was represented by cousel; see *R* v. *Shimmin* (1882) 15 Cox C. C. 122, *R* v. *Doherty* (1887) 16 Cox C. C. 306–310, and Zelman Cowen, and P. B. Carter, *Essays on the Law of Evidence* (Oxford: Clarendon Press, 1956), pp. 205–218. The right to make an unsworn statement was expressly preserved by s. 1 (h) of the *Criminal Evidence Act* (1898) which gave the prisoner the right to present his testimony on oath.

60 Cairns, *Advocacy*, pp. 118–119.

61 Langbein, III, 1048.

62 The old format of pre-trial examination familiar to Fielding had been replaced in 1848 (11 & 12 Vict., c. 42) with a procedure which ensured that 'the prisoner [was] protected against all judicial questioning before or at the trial': James Fitzjames Stephen, *A History of the Criminal Law of England*, 3 vols. (London: Macmillan, 1883), vol. I, p. 441.

63 For the role of inference in the assessment of intent, see Welsh, *Strong Representations*, pp. 37–39.

64 19 & 20 Vict. c. 16; see also *R* v. *Palmer* (1856) 103 Revised Reports 845–849, which discusses the implementation of the Act. For reports of the trial, see *R* v. *Palmer: Verbatim Report of the Trial of William Palmer, at the Central Criminal Court, Old Bailey, London, May 14 & following days, 1856, before Lord Campbell, Mr Justice Creswell & Mr Baron Aldeson. Transcribed from the Short-hand Notes of Mr Angelo Bennett, of Rolls Chambers, Chancery Lane* (London: J. Allen, 1856); also *The Times Report of the Trial of William Palmer for Poisoning John Parsons Cook at Rugeley. From the Short-hand Notes taken in the Court from Day to Day* (London: Ward & Lock, 1856). For legal analysis of Palmer's case, see Stephen, *General View*, pp. 357–390; and also Cairns, *Advocacy*, chs. 6 and 7.

65 *R* v. *Palmer: Verbatim Report*, p. 175.

66 Ibid., p. 306.

67 'The Advocate's Licence', *The Examiner*, 24 May 1856, p. 321.

68 *R* v. *Palmer: Verbatim Report*, pp. 307–308.

69 For discussion of the prosecutorial urge which was seen as necessary to stem the tide of audacious poisoning cases, see *The Examiner*, 29 March 1845 (discussing the cases of *Belaney* and *Tawell*), *The Examiner*, 28 June 1856, 26 July 1856 & 16 August 1856 (discussing a Spanish incident and the notorious cases of *Dove* and *Palmer*), and *The Times*, 29 September 1862 (discussing the case of *Wilson*, arguably another multiple offender).

70 Sutherland, 'Origins of the Sensation Novel', 243–258.

71 'Palmer's End', *The Examiner*, 21 June 1856, p. 386.

72 See *The Examiner*, 12 April 1845 for the report of Hocker's trial, then 19 April, 26 April and 3 May 1845 for analysis of the case and an account of his execution.

73 For analysis of the close editorial control Dickens exercised over *Household Words*, see Kaplan, *Dickens*, pp. 263–268.

74 [Henry Morley], 'A Criminal Trial', *Household Words*, 21 June 1856. The article is unsigned but the attribution is traced by Ann Lohrli in her study of the *Household Words* office book entitled *Household Words: A Weekly Journal 1850–1859 Conducted by Charles Dickens* (University of Toronto Press, 1973), p. 154.

75 Welsh makes the same point, but insists that it results from the dominance of circumstantial evidence as a narrative paradigm: *Strong Representations*, p. 48.

76 Anthony Trollope, *Orley Farm* (London: Folio, 1993), p. 617. Other references to this edition are included in the text. On the representation of Chaffanbrass, and Trollope's changing attitudes towards legal advocacy, see McMaster, *Trollope and the Law*, ch. 3.

77 George Eliot, *Felix Holt*, ed. by Fred C. Thomson (Oxford: Clarendon Press, 1980), ch. xxvii, p. 222. Other references to this edition are included in the text.

78 Charlotte Yonge, *The Trial: More Links of the Daisy Chain* (London: Macmillan, 1864), p. 303.

79 Gordon S. Haight, *George Eliot: A Biography* (Oxford: Clarendon Press, 1968), p. 320. See also Eliot, *The George Eliot Letters*, ed. by Gordon S. Haight, 9 vols. (New Haven: Yale University Press, 1954–1978), vol. III, p. 246, pp. 262–267.

80 Haight, *Biography*, p. 383. She was to consult Harrison again in 1874 with respect to the plot of *Daniel Deronda*: Haight, *Biography*, p. 476; *Letters*, vol. VI, pp. 110, 126, 148–153, vol. IX, p. 355. Eliot knew Fitzjames Stephen; *Letters*, vol. III, p. 438; vol. IV, p. 192. She also knew Sir Henry Maine, author of *Ancient Law* (1861): *Letters*, vol. V, p. 237; vol. VII, p. 176. On her legal reading, see Joseph Weisenfarth, (ed.), *A Writer's Notebook 1854–1879* (Charlottesville: University Press of Virginia, 1981), pp. 53–54; William Baker, (ed.), *Some George Eliot Notebooks: Volume I – MS 707* (University of Salzburg Press, 1976), pp. 193–207, which includes notes on the 'arithmetical mode of estimating evidence' made from her

reading of the sixth edition of Best's *Principles of the Law of Evidence* (1875), (p. 193), together with maxims from the work of Bentham, Austin, and Juvenal and information on military law derived from Charles Clode's *Military Forces of the Crown* (1869); J. Pratt and V. Neufeldt (eds.), *George Eliot's Middlemarch Notebooks*, pp. 202–207, pp. 259–264; and Jane Irwine (ed.), *George Eliot's 'Daniel Deronda' Notebooks* (Cambridge University Press, 1997), pp. 327–328.

81 See Eliot, *Letters*, vol. IV, pp. 214–262.

82 For Eliot's exchanges with Harrison on the Prisoners' Counsel Act, see Eliot, *Letters*, vol. IV, pp. 259–261.

83 After the enactment of the Prisoners' Counsel Act, there was some confusion as to the weight to be given to an accused's unsworn statement. In *R* v. *Beard* (1837) 8 Car. & P. 142, Justice Coleridge seemed to indicate that an unsworn statement could provide probative evidence of the facts contained within it, but in *R* v. *Rider* (1838) 8 Car. & P. 539, Justice Patteson held that an unsworn statement could not be considered by a jury as evidence that the events took place as the accused described, and he asserted that unless the prisoner's narrative is supported by probative, corroborative evidence, the jury should 'dismiss [his] statement from their minds'. Much later, in *R* v. *Shimmin*, where the prisoner was allowed to offer an unsworn statement even though he enjoyed the benefit of legal representation, Justice Cave reasoned that although the prisoner's story was not made on oath and not subject to the rigours of cross-examination and 'was therefore not entitled to the same weight as sworn testimony', it was 'entitled to such consideration as the jury might think it deserved'. He stated that '[w]henever a prisoner had made a statement when before the magistrates, his (his Lordship's) practice was to inquire of the prosecution if they had made inquiry into its truth, and if they had either omitted to do so, or, having done so, had been unable to shake it, he was accustomed to treat it as true, and so to direct the jury': *R* v. *Shimmin* (1882) 15 Cox C. C. 122 at p. 124.

84 An alternative view which diminishes the role of intention in the appraisal of culpability is suggested in Charles Bray's *The Philosophy of Necessity; or the Law of Consequences; as Applicable to Mental, Moral, and Social Sciences*, 2 vols. (London: Longman, Orme, Brown, Green & Longmans, 1841), vol. I, pp. 176–177. Haight suggests that Eliot had read this by New Year's Day 1842: Haight, *Biography*, p. 40.

85 Harrison to George Eliot, 26 May 1866; Eliot, *Letters*, vol. IV, p. 260.

86 Haight records that Eliot and Lewes were reading *Mary Barton* aloud on their travels in Germany in 1858; *Biography*, p. 258. See also, Christine L. Krueger, 'Witnessing Women: Trial Testimony in Novels by Tonna, Gaskell, and Eliot', in Heinzelman and Wiseman (eds.), *Representing Women*, pp. 337–355.

87 Yonge, *The Trial*, p. 305.

88 In this sense, his early work *Barnaby Rudge* (1841) may be seen as an ambitious attempt to recover a lost voice and to enable a marginalised figure – the intellectually disabled Barnaby (whose handicap providentially results from his father's commission of a capital offence on the night of his birth and is thus in substitution for his father's evasion of responsibility) – to occupy the focal point of the narrative. Again, this study of criminal capacity is particularly topical, as the laws relating to insanity were under close scrutiny at the time of the novel's composition as a consequence of the case of *R* v. *Oxford* (1840) 9 Car. & P. 525, in which an insane accused had allegedly attempted to assassinate Queen Victoria. Collins provides several references to Dickens's knowledge of the *Oxford* case: Collins, *Dickens and Crime*, pp. 229 & 344. Yet the success of Dickens's fictional narrative has been the subject of much criticism, and it has been suggested that Barnaby's inability to maintain prominence in the novel bearing his name is perhaps itself evidence of the oppressive powers of the articulate community to silence the less fortunate: see Natalie McKnight, *Idiots, Madmen, and Other Prisoners in Dickens* (New York: St Martin's Press, 1993), pp. 90–91.

89 K. J. Fielding and W. Brice, 'Charles Dickens on "The Exclusion of Evidence" – I', *The Dickensian* 64 (1968), 131–140, at 138. The conclusion of the article appears as 'Charles Dickens on "The Exclusion of Evidence" – Concluded', *The Dickensian* 65 (1969), 35–41.

90 *The Examiner*, 12 January 1850.

91 *Household Words*, 26 February – 27 March 1852, at 64.

92 Ibid., 50.

93 James Fitzjames Stephen, 'Oaths', *Cornhill Magazine* 7 (1863), 516–529, at 516. The article is unsigned, but attributed to Stephen by *The Wellesley Periodical Index*, vol. I, p. 334.

94 Charles Dickens, *David Copperfield* (Harmondsworth: Penguin, 1994), p. 21.

95 Also discussed in Fielding and Brice, 'The Exclusion of Evidence – I' 133–135.

96 Stephen, 'Oaths', 527–528.

97 *Adam Bede*, 2 vols., in *The Cabinet Edition of the Works of George Eliot* (Edinburgh: Blackwood, 1878–1880), vol. I, ch. xvii, pp. 265–266. Other references to this edition are included in the text.

98 Similarly, George Henry Lewes observes, in a letter to John Blackwood:

[Sheard has] promised to see that her law is all right. She is as fidgety about minute accuracy as if she were on oath.

19 January 1860, Eliot, *Letters*, vol. III, p. 263.

99 Davis, *Factual Fictions*, ch. 7.

100 Stephen, 'The License of Modern Novelists', 130.

101 Percy Bysshe Shelley, 'The Defence of Poetry', in Alasdair D. F. Macrae (ed.), *Percy Bysshe Shelley: Selected Poetry and Prose* (London: Routledge, 1991), pp. 204–233, at p. 233.
102 Stephen, 'The License of Modern Novelists', 156.
103 [Denman], 'Law of Evidence', 170.
104 Ibid., 202.
105 Thackeray, *The Newcomes*, p. 760.
106 Richard D. Altick, *Victorian Studies in Scarlet* (London: Dent, 1970), pp. 73–74.
107 See Albert Borowitz, *The Thurtell-Hunt Murder Case* (London, 1987), p. 166 and p. 171.
108 Stephen, 'The Morality of Advocacy', *Cornhill Magazine* 3 (1861), 447–459, at 453. This article is unsigned, but attributed to Stephen by *The Wellesley Periodical Index*, vol. 1, p. 328.
109 Ibid., 454.
110 On Stephen's assessment of Dickens's work, see K. J. M. Smith, *James Fitzjames Stephen: Portrait of a Victorian Rationalist* (Cambridge University Press, 1988), ch. 2.
111 'Why?', *Household Words*, Saturday, 1 March 1856. The article is unsigned, but attributed to Dickens by Lohrli, *Household Words*, p. 150.
112 Stephen, *History of the Criminal Law of England*, vol. 1, p. 442.
113 Weisberg, *Poethics*, p. 71.
114 Dickens, *A Tale of Two Cities* (Oxford University Press, 1949; repr. 1987), Book II, ch. iii. Grossman, 'The Art of Alibi', p. 45; also Bender, *Imagining the Penitentiary*, p. 177, and Welsh, *Strong Representations*, p. 58.
115 Ricoeur, *Time and Narrative*, vol. II, p. 90.
116 Charles Dickens, 'The Demeanour of Murderers', *Household Words*, 14 June 1856. The article is unsigned, but attributed to Dickens by Lohrli, *Household Words*, p. 154.

4 THE MARTYR AS WITNESS: INSPIRATION AND THE APPEAL TO INTUITION

1 Ricoeur, 'The Hermeneutics of Testimony', pp. 135–136.
2 James, *Varieties of Religious Experience*, p. 24.
3 Stone, *Evidence*, p. 2.
4 Ricoeur, 'The Hermeneutics of Testimony', p. 138, citing John 18: 37.
5 Ibid., pp. 140–141.
6 Cover, *Narrative, Violence and the Law*, p. 207.
7 George Levine, 'Scientific Discourse as an Alternative to Faith', in *Victorian Faith in Crisis: Essays on Continuity and Change in Nineteenth-Century Religious Belief*, ed. by Richard Helmstadter and Bernard Lightman (Basingstoke: Macmillan, 1990), pp. 225–261, at p. 242.
8 Newman, *John Henry Newman: Autobiographical Writings*, ed. by Henry Tristram (New York: Sheed & Ward, 1955), p. 83.

9 Ian Ker, *John Henry Newman: A Biography* (Oxford: Clarendon Press, 1988), p. 29.
10 John Henry Newman, *Apologia pro Vita Sua*, ed. by Martin J. Svaglic (Oxford: Clarendon Press, 1967), pp. 35–36.
11 Newman, 'Milman's View of Christianity', in *Essays Critical and Historical*, 2 vols. (London: Basil Montagu Pickering, 1872), vol. II, p. 250.
12 Newman, *Essays*, vol. I, p. 252.
13 Letter to John Stanislas Flanagan, 15 February 1868, in Newman, *The Theological Papers of John Henry Newman on Biblical Inspiration and Infallibility*, ed. by J. Derek Holmes (Oxford: Clarendon Press, 1979), p. 158.
14 John Henry Newman, *An Essay on the Development of Christian Doctrine* (Notre Dame: University of Notre Dame Press, 1989; repr. of revised text of 1878), p. 382. Newman is here quoting from his earlier *Essays*, vol. II, p. 231.
15 Newman, *Development of Christian Doctrine*, p. 344.
16 Letter to E. B. Pusey, 13 April 1858 in Newman, *Letters and Diaries*, 33 vols., ed. by Charles Dessain, Thomas Gornall *et al.*, I–VIII, XXIII–XXXI (Oxford: Clarendon Press, 1973–1995), and IX–XXII (London: Nelson, 1961–1972); vol. XVIII, p. 322.
17 Newman, *Development of Christian Doctrine*, p. 336.
18 Newman, *Apologia*, pp. 218–219.
19 Newman, *Development of Christian Doctrine*, p. 342.
20 Letter to Pusey, 13 April 1858: *Letters and Diaries*, vol. XVIII, p. 322.
21 Ker, *John Henry Newman*, p. 735.
22 Ibid., p. 496. Historians agree that the two fundamental tenets of orthodoxy most threatened by the controversy over the publication of *Essays and Reviews*, and the subsequent trials of Williams and Wilson, were the doctrine of inspiration and the idea of the eternal punishment of the non-believer. See for example, Owen Chadwick, *The Victorian Church*, 2 vols. (London: A. & C. Black, 1966–1970), vol. II, pp. 75–85, Ellis, *Seven Against Christ*, ch. 4, and Altholz, *Anatomy of a Controversy*, ch. 10. This impression is confirmed by a reading of Stephen's defence of Dr Rowland Williams before the Court of Arches in 1862. He dwells at great length on conflicting conceptions of inspiration and he sees contrasting attitudes to the infallibility of the Scriptural text as at the heart of the prosecution. The orthodox apologists cling to the idea of the Bible as constituting the (dictated) word of God and consequently the charges against Dr Williams were 'an attempt to tie down the clergy of the Church of England to the weapons of defence which were used 100 years ago, at a time when history and criticism were in their infancy, when language was most imperfectly studied, and when physical science was little understood; when the rules of evidence themselves adopted in courts of justice were hampered by absurdities which have since been removed by legislation': *Defence*, p. 275.
23 Newman, 'The Inspiration of Scripture' (1861), in *Theological Papers*, p. 72.

24 Ibid., p. 74.
25 Benjamin Jowett, 'On the Interpretation of Scripture', in *Essays and Reviews*, pp. 330–433, at p. 348.
26 Stephen, *Defence*, pp. 97, 127–128, 149.
27 Ibid., p. 142.
28 Connop Thirlwall, 'Introduction' to Schleiermacher, *A Critical Essay on the Gospel of St. Luke*, p. vii. Other references to this essay are included in the text.
29 Stephen, *Defence*, p. 284.
30 Schleiermacher, *Essay on St. Luke*, p. 163.
31 Strauss, *Life of Jesus*, vol. II, p. 124.
32 Newman, *Callista: A Sketch of the Third Century* (London: Burns, Oates, 1881), p. 361. Other references to this edition are included in the text.
33 Jowett, 'On the Interpretation of Scripture', p. 337.
34 Ibid., p. 377.
35 Newman, *Development of Christian Doctrine*, p. 339.
36 Ker, *John Henry Newman*, pp. 735–736.
37 Newman, 'The Inspiration of Scripture' (1861), in *Theological Papers*, pp. 80–81.
38 John Henry Newman, 'On the Inspiration of Scripture', *The Nineteenth Century* 15 (1884), 185–199, at 192. See also the discussion of this article in Newman's *On the Inspiration of Scripture*, ed. by J. Derek Holmes and Robert Murray (London: Geoffrey Chapman, 1967).
39 Newman, 'On the Inspiration of Scripture', 192 and 194–196.
40 Letter to Flanagan, 15 February 1868, in *Theological Papers*, p. 156. Newman then went on to equate the authority of the Church on questions of Scriptural interpretation with that of the Apostles rather than that of the Fathers:

> [The Fathers] were not individually perfect theologians; why is an Apostle, why is the Church able to decide the point? Because each, in his or her own way, is a perfect theologian – the difference between them being that the Apostle answers promptly, the Church uncertainly, at intervals, for what the Apostle is in his own person, that the Church is in her whole evolution of ages, per modium unius, a living, present treasury of the Mind of the Spirit of Christ. (pp. 157–158)

41 Newman, *Autobiographical Writings*, pp. 272–273.
42 Newman, 'On the Inspiration of Scripture', 193.
43 Ibid., footnote to 195–196.
44 Hennell, *Inquiry*, p. 214.
45 Stephen, *Defence*, p. 206.
46 Ibid., pp. 210–211.
47 Levine, *The Boundaries of Fiction*, p. 228.
48 Strauss, *Life of Jesus*, vol. II, p. 183.
49 Stephen Prickett, *Origins of Narrative; The Romantic Appropriation of the Bible* (Cambridge University Press, 1996), pp. 266–267.

50 Cover, *Narrative, Violence, and the Law*, p. 207.
51 See for example, Yonge, *The Trial*, p. 262 and p. 276.
52 See Prickett, *Origins of Narrative*, p. 15.
53 Ricoeur, 'The Hermeneutics of Testimony', pp. 121–122.
54 Prickett, *Origins of Narrative*, p. 242.
55 Ricoeur, 'The Hermeneutics of Testimony', p. 129.
56 Ibid., p. 131.
57 Newman, *An Essay in Aid of a Grammar of Assent*, ed. by I. T. Ker (Oxford: Clarendon Press, 1985), pp. 65–66. Newman is here citing notes from an earlier work (1841).
58 Newman, *Grammar of Assent*, p. 36.
59 Newman, *Loss and Gain*, p. 362.
60 George Eliot, *Romola* (Oxford: Clarendon Press, 1993), ch. lxvi, p. 546. Other references to this edition are included in the text.
61 David Carroll, *George Eliot and the Conflict of Interpretations* (Cambridge University Press, 1992), p. 195.
62 Ibid., pp. 197–198.
63 Ibid., p. xi.
64 John Coulson, *Religion and Imagination* (Oxford: Clarendon Press, 1981), pp. 107–108.
65 Robert Browning, 'A Death in the Desert', in *Poetical Works 1833–1864*, pp. 818–836, at pp. 818–819. Other references to this edition are included in the text.
66 As Michael Wheeler has pointed out, the comforting slippage between 'death' and 'sleep' in the account of the raising of Lazarus came under increasing stress in mid-Victorian times as the narrative was demythologized by the higher critics; ' "Can These Dry Bones Live?": Questions of Belief in a Future Life', in *The Critical Spirit and the Will to Believe*, ed. by David Jasper and T. R. Wright (Basingstoke: Macmillan, 1989), pp. 23–36. Wheeler then examines the disintegration of this archetypal account in his analysis of death-bed scenes in Victorian fiction; *Death and the Future Life in Victorian Literature and Theology* (Cambridge University Press, 1990), pp. 28–47, with particular reference to Lazarus at pp. 16–21.
67 Shaffer, *'Kubla Khan'*, p. 198.
68 Ibid., p. 206. See also Renan, *Life of Jesus*, p. 18.
69 Shaffer, *'Kubla Khan'*, p. 213.
70 Ibid., p. 209.
71 Robert Browning, *The Ring and the Book*, ed. by Richard D. Altick (New Haven: Yale University Press, 1981), Book 1, lines 839–845. Other references to this edition (by book and line number) are included in the text.
72 John Marshall Gest, *The Old Yellow Book* (Boston: Chipman Law, 1925), p. 608.
73 See Introduction, p. 15.

74 Browning's hatred of 'buffoon' lawyers is revealed in several letters to Julia Wedgwood, e.g. 19 November 1868, 21 January 1869 and 1 February 1869: *Robert Browning and Julia Wedgwood*, ed. by Richard Curle (London: John Murray & Jonathan Cape, 1937), pp. 160, 167 and 176–177.

75 The presumption of veracity in speech at the time of death is discussed by both parties to the proceedings in the *Old Yellow Book*; see Gest, pp. 246–248, p. 587 for the application of this presumption to Pompilia's testimony, and Gest, pp. 183–187 for the argument that the weight of her testimony should not be bolstered by reference to this presumption. A Victorian statement of a similar rule is to be found in Best's treatise:

> On trials for homicide the general rule of law which rejects second-hand or hearsay evidence is suspended, so far as to render receivable declarations made by the deceased as to the cause of his death, provided they are made by him at a time when he has given up all hope of recovery. This exception has been allowed, partly from necessity and partly on the ground that the situation of the party may fairly be taken as conferring a religious sanction on what he says, at least equal to that supplied by an oath.

Best, *Evidence*, p. 179, footnote omitted. Thayer identified this exception to the usual inadmissibility of hearsay material as one of the oldest rules of evidence; Thayer, *Evidence*, pp. 519–520.

76 Newman, *Grammar of Assent*, p. 57.

77 Coulson, *Religion and Imagination*, p. 145.

CONCLUSION

1 Mary Augusta Ward, *Robert Elsmere*, 3 vols. (London: Smith, Elder, 1888), vol. II, p. 174. Other references to this edition are included in the text.

2 W. E. Gladstone, ' "Robert Elsmere" and the Battle of Belief', *The Nineteenth Century* 23 (1888), 766–788, at 769.

3 Ibid., 778.

4 Baden Powell, *Order of Nature*, p. 145.

5 John Henry Newman, *Two Essays on Scripture Miracles and on Ecclesiastical*, 2nd edn (London: Basil Montagu Pickering, 1870), p. 74.

6 Newman, *Apologia*, p. 31.

7 Newman, *Grammar of Assent*, p. 36.

8 Ibid., p. 240.

9 Ibid., pp. 264–265.

10 Colin Moran, 'Cardinal Newman and Jury Verdicts: Reason, Belief, and Certitude', *Yale Journal of Law and the Humanities* 8 (1996), 1, 63–91, at 85.

11 Ibid., 86.

12 Newman, *Grammar of Assent*, p. 266.

13 Moran, 'Newman and Jury Verdicts', 87.
14 Smith, *Fitzjames Stephen*, pp. 44–46.
15 Stephen, 'Dr. Newman's "Apologia"', *Fraser's Magazine* 70 (1864), 265–303, at 272. This article is unsigned, but attributed to Stephen by *The Wellesley Periodical Index*, vol. II, p. 462.
16 Ibid., 274.
17 Ibid., 283.
18 Ibid., 291.
19 Stephen, 'On Certitude in Religious Assent', *Fraser's Magazine* NS 5 (1872), 23–42, at 37. This article is unsigned, but attributed to Stephen by *The Wellesley Periodical Index*, vol. II, p. 486.
20 Ibid., 32.
21 Ibid., 40.
22 Ibid., 30.
23 Mansel, *Bampton Lectures*, pp. 24–25.
24 James, *Varieties*, p. 341 and pp. 345–346.
25 Ibid., pp. 383–384.
26 Ibid., p. 266.
27 George L. Craik, (ed.), *English Causes Célèbres; or, Reports of Remarkable Trials* (London: Charles Knight, 1840), vol. I, p. v.
28 Stephen, 'The Relation of Novels to Life', *Cambridge Essays* (London: Parker, 1855), pp. 148–192, at p. 155.
29 See Chapter 1, p. 30.
30 Stephen, 'Relation of Novels', pp. 155–156.
31 Ibid., p. 187.
32 Ibid., p. 189.
33 Theodore Ziolkowski, *The Mirror of Justice: Literary Reflections of Legal Crises* (Princeton University Press, 1997), p. 63.
34 Frank Kermode, *The Sense of an Ending: Studies in the Theory of Fiction* (Oxford University Press, 1967), p. 132.
35 Ibid., p. 167.
36 See Welsh, *Strong Representations*, pp. 198–201, and Shapiro, 'Circumstantial Evidence', 229.
37 Blackstone, *Commentaries*, vol. IV, p. 352. The image of the 'golden thread' is to be found in Viscount Sankey's famous judgement in the case of *Woolmington v. DPP* [1935] AC 462: 'Throughout the web of the English criminal law one golden thread is always to be seen, that it is the duty of the prosecution to prove the prisoner's guilt . . .' (at pp. 481–882).
38 Paley, *Moral and Political Philosophy*, pp. 552–553.
39 [Denman], 'Law of Evidence', 180.
40 Ibid., 179.
41 Ibid., 186.
42 Elizabeth Gaskell, *Mary Barton* (Oxford University Press, 1906; repr. 1991), p. 261.

43 See Chapter 2, p. 77 and pp. 98–99.
44 Shelley, *Frankenstein*, pp. 80–83.
45 Welsh notes that nineteenth-century protagonists rarely felt innocent even when acquitted of a crime; this, Welsh argues, is the psychological burden of participation in the social contract: see *Strong Representations*, pp. 91–99.
46 See Chapter 2, pp. 95–97.
47 See Hollingsworth, *The Newgate Novel*, chs. 5 and 6.

Bibliography

PRIMARY SOURCES

Books, articles, and newspapers

Anon., *The Life of Mr. Woolston, with an Impartial Account of his Writings* (London: Roberts, 1733).

Austin, John, *The Province of Jurisprudence Determined*, 2nd edn (London: John Murray, 1861).

Bathurst, Earl, *The Theory of Evidence* (London: Bathurst, 1761).

Bentham, Jeremy, *A Rationale of Judicial Evidence, Specially Applied to English Practice*, 5 vols. (London: Hunt & Clarke, 1827).

A Treatise on Judicial Evidence (London: Baldwin, Cradock & Joy, 1825).

Best, W. M., *A Treatise on the Principles of Evidence* (London: S. Sweet, 1849).

Blackstone, William, *Commentaries on the Laws of England*, 4 vols. (Oxford: Clarendon Press, 1765–1769).

Bray, Charles, *The Philosophy of Necessity; or the Law of Consequences; as Applicable to Mental, Moral, and Social Sciences*, 2 vols. (London: Longman, Orme, Brown, Green & Longmans, 1841).

Browning, Robert, *Robert Browning and Julia Wedgwood*, ed. by Richard Curle (London: John Murray & Jonathan Cape, 1937).

Poetical Works 1833–1864, ed. by Ian Jack (Oxford University Press, 1970; repr. 1980).

The Ring and the Book, ed. by Richard D. Altick (New Haven: Yale University Press, 1981).

Butler, Joseph, *The Analogy of Religion, Natural and Revealed, to the Course and Constitution of Nature* (London: Knapton, 1736).

Coleridge, Samuel Taylor, *Lectures 1795 on Politics and Religion*, ed. by Lewis Patton and Peter Mann (London: Routledge & Kegan Paul, 1971).

Aids to Reflection, ed. by John Beer (London: Routledge, 1993).

Collins, Wilkie, *The Moonstone*, 3 vols. (London: Tinsley, 1868).

The Woman in White (Oxford University Press, 1996).

Craik, George L. (ed.), *English Causes Célèbres; or, Reports of Remarkable Trials* (London: Charles Knight, 1840).

Defoe, Daniel, *The Life and Adventures of Robinson Crusoe*, ed. by Angus Ross (Harmondsworth: Penguin, 1965; repr. 1985).

Moll Flanders, ed. by G. A. Starr (Oxford University Press, 1981; repr. 1991).

[Denman, Lord Thomas], 'Law of Evidence – Criminal Procedure – Publicity', *Edinburgh Review* (1824), lxxix, 169–207.

Dickens, Charles, *The Posthumous Papers of the Pickwick Club* (London: Oxford University Press, 1937; repr. 1959).

Bleak House (Oxford University Press, 1948; repr. 1978).

A Tale of Two Cities (Oxford University Press, 1949; repr. 1987).

Our Mutual Friend (Oxford University Press, 1952; repr. 1992).

Barnaby Rudge (London: Oxford University Press, 1954).

Sketches by Boz (London: Oxford University Press, 1957).

The Letters of Charles Dickens, ed. by Madeline House and Graham Storey, 7 vols. (Oxford: Clarendon Press, 1965–1981).

Oliver Twist, ed. by K. Tillotson (Oxford: Clarendon Press, 1966).

Little Dorrit, ed. by Harvey Peter Sucksmith (Oxford: Clarendon Press, 1979).

Martin Chuzzlewit, ed. by Margaret Cardwell (Oxford: Clarendon Press, 1982).

Selected Letters of Charles Dickens, ed. by David Paroissien (Basingstoke: Macmillan, 1985).

David Copperfield (Harmondsworth: Penguin, 1994).

Hard Times (Harmondsworth: Penguin, 1995).

The Old Curiosity Shop, ed. by Elizabeth M. Brennan (Oxford: Clarendon Press, 1997).

Eliot, George, *Adam Bede*, 2 vols., in *The Cabinet Edition of the Works of George Eliot* (Edinburgh: Blackwood, 1878–1880).

The George Eliot Letters, ed. by Gordon S. Haight, 9 vols. (New Haven: Yale University Press, 1954–1978).

Felix Holt, ed. by Fred C. Thomson (Oxford: Clarendon Press, 1968).

Daniel Deronda, ed. by Graham Handley (Oxford: Clarendon Press, 1984).

Scenes of Clerical Life, ed. by Thomas A. Noble (Oxford: Clarendon Press, 1985).

Romola, ed. by Andrew Brown (Oxford: Clarendon Press, 1993).

George Eliot's 'Daniel Deronda' Notebooks, ed. by Jane Irwin (Cambridge University Press, 1997).

Essays and Reviews (London: John W. Parker, 1860).

The Examiner, Selections from 1840–1856.

Fielding, Henry, *Journal of a Voyage to Lisbon*, ed. by Austin Dobson (London: Henry Frowde & Oxford University Press, 1907).

Joseph Andrews, ed. by Martin C. Battestin (Oxford: Clarendon Press, 1967).

The History of Tom Jones: A Foundling, ed. by Martin C. Battestin and Fredson Bowers, 2 vols. (Oxford: Clarendon Press, 1974).

Shamela, in *Joseph Andrews and Shamela* (Oxford University Press, 1980).

Amelia, ed. by Martin C. Battestin (Oxford: Clarendon Press, 1983).

An Enquiry into the Causes of the Late Increase of Robbers and Related Writings, ed. by Malvin R. Zirker (Oxford: Clarendon Press, 1988).

Jonathan Wild, ed. by David Nokes (Harmondsworth: Penguin, 1994).

Feuerbach, Ludwig, *The Essence of Christianity*, trans. by George Eliot (London: John Chapman, 1854).

Forsyth, William, *Hortensius: An Historical Essay on the Office and Duties of an Advocate* (London: John Murray, 1849).

Frank, Anne, *The Diary of a Young Girl: The Definitive Edition*, trans. by Susan Massotty (London: Viking, 1997).

Gaskell, Elizabeth, *Mary Barton* (Oxford University Press, 1906; repr. 1991).

Gilbert, Geoffrey, *The Law of Evidence*, 2nd edn (London: Owen, 1760).

The Law of Evidence, ed. by Capel Lofft, 4 vols. (London: Rivington, Longman, Dilly, Clarke & Otridge, 1791–1792).

Gladstone, William, '"Robert Elsmere" and the Battle of Belief', *The Nineteenth Century*, 23 (1888), 766–788.

Godwin, William, *An Enquiry Concerning Political Justice, and its Influence on General Virtue and Happiness*, 2 vols. (London: Robinson, 1793).

Cursory Strictures on the Charge Delivered by Lord Chief Justice Eyre to the Grand Jury (London: Eaton, 1794).

Caleb Williams (Harmondsworth: Penguin, 1988).

Green, Thomas Hill, *Works of Thomas Hill Green*, ed. by R. L. Nettleship, 3 vols. (London: Longmans, Green 1885–1888).

Hale, Matthew, *The History of the Common Law of England* (London: Walthoe, 1713).

Hawkins, William, *A Treatise of the Pleas of the Crown*, 2nd edn (London: Walthoe, 1724).

[Hawles, John], *The English-man's Right. A Dialogue between a Barrister at Law and a Jury-man: Plainly setting forth I. The Antiquity II. The excellent designed use III. The Office and just Priviledges, of Juries, by the Law of England* (London: Fineway, 1680).

Hazlitt, William, 'On the English Novelists' in *Lectures on the English Comic Writers, and Fugitive Writings* (London: Dent, 1963).

Hennell, Charles, *An Inquiry Concerning the Origins of Christianity* (London: Smallfield, 1838).

Household Words, ed. by Charles Dickens, March 1852.

Household Words, ed. by Charles Dickens, 1856.

Hume, David, *Enquiries Concerning Human Understanding and Concerning the Principles of Morals*, ed. by L. A. Selby-Bigge, 3rd edn (Oxford: Clarendon Press, 1975).

Huxley, Thomas H., *Science and the Christian Tradition* (London: Macmillan, 1895).

Illustrated Life and Career of William Palmer of Rugeley: containing details of his conduct as school-boy, medical student, racing-man and poisoner; with original letters of William and Anne Palmer, and other authentic documents (London: Ward & Lock, 1856).

James, William, *The Varieties of Religious Experience: A Study in Human Nature, Being the Gifford Lectures on Natural Religion Delivered at Edinburgh in 1901–1902* (Cambridge, MA: Harvard University Press, 1985).

Jameson, Anna Brownell, *Sacred and Legendary Art*, 3rd edn, 2 vols. (London: Longman, Brown, Green, Longmans & Roberts, 1857).

Jowett, Benjamin, *Commentaries on the Epistles of St. Paul to the Thessalonians, Galatians, Romans*, 2 vols. (London: John Murray, 1855).

Theological Essays of the Late Benjamin Jowett, ed. by Lewis Campbell (London: Henry Frowde, 1906).

Joy, Henry, *On the Admissibility of Confessions and Challenge of Jurors in Criminal Cases in England and Ireland* (Dublin: Milliken, 1842).

Kingsley, Charles, *Hypatia*, 2 vols. (London: John W. Parker, 1853).

Poems of Charles Kingsley (Oxford University Press, 1913).

Alton Locke, ed. by Elizabeth A. Cripps (Oxford University Press, 1983).

The Law Times, 1845.

The Law Magazine, 1845.

Liddon, Henry Parry, *The Divinity of our Lord and Saviour Jesus Christ: Eight Lectures Preached before the University of Oxford in the Year 1866* (London: Rivingtons, 1867).

Mansel, Henry Longueville, *The Limits of Religious Thought Examined in Eight Lectures, Preached before the University of Oxford, in the Year 1858* (Oxford: John Murray, 1858).

Mill, J. S., *Collected Works*, ed. by J. M. Robson and J. Stillinger et al., 33 vols. (University of Toronto Press, 1977–1991).

The Morning Chronicle, June and October 1836.

Newman, John Henry, *Loss and Gain* (London: Burns, 1848).

Two Essays on Scripture Miracles and on Ecclesiastical, 2nd edn (London: Basil Montagu Pickering, 1870).

Essays Critical and Historical, 2 vols. (London: Basil Montague Pickering, 1872).

An Essay on the Development of Christian Doctrine, ed. by I. T. Ker (University of Notre Dame Press, 1989; repr. of rev. text of 1878).

Callista: A Sketch of the Third Century (London: Burns, Oates & Co., 1881).

'On the Inspiration of Scripture', *The Nineteenth Century* (1884), 185–199.

John Henry Newman: Autobiographical Writings, ed. by Henry Tristram (New York: Sheed & Ward, 1955).

On the Inspiration of Scripture, ed. by J. Derek Holmes and Robert Murray (London: Geoffrey Chapman, 1967).

Apologia pro Vita Sua, ed. by Martin J. Svaglic (Oxford: Clarendon Press, 1967).

Letters and Diaries, ed. by Charles Dessain, Thomas Gornall et al., vols. 33, I–VIII, XXIII–XXXI (Oxford: Clarendon Press, 1973–1995), vols. IX–XXII (London: Nelson, 1961–1972).

The Theological Papers of John Henry Newman on Biblical Inspiration and Infallibility, ed. by J. Derek Holmes (Oxford: Clarendon Press, 1979).

An Essay in Aid of a Grammar of Assent, ed. by I. T. Ker (Oxford: Clarendon Press, 1985).

Oxford Essays (London: John W. Parker, 1857).

Paley, William, *The Principles of Moral and Political Philosophy* (London: Faulder, 1785).

A View of the Evidences of Christianity, 2 vols. (London: Faulder, 1794).

Natural Theology: or, Evidences of the Existence and Attributes of the Deity, collected from the Appearances of Nature (London: Faulder, 1802).

Parliamentary Debates, 20 March 1826–31 May 1826, 15 (London: Hansard, 1827).

Parliamentary Papers: Reports from Commissioners: Church, Education, Law, etc. 36 (London, 1836).

Powell, Baden, *The Order of Nature Considered in Reference to the Claims of Revelation* (London: Longman, Brown, Green, Longmans & Roberts, 1859).

Punch, 1841–1850.

Ray, Thomas, *A Vindication of the Miracles of our Saviour, or a Compleat Answer to all Mr. Woolston's Discourses*, 2nd edn (London: John Marshall, 1731).

Renan, Ernest, *The Life of Jesus*, trans. by anon. (London: Trubner, 1864).

Richardson, Samuel, *Clarissa: Preface, Hints of Prefaces, and Postscript* (Los Angeles: William Andrews Clark Memorial Library, 1964, Augustan Reprints Society, no. 103).

Pamela: or, Virtue Rewarded, ed. by Peter Sabor (Harmondsworth: Penguin, 1980; repr. 1985).

Clarissa: or The History of a Young Lady, ed. by Angus Ross (Harmondsworth: Penguin, 1985).

Schleiermacher, Friedrich, *A Critical Essay on the Gospel of St. Luke*, trans. by Connop Thirlwall (London: John Taylor, 1825).

Christmas Eve: Dialogue on the Incarnation, trans. by Terrence N. Rice (Richmond: John Knox, 1967).

The Life of Jesus, trans. by S. MacLean Gilmour (Philadelphia: Fortress Press, 1975).

Scott, Walter, *Waverley; or, 'Tis Sixty Years Since*, ed. by Claire Lamont (Oxford: Clarendon Press, 1981).

The Heart of Midlothian, ed. by Claire Lamont (Oxford University Press, 1982).

Ivanhoe, ed. by A. N. Wilson (Harmondsworth: Penguin, 1982).

Shelley, Mary, *Frankenstein: or, the Modern Prometheus* (Harmondsworth: Penguin, 1985; repr. 1992).

Shelley, Percy Bysshe, *Percy Bysshe Shelley: Selected Poetry and Prose*, ed. by Alasdair D. F. Macrae (London: Routledge, 1991).

Sherlock, Thomas, *The Tryal of the Witnesses of the Resurrection of Jesus* (London: Roberts, 1729).

Smith, P. A., *A History of Education for the English Bar* (London: Butterworths, 1860).

Stanley, Arthur Penrhyn, *Sermons and Essays on the Apostolical Age* (Oxford: John Henry Parker, 1847).

Starkie, Thomas, *A Practical Treatise on the Law of Evidence*, 3 vols. (London: Clarke, 1824).

Stephen, James Fitzjames, 'On the Relation of Novels to Life', *Cambridge Essays* (London: Parker, 1855), 148–192.

'The License of Modern Novelists', *Edinburgh Review* 106 (1857), 124–156.

'The Morality of Advocacy', *Cornhill Magazine* 3 (1861), 447–459.

Defence of the Rev. Rowland Williams, D. D., in the Arches' Court of Canterbury (London: Smith, Elder, 1862).

'Oaths', *Cornhill Magazine* 7 (1863), 516–529.

A General View of the Criminal Law of England (London: Macmillan, 1863).

'Dr. Newman's "Apologia" ', *Fraser's Magazine* 70 (1864), 265–303.

The Indian Evidence Act with an Introduction on the Principles of Judicial Evidence (Calcutta: Thacker, Spink, 1872).

'On Certitude in Religious Assent', *Fraser's Magazine*, NS 5 (1872), 23–42.

A History of the Criminal Law of England, 3 vols. (London: Macmillan, 1883).

'Prisoners as Witnesses', *The Nineteenth Century* 20 (1886), 453–472.

Stephen, Leslie, and Sidney Lee, (eds.), *Dictionary of National Biography*, 69 vols. (London: Smith, Elder, 1885–1912).

Strauss, David Friedrich, *The Life of Jesus Critically Examined*, trans. by George Eliot, 3 vols. (London: Chapman, 1846).

[Talfourd, Thomas Noon], 'On the Principle of Advocacy as Developed in the Practice of the Bar', *The Law Magazine* 4 (1846), 1–34.

Thackeray, William, 'Going to see a Man Hanged', *Fraser's Magazine* (1840), 150–158.

The History of Henry Esmond (Harmondsworth: Penguin, 1985).

Vanity Fair (Harmondsworth: Penguin, 1985).

The History of Pendennis (Harmondsworth: Penguin, 1986).

The Newcomes (Harmondsworth: Penguin, 1996).

Thayer, James Bradley, *A Preliminary Treatise on Evidence at the Common Law* (London: Sweet & Maxwell, 1898).

The Times, Selections from 1845–1862.

Trollope, Anthony, *Orley Farm* (London: Folio, 1993).

Venn, Henry, *Man a Condemned Prisoner and Christ the Strong Hold to Save Him: Being the Substance of a Sermon preached at the Assizes held at Kingston, in Surry (sic) before the Hon. Sir Sidney Stafford Smythe, one of the Barons of His Majesty's Court of Exchequer, on Thursday March 16, 1769* (London: E. & C. Dilly, 1769).

Ward, Mary Augusta, *Robert Elsmere*, 3 vols. (London: Smith, Elder, 1888).

Helbeck of Bannisdale (Harmondsworth: Penguin, 1983).

Whately, Richard, *Historic Doubts Relative to Napoleon Buonaparte* (London: Hatchard, 1819).

Wilson, Walter, *Memoirs of the Life and Times of Daniel De Foe*, 3 vols. (London: Hurst, Chance, 1830).

Woolston, Thomas, *A Discourse on the Miracles of our Saviour, in View of the Present Controversy between Infidels and Apostates*, 6th edn (London, 1729).
Yonge, Charlotte, *The Trial; More Links in the Daisy Chain* (London: Macmillan, 1864).

Cases

Hutchinson v. *Stephens* (1837) 1 Keen 665.
Mortimer v. *Mortimer* (1820) 2 Hag. Con. 310.
Omychund v. *Barker* (1744) 1 Atk. 22.
R v. *Atwood & Robbins* (1788) 1 Leach 464.
R v. *Barbot* (1753) 18 *State Trials* 1230.
R v. *Beard* (1837) 8 Car. & P. 142.
R v. *Blandy* (1752) 18 *State Trials* 1118.
R v. *Boucher* (1837) 8 Car. & P. 141.
R v. *Brasier* (1779) 1 Leach 199.
R v. *Dyer* (1844) 1 Cox C. C. 113.
R v. *Hardy* (1794) 24 *State Trials* 199.
R v. *Malings* (1838) 8 Car. & P. 242.
R v. *Oxford* (1840) 9 Car. & P. 525.
R v. *Palmer* (1856) 103 Revised Reports 845–849.
R v. *Palmer: Verbatim Report of the Trial of William Palmer, at the Central Criminal Court, Old Bailey, London, May 14 & following days, 1856, before Lord Campbell, Mr Justice Cresswell, and Mr Baron Alderson. Transcribed from the short-hand notes of Mr Angelo Bennett, of Rolls Chambers, Chancery Lane* (London: J. Allen, 1856).
The Times Report of the Trial of William Palmer for poisoning John Parsons Cook at Rugeley. From the short-hand notes taken in the Central Criminal Court from day to day (London: Ward & Lock, 1856).
R v. *Rider* (1838) 8 Car. & P. 539.
R v. *Shimmin* (1882) 15 Cox CC 122.
R v. *Walking* (1838) 8 Car. & P. 243.
R v. *Warickshall* (1778) 1 Leach 263.
R v. *Williams* (?1833) 7 Car. & P. 321.
R v. *Woodcock* (1789) 1 Leach 500.
Walton v. *Shelley* (1786) 1 T. R. 296.
Williams v. *Williams* (1798) 1 Hag. Con. 299.
Woolmington v. *DPP* [1935] AC 462.
Wright v. *Doe dem. Sandford Tatham* (1837) 7 AD & E 313.

Statutes

25 Edw. III, st. 5, c. 2.
2 & 3 Phil. & Mar., c. 10.
7 & 8 Gul. III, c. 3.

1 Ann st. 2, c. 9.
9 Geo. IV, c. 32.
3 & 4 Will. IV, c. 49.
6 & 7 Will. IV, c. 114: Prisoners' Counsel Act (1836).
6 & 7 Vict., c. 85.
14 & 15 Vict., c. 99.
61 & 62 Vict., c. 36: Criminal Evidence Act (1898).

SECONDARY SOURCES

Allen, Christopher, *The Law of Evidence in Victorian England* (Cambridge University Press, 1997).

Altholz, Joseph, *Anatomy of a Controversy: The Debate over 'Essays and Reviews' 1860–1864* (Aldershot: Scolar Press, 1994).

Altick, Richard D., *Victorian Studies in Scarlet* (London: Dent, 1970).

Altick, Richard D. and James F. Loucks, *Browning's Roman Murder Story* (University of Chicago Press, 1968).

Amory, Hugh, 'Magistrate or Censor?: The Problem of Authority in Fielding's Later Writings', *Studies in English Literature* 12 (1972), 503–515.

Baker, J. H., 'Counsellors and Barristers', *Cambridge Law Journal* (1969), 205–229.

An Introduction to English Legal History, 3rd edn (London: Butterworths, 1990).

Baker, William, *Some George Eliot Notebooks: Volume 1 – MS 707* (University of Salzburg Press, 1976).

Barrell, John, *The Birth of Pandora and the Division of Knowledge* (Basingstoke: Macmillan, 1992).

Battestin, Martin C., *Henry Fielding: A Life* (London: Routledge, 1989; repr. 1993).

Beattie, J. M., *Crime and the Courts in England 1660–1800* (Oxford: Clarendon Press, 1986).

'Scales of Justice: Defense Counsel and the English Criminal Trial in the Eighteenth and Nineteenth Centuries', *Law and History Review* 9 (1991), 221–267.

Beer, Gillian, *Darwin's Plots* (London: Routledge & Kegan Paul, 1983).

Arguing with the Past: Essays in Narrative from Woolf to Sydney (London: Routledge, 1989).

Bell, Ian A., *Literature and Crime in Augustan England* (London: Routledge & Kegan Paul, 1991).

Henry Fielding: Authorship and Authority (Harlow: Longman, 1994).

Bender, John, *Imagining the Penitentiary: Fiction and the Architecture of Mind in Eighteenth-Century England* (University of Chicago Press, 1987).

Bentley, David, *English Criminal Justice in the Nineteenth Century* (London: Hambledon, 1998).

Bonaparte, Felicia, *The Tryptych and the Cross: The Central Myths of George Eliot's Poetic Imagination* (Brighton: Harvester Press, 1979).

Borowitz, Albert, *The Thurtell-Hunt Murder Case* (London, 1987).

Bradley, Ian, *The Call to Seriousness: The Evangelical Impact on the Victorians* (London: Jonathan Cape, 1976).

Brooks, Peter and Paul Gewirtz, (eds.), *Law's Stories: Narrative and Rhetoric in the Law* (New Haven: Yale University Press, 1996).

Brown, David, *Walter Scott and the Historical Imagination* (London: Routledge & Kegan Paul, 1979).

Buckler, William E., *Poetry and Truth in Robert Browning's 'The Ring and the Book'* (New York University Press, 1985).

Butt, John, '*Bleak House* in the Context of 1851', *Nineteenth-Century Fiction* 10 (1955), 1–21.

Cairns, David, *Advocacy and the Making of the Adversarial Criminal Trial 1800–1865* (Oxford: Clarendon Press, 1998).

Canfield, J. Douglas, *Word as Bond in English Literature from the Middle Ages to the Restoration* (Philadelphia: University of Pennsylvania Press, 1989).

Carroll, David, *George Eliot and the Conflict of Interpretations* (Cambridge University Press, 1992).

Castle, Terry, *Clarissa's Ciphers: Meaning and Disruption in Richardson's 'Clarissa'* (Ithaca: Cornell University Press, 1982).

Chadwick, Owen, *The Victorian Church*, 2 vols. (London: A. & C. Black, 1966–1970).

Clark, Cumberland, *Talfourd and Dickens* (London: Chiswick Press, 1919).

Clemit, Pamela, *The Godwinian Novel: The Rational Fictions of Godwin, Brockden Brown, Mary Shelley* (Oxford: Clarendon Press, 1993).

Coady, C. A. J., *Testimony: A Philosophical Study* (Oxford: Clarendon Press, 1992).

Cocks, Raymond, *Foundations of the Modern Bar* (London: Sweet & Maxwell, 1983).

Collins, Phillip, *Dickens and Crime*, 3rd edn (Basingstoke: Macmillan, 1962; repr. 1994).

Cornett, Judy M., 'The Treachery of Perception: Evidence and Experience in *Clarissa*', *University of Cincinnati Law Review* 63 (1994), 1, 165–193.

Cornish, W. R., *Crime and Law in Nineteenth Century Britain* (Dublin: Irish University Press, 1978).

Coulson, John, *Religion and Imagination* (Oxford: Clarendon Press, 1981).

Cover, Robert, *Narrative, Violence, and the Law: The Essays of Robert Cover*, ed. by Martha Minow et al. (Ann Arbor: University of Michigan Press, 1993).

Cowen, Zelman and P. B. Carter, *Essays on the Law of Evidence* (Oxford: Clarendon Press, 1956).

Cromartie, Alan, *Sir Matthew Hale 1609–1676: Law, Religion and Natural Philosophy* (Cambridge University Press, 1995).

Cross, Rupert, *Evidence*, 4th edn (London: Butterworths, 1974).

Cross, Rupert, and Colin Tapper, *Evidence*, 7th edn (London: Butterworths, 1990).

Cunningham, Valentine, *Everywhere Spoken Against: Dissent in the Victorian Novel* (Oxford: Clarendon Press, 1975).

Dale, Peter Allen, *In Pursuit of a Scientific Culture: Science, Art, and Society in the Victorian Age* (Madison: University of Wisconsin Press, 1989).

Dart, Gregory, *Rousseau, Robespierre and English Romanticism* (Cambridge University Press, 1999).

Davis, Lennard J., *Factual Fictions: The Origins of the English Novel* (New York: Columbia University Press, 1983).

Davis, Nuel Pharr, *The Life of Wilkie Collins* (Urbana: University of Illinois Press, 1956).

Decicco, Lynne Marie, *Women and Lawyers in the Mid-Nineteenth Century Novel: Uneasy Alliances and Narrative Misrepresentation* (Lewiston: Edwin Mellen, 1996).

Duman, Daniel, 'Pathway to Professionalism: The Legal Profession in the Nineteenth Century', *Journal of Social History* 13 (1980), 615–628.

Dunlop, C. B. R., 'Literature Studies in Law Schools', *Cardozo Studies in Law and Literature* 3 (1991), 63–110.

Eggleston, Richard, *Evidence, Proof and Probability*, 2nd edn (London: Weidenfeld & Nicolson, 1983).

Ellis, Ieuan, *Seven Against Christ: A Study of Essays and Reviews* (Leiden: E. J. Brill, 1980).

Epstein, James A., *Radical Expression: Political Language, Ritual, and Symbol in England, 1790–1850* (Oxford & New York: Oxford University Press, 1994).

Faller, Lincoln B., *Turned to Account: The Forms and Functions of Criminal Biography in Late Seventeenth- and Early-Eighteenth Century England* (Cambridge University Press, 1987).

Felman, Shoshana, and Lori Daub, *Testimony: Crises of Witnessing in Literature, Psychoanalysis, and History* (New York: Routledge, 1992).

Fielding, K. J. and W. Brice, 'Charles Dickens on "The Exclusion of Evidence" – 1', *The Dickensian* 64 (1968), 131–140.

'Charles Dickens on "The Exclusion of Evidence" – Concluded', *The Dickensian* 65 (1969), 35–41.

Fish, Stanley, *Is there a Text in this Class?: The Authority of Interpretive Communities* (Cambridge, MA: Harvard University Press, 1980).

Fisichelli, Glynn-Ellen, 'The Language of Law and Love: Anthony Trollope's *Orley Farm*', *ELH* 61 (1994), 3, 635–653.

Foucault, Michel, *Discipline and Punish: The Birth of the Prison*, trans. by Alan Sheridan (London: Allen Lane, 1977).

Gatrell, V. A. C., *The Hanging Tree: Execution and the English People 1770–1868* (Oxford University Press, 1994).

Gest, John Marshall, *The Old Yellow Book* (Boston: Chipman Law, 1925).

Goldstein, Laurence, (ed.), *Precedent in Law* (Oxford: Clarendon Press, 1991).

Goodrich, Peter, *Law in the Courts of Love: Literature and Other Minor Jurisprudences* (London and New York: Routledge, 1996).

Green, Thomas A., *Verdict According to Conscience: Perspectives on the English Criminal Trial Jury 1200–1800* (University of Chicago Press, 1985).

Green, Thomas A., and J. S. Cockburn, (eds.), *Twelve Good Men and True: The Criminal Trial Jury in England, 1200–1800* (Princeton University Press, 1988).

Grossman, Jonathan H., 'The Art of Alibi' (Unpublished PhD thesis, University of Pennsylvania, 1996).

'Representing Pickwick: The Novel and the Law Courts', *Nineteenth-Century Literature*, September 1997, 171–197.

Hacking, Ian, *The Emergence of Probability* (Cambridge University Press, 1975).

Haight, Gordon S., *George Eliot: A Biography* (Oxford: Clarendon Press, 1968).

Hamaoui, Lea Fridman, 'Art and Testimony: The Representation of Historical Horror in Literary Works by Piotr Rawicz and Charlotte Delbo', *Cardozo Studies in Law and Literature* 3 (1991), 243–259.

Handwerk, Gary, 'Of Caleb's Guilt and Godwin's Truth: Ideology and Ethics in *Caleb Williams*', *ELH* 60 (1993) 4, 939–960.

Harden, Edgar F., *A Checklist of Contributions by William Makepeace Thackeray to Newspapers, Periodicals, Books, and Serial Part Issues 1828–1864* (University of Victoria: English Literature Studies, 1996).

Hardy, Barbara, (ed.), *Critical Essays on George Eliot* (London: Routledge & Kegan Paul, 1970).

Hatton, Thomas, and Arthur H. Cleaver, *A Bibliography of the Periodical Works of Charles Dickens* (London: Chapman & Hall, 1933).

Hay, Douglas, 'Property, Authority and the Criminal Law', in Hay et al., *Albion's Fatal Tree: Crime and Society in Eighteenth Century England* (London: Allen Lane, 1975).

Heinzelman, Susan Sage, 'Guilty in Law, Implausible in Fiction; Jurisprudential and Literary Narratives in the Case of Mary Blandy, Parricide', in Susan Sage Heinzelman and Zipporah Batshaw Wiseman, (eds.), *Representing Women: Law, Literature, and Feminism* (Durham: Duke University Press, 1994).

Helfield, Randa, 'Constructive Treason and Godwin's Treasonous Constructions', *Mosaic* 28 (1995) 2, 43–62.

Helmstadter, Richard J., and Bernard Lightman, (eds.), *Victorian Faith in Crisis: Essays on Continuity and Change in Nineteenth-Century Religious Belief* (Basingstoke: Macmillan, 1990).

Heyns, Michiel, *Expulsion and the Nineteenth-Century Novel: The Scapegoat in English Realist Fiction* (Oxford: Clarendon Press, 1994).

Hill, Christopher, *Society and Puritanism in Pre-Revolutionary England* (London: Secker & Warburg, 1964).

Hillis Miller, J., *The Disappearance of God: Five Nineteenth-Century Writers* (Cambridge, MA: Belknap Press, 1975).

Holdsworth, William, *Charles Dickens as a Legal Historian* (New Haven: Yale University Press, 1929).

Hollingsworth, Keith, *The Newgate Novel 1830–1847: Bulwer, Ainsworth, Dickens, and Thackeray* (Detroit: Wayne State University Press, 1963).

Houghton, Walter E., et al., (eds.), *The Wellesley Index to Victorian Periodicals*, 5 vols. (University of Toronto Press; London: Routledge & Kegan Paul, 1966–1989).

Hynes, Peter, 'Curses, Oaths, and Narrative in Richardson's *Clarissa*', *ELH* 56 (1989), 2, 311–326.

Irvine, William and Park Honan, *The Book, the Ring and the Poet: A Biography of Robert Browning* (London: Bodley Head, 1974).

Jack, Ian, *Browning's Major Poetry* (Oxford: Clarendon Press, 1973).

Jay, Elisabeth, *Faith and Doubt in Victorian Britain* (Basingstoke: Macmillan, 1986).

Kaplan, Fred, *Dickens: A Biography* (London: Hodder & Stoughton, 1988).

Kaplan, M. Lindsay, *The Culture of Slander in Early Modern England* (Cambridge University Press, 1997).

Kent, Christopher, 'Probability, Reality and Sensation in the Novels of Wilkie Collins', *Dickens Studies Annual: Essays in Victorian Fiction* 20 (1991), 259–280.

Ker, Ian, *John Henry Newman: A Biography* (Oxford: Clarendon Press, 1988).

Kermode, Frank, *The Sense of an Ending: Studies in the Theory of Fiction* (Oxford University Press, 1967).

Kornstein, Daniel, *Kill All the Lawyers? Shakespeare's Legal Appeal* (Princeton University Press, 1994).

Knoepflmacher, U. C., *Religious Humanism and the Victorian Novel: George Eliot, Walter Pater and Samuel Butler* (Princeton University Press, 1965).

Landsman, Stephan, 'The Rise of the Contentious Spirit: Adversary Procedure in Eighteenth-Century England', *Cornell Law Review* 75 (1990), 497–609.

Langbein, John, 'The Criminal Trial before the Lawyers', *University of Chicago Law Review* 45 (1978), 263–316.

'*Albion's* Fatal Flaws', *Past and Present* 98 (1983), 96–120.

'Shaping the Eighteenth-Century Criminal Trial: A View from the Ryder Sources', *University of Chicago Law Review* 50 (1983), 1–136.

'The Historical Origins of the Privilege Against Self-Incrimination at Common Law', *Michigan Law Review* 92 (1993–1994), 1047–1085.

Lansbury, Coral, *The Reasonable Man: Trollope's Legal Fiction* (Princeton University Press, 1981).

Lawton, David, *Blasphemy* (Hemel Hempstead: Harvester Wheatsheaf, 1993).

Lemmings, David, *Gentlemen and Barristers: The Inns of Court and the English Bar 1680– 1730* (Oxford: Clarendon Press, 1990).

Levine, George, *The Boundaries of Fiction: Carlyle, Macaulay, and Newman* (Princeton University Press, 1968).

Darwin and the Novelists: Patterns of Science in Victorian Fiction (Cambridge, MA: Harvard University Press, 1988).

Levy, Leonard W., *Treason Against God: A History of the Offense of Blasphemy* (New York: Schocken, 1981).

Lewis, J. R., *The Victorian Bar* (London: Hale, 1982).

Lohrli, Ann, *Household Words: A Weekly Journal 1850–1859 Conducted by Charles Dickens; Table of Contents, List of Contributors and their Contributions* (University of Toronto Press, 1973).

Loncar, Kathleen, *Legal Fiction: Law in the Novels of Nineteenth-Century Women Novelists* (London: Minerva, 1995).

McKeon, Michael, *The Origins of the English Novel 1600–1740* (Baltimore: Johns Hopkins University Press, 1987).

McKnight, Natalie, *Idiots, Madmen, and other Prisoners in Dickens* (New York: St Martin's Press, 1993).

McMaster, R. D., *Trollope and the Law* (Basingstoke: Macmillan, 1986).

Moran, Colin, 'Cardinal Newman and Jury Verdicts: Reason, Belief, and Certitude', *Yale Journal of Law and the Humanities* 8 (1996), 1, 63–91.

Morano, Anthony, 'A Re-examination of the Development of the Beyond Reasonable Doubt Rule', *Boston University Law Review* 55 (1975), 507–528.

Neel, Bege Bowers, 'Lawyers on Trial: Attitudes Towards the Lawyers' Use and Abuse of Rhetoric in Nineteenth-Century England' (Unpublished PhD thesis, University of Tennessee, 1984).

Patey, Douglas, *Probability and Literary Form: Philosophic Theory and Literary Practice in the Augustan Age* (Cambridge University Press, 1984).

Peterson, William S., *Victorian Heretic: Mrs Humphry Ward's 'Robert Elsmere'* (Leicester University Press, 1976).

Pitkin, Hanna Fenichel, *The Concept of Representation* (Berkeley: University of California Press, 1967).

Posner, Richard, *Law and Literature: A Misunderstood Relation* (Cambridge, MA: Harvard University Press, 1988).

Prest, Wilfrid R., *The Rise of the Barristers: A Social History of the English Bar 1590–1640* (Oxford: Clarendon Press, 1986).

Prickett, Stephen, *Words and the Word* (Cambridge University Press, 1986).

Origins of Narrative: The Romantic Appropriation of the Bible (Cambridge University Press, 1996).

Pritchard, Allan, 'The Urban Gothic of *Bleak House*', *Nineteenth Century Fiction* 45 (1991), 432–452.

Richardson, Ruth, *Death, Dissection and the Destitute* (London: Routledge & Kegan Paul, 1987).

Ricoeur, Paul, *Essays on Biblical Interpretation*, ed. by Lewis S. Mudge (London: SPCK, 1981).

Time and Narrative, trans. by Kathleen Blamey, Kathleen McLaughlin and David Pellauer, 3 vols. (University of Chicago Press, 1984–1988).

From Text to Action: Essays in Hermeneutics II, trans. by Kathleen Blamey and John B. Thompson (London: Athlone Press, 1991).

Oneself as Another, trans. by Kathleen Blamey (University of Chicago Press, 1992).

Rorty, Richard, *Contingency, Irony and Solidarity* (Cambridge University Press, 1989).

Sage, Victor, *Horror Fiction in the Protestant Tradition* (Basingstoke: Macmillan, 1988).

Schaffer, Simon, 'Defoe's Natural Philosophy and the Worlds of Credit', in John Christie and Sally Shuttleworth, (eds.), *Nature Transfigured: Science and Literature, 1700– 1900* (Manchester University Press, 1989).

Secor, Marie, 'Jeanie Deans and the Nature of True Eloquence', in Don H. Bialostosky and Lawrence D. Needham, (eds.), *Rhetorical Traditions and British Romantic Literature* (Bloomington & Indiana: Indiana University Press, 1995).

Shaffer, Elinor, *'Kubla Khan' and the Fall of Jerusalem: The Mythological School in Biblical Criticism and Secular Literature 1770–1880* (Cambridge University Press, 1975).

Shapin, Steven, *A Social History of Truth: Civility and Science in Seventeenth-Century England* (University of Chicago Press, 1994).

Shapiro, Barbara, *Probability and Certainty in Seventeenth-Century England: A Study of the Relationships between Natural Science, Religion, History, Law, and Literature* (Princeton University Press, 1983).

'Beyond Reasonable Doubt' and 'Probable Cause' (Berkeley: University of California Press, 1991).

'Circumstantial Evidence: Of Law, Literature, and Culture', *Yale Journal of Law and the Humanities* 5 (1993), 1, 219–241.

'The Concept "Fact": Legal Origins and Cultural Diffusion', *Albion* 26 (1994), 2, 227–252.

Shuttleworth, Sally, *George Eliot and Nineteenth-Century Science: The Make-Believe of a Beginning* (Cambridge University Press, 1984).

Simpson, K. G., (ed.), *Henry Fielding: Justice Observed* (London: Vision Press, 1985).

Smith, K. J. M., *James Fitzjames Stephen: Portrait of a Victorian Rationalist* (Cambridge University Press, 1988).

Stewart, Garrett, *Death Sentences: Styles of Dying in British Fiction* (Cambridge, MA: Harvard University Press, 1985).

Stone, Julius, *Evidence: Its History and Policies*, rev. by W. A. N. Wells (Sydney: Butterworths, 1991).

Sutherland, John, *The Longman Companion to Victorian Fiction* (London: Longman, 1988; repr. 1990).

'Wilkie Collins and the Origins of the Sensation Novel', *Dickens Studies Annual: Essays on Victorian Fiction* 20 (1991), 243–258.

The Life of Walter Scott: A Critical Biography (Oxford: Blackwell, 1995).

Swan, Beth, *Fictions of Law: An Investigation of the Law in Eighteenth-Century English Fiction* (Frankfurt: Peter Lang, 1997).

Symondson, Anthony, (ed.), *The Victorian Crisis of Faith* (London: SPCK, 1970).

Tucker, E. F. J., *Intruder into Eden: Representations of the Common Lawyer in English Literature 1350–1750* (Columbia: Camden House, 1984).

    Coram Paribus: Images of the Common Lawyer in Romantic and Victorian Literature (Charleston: Citadel, 1986).

Twining, William, *Rethinking Evidence: Exploratory Essays* (Oxford: Blackwell, 1990).

Vance, Norman, 'Law, Religion and the Unity of *Felix Holt*', in *George Eliot: Centenary Essays*, ed. by Anne Smith (London: Vision Press, 1980).

Vargish, Thomas, *The Providential Aesthetic in Victorian Fiction* (Charlottesville: University of Virginia Press, 1985).

Ward, Ian, *Law and Literature: Possibilities and Perspectives* (Cambridge University Press, 1995).

    'The Jurisprudential *Heart of Midlothian*', *Scottish Literary Journal* 24 (1997), 1, 25–39.

Watt, Ian, *The Rise of the Novel* (London: Chatto & Windus, 1957).

Weisberg, Richard, *The Failure of the Word: The Protagonist as Lawyer in Modern Fiction* (New Haven: Yale University Press, 1984).

    Preface 'Testimony', *Cardozo Studies in Law and Literature* 3 (1991), 2, i–iii.

    Poethics; And Other Strategies of Law and Literature (New York: Columbia University Press, 1992).

Weisel, Elie, (ed.), *Dimensions of the Holocaust* (Evanston: Northwestern University Press, 1977).

Weisenfarth, Joseph, (ed.), *George Eliot: A Writer's Notebook 1854–1879* (Charlottesville: University Press of Virginia, 1981).

Welsh, Alexander, *George Eliot and Blackmail* (Cambridge, MA: Harvard University Press, 1985).

    Strong Representations: Narrative and Circumstantial Evidence in England (Baltimore: Johns Hopkins University Press, 1992).

West, Robin, 'Adjudication is not Interpretation', *Tennessee Law Review* 54 (1987), 203–278.

    Narrative, Authority, and Law (Ann Arbor: University of Michigan Press, 1993).

    Caring for Justice (New York University Press, 1997).

Wheeler, Michael, ' "Can These Dry Bones Live?" Questions of Belief in a Future Life', in *The Critical Spirit and the Will to Believe*, ed. by David Jasper and T. R. Wright (Basingstoke: Macmillan, 1989).

    Death and the Future Life in Victorian Literature and Theology (Cambridge University Press, 1990).

White, James Boyd, *The Legal Imagination: Studies in the Nature of Legal Thought and Expression* (Boston: Little, Brown & Co., 1973).

Wiener, Martin J., *Reconstructing the Criminal: Culture, Law, and Policy in England 1830– 1914* (Cambridge University Press, 1990).

Williams, Glanville, *The Proof of Guilt: A Study of the English Criminal Trial* (London: Stevens, 1955).

Witemeyer, Hugh, *George Eliot and the Visual Arts* (New Haven: Yale University Press, 1979).

Ziolkowski, Theodore, *The Mirror of Justice: Literary Reflections of Legal Crises* (Princeton University Press, 1997).

Zomchick, John P., *Family and the Law in Eighteenth-Century Fiction: The Public Conscience in the Private Sphere* (Cambridge University Press, 1993).

Index

Romanticism, 29, 161, 162, 186, 190

St John, 39, 41–42, 145, 165–169, 200 n. 48
St Luke, 40–41, 153
St Paul, 27, 49, 147
Schleiermacher, Frederic, 39–41, 43, 47, 152–153
Scott, Walter, 68
  Heart of Midlothian, 23, 31, 72, 95–98, 131, 134, 184
  Waverley, 127
Shaffer, Elinor, 38, 39–40, 42, 45, 168–169
Shapin, Steven, 26–27, 68–69
Shapiro, Barbara, 5, 19, 26–27, 53, 58, 60, 68
Shee, William, 123, 126
Shelley, Mary, *Frankenstein*, 189, 206 n. 158
Sherlock, Thomas, 32–33
Starkie, Thomas, 28, 187, 208 n. 20
Stephen, James Fitzjames, 60, 103–104, 180, 183, 184, 185, 188
  'Certitude', 172
  Defence of Dr Williams, 151–152
  General View of the Criminal Law, 63, 108–109, 121, 125, 177–178
  Indian Evidence Act, 60–61
  'License of Modern Novelists', 104, 110, 139–140, 141, 181
  'Newman's "Apologia"', 178–179
  'Novels in Relation to Real Life', 181–182
  'Oaths', 136–138
  and Charles Dickens, 104, 139–141
  and John Henry Newman, 177–179
Strauss, David, 39, 41, 42–43, 152–153, 158
Sutherland, John, 2, 124

Talfourd, Thomas Noon, 112, 117, 213 n. 51
testimony, definition 28–29, 194 n. 19
  and the Holocaust, 3–4, 194 n. 16
  and religion, 22, 27–29, 39–40, 42, 46–48, 145–149, 154, 161, 162, 163–164, 174–176, 180
  in science, 5, 26–27, 53
  in courts of law, 73–74
  in fiction, 138–144
  in *Amelia*, 81–82
  in *Bleak House*, 118–119, 134–136
  in *Caleb Williams*, 92–93
  in *Callista*, 154–156, 159–162, 165
  in *Clarissa*, 84–85
  in 'A Death in the Desert', 165–169

  in *Felix Holt*, 132–134
  in *Heart of Midlothian*, 96–97
  in *Orley Farm*, 128–129
  in *The Ring and the Book*, 169–172
  in *Robert Elsmere*, 174–175
  in *Romola*, 162–164
  in *Tom Jones*, 76–80
  of accomplices, 75–76
  of guilt, 190–191
  of innocence, 187–190
  of women, 69, 190
Thackeray, William Makepeace, 31, 183, 185
  Henry Esmond, 92
  History of Pendennis, 13–14, 92, 128, 140
  The Newcomes, 31, 117, 128, 185
  Vanity Fair, 110–111, 185
Thayer, James Bradley, 1, 55, 222 n. 75
Thirlwall, Connop, 152–153
treason, 54, 89–90, 99, 102
trials,
  history of, 2, 6, 21, 48–66, 73–76, 105–109, 113, 115–118, 119–120, 121, 123–124, 125
  and literature, 4, 6, 30, 79–80, 91–94, 96–98, 110–115, 118–119, 121–134, 139, 140–144, 154, 169–171, 181–184, 186–192
  in religion, 22, 32–34, 148, 154, 159–160, 162, 175, 176, 179
  State, 24, 58–59, 63, 89–90, 181–182
Trollope, Anthony, 11, 23
  Orley Farm, 7, 122, 127–130, 143, 159, 185, 188, 189–190

Ward, Mrs Humphry, *Robert Elsmere*, 34, 174–175, 184
  Helbeck of Bannisdale, 184
Watt, Ian, 24, 25–26
Weisberg, Richard, 3–4 , 8–9
Welsh, Alexander, *Strong Representations*, 8, 19–22, 25, 58, 60, 61, 68, 72–73, 76–79, 84, 95, 98–99, 108, 143, 171, 183, 185, 188, 191, 192
West, Robin, 8–10
Woolston, Thomas, 32, 199 n. 29

Yonge, Charlotte, 105, 122, 127, 130, 133, 159–160, 185

Zomchick, John, 7, 80, 84, 85, 93–94

CAMBRIDGE STUDIES IN NINETEENTH-CENTURY
LITERATURE AND CULTURE

General editor
Gillian Beer, *University of Cambridge*

Titles published

Lightning Source UK Ltd.
Milton Keynes UK
UKOW052229130112

185344UK00001B/65/A